The Economics of Market Disequilibrium

This is a volume in
ECONOMIC THEORY, ECONOMETRICS, AND MATHEMATICAL
ECONOMICS

A Series of Monographs and Textbooks

Consulting Editor: KARL SHELL

A complete list of titles in this series appears at the end of this volume.

The Economics of
Market Disequilibrium

Jean-Pascal Benassy

Centre d'Études Prospectives d'Économie Mathématique
Appliquées à la Planification
Paris, France

1982

ACADEMIC PRESS

A Subsidiary of Harcourt Brace Jovanovich, Publishers

New York   London
Paris   San Diego   San Francisco   São Paulo   Sydney   Tokyo   Toronto

ACADEMIC PRESS, INC.
111 Fifth Avenue, New York, New York 10003

United Kingdom Edition published by
ACADEMIC PRESS, INC. (LONDON) LTD.
24/28 Oval Road, London NW1 7DX

Library of Congress Cataloging in Publication Data

Benassy, Jean-Pascal.
   The economics of market disequilibrium.

   (Economic theory, econometrics, and mathematical
economics)
   Includes index.
   1. Equilibrium (Economics) I. Title. II. Series.
HB145.B45   339.5   82-6695
ISBN 0-12-086420-7   AACR2

PRINTED IN THE UNITED STATES OF AMERICA

82 83 84 85   9 8 7 6 5 4 3 2 1

to my Parents

Contents

3. Effective Demand: A First Approach

4. Effective Demand and Spillover Effects

5. Price Making

Part II. Non-Walrasian Equilibrium Concepts

6. The General Framework

Part III.   Macroeconomics

11. A Model of Unemployment

12. Unemployment and Expectations

13. A Model of Unemployment with Flexible Price

14. A Model of Inflation

Appendixes

Preface

The purpose of this book is to construct an economic theory of market disequilibrium that will enable us to describe the functioning of an economy when supply and demand do not match on some markets. The stimulating contributions of Clower (1965) and Leijonhufvud (1968) have made quite clear that such a theory is a necessary step toward the integration of microeconomics and macroeconomics in the Keynesian tradition. They showed indeed that Keynesian Economics, which was totally disconnected from standard microeconomic theory, either Marshallian or Walrasian, could be made consistent with a more general theory allowing individual markets to be in disequilibrium. This book should thus be of interest both to macroeconomists desiring some microeconomic foundations for model construction pertinent to the analysis of policy problems, and to microeconomists who feel the need for an extended microeconomic theory allowing them to deal with states of market disequilibrium and thus with such important problems as involuntary unemployment.

The book provides a self-contained and comprehensive treatment of the theory, dealing with both the microeconomic and the macroeconomic aspects. The microeconomic theory of market disequilibrium is built progressively, starting with the basic microeconomics of individual markets and agents and continuing with more sophisticated multimarket models that extend the traditional Walrasian framework to deal with market disequilibrium, quantity signals, noncompetitive price making, and expectations. In the macroeconomic part of the book some simple synthetic models of unemployment and inflation and the associated problems of economic policy are studied in a framework as close as possible to that of standard macroeconomic theory.

The book draws together work that I have done over several years. My thinking on the subject started with my doctoral dissertation, under the patient and helpful guidance of my adviser Gérard Debreu. At that time I had many stimulating conversations with Bent Hansen. I am also grateful to the many people who made useful comments on my thesis and on my subsequent articles on the topic, among whom I would like to mention Michael Allingham, Robert Clower, Jacques Drèze, Jean-Michel Grandmont, Roger Guesnerie, Frank Hahn, Werner Hildenbrand, Peter Howitt, Serge-Christopher Kolm, Guy Laroque, Axel Leijonhufvud, Pierre Malgrange, Thomas Marschak, Takashi Negishi, Joseph Ostroy, and Yves Younès.

My greatest debt is to those who read the manuscript at its different stages and commented extensively on it: Richard Arnott, Michael Blad, Robert Boyer, Roy Gardner, and Reinhard John, whose suggestions led to innumerable improvements in the text. However, I remain solely responsible for the opinions expressed and for any errors made. Last but not least, Josselyne Bitan cheerfully and efficiently typed the successive drafts of the manuscript.

The Economics of Market Disequilibrium

Introduction

The Problem

For about 40 years now, economics has been split between two partial and conflicting representations of the functioning of market economies. The first, exemplified by general equilibrium models, is essentially concerned with the allocation of factors (assumed fully employed and thus "scarce") and the determination of relative prices. The second, exemplified by macroeconomic models in the Keynesian tradition, deals chiefly with the degree of utilization of factors at an aggregated level (notably, employment) and with the determination of the price level. In spite of numerous attempts at reconciliation, it has become increasingly clear that these two representations correspond to two different classes of economic models with quite different structures.

The Economics of Market Equilibrium

Ever since Adam Smith, classical and then neoclassical economics have been dominated by what we shall call the *economics of market equilibrium* or, briefly, *equilibrium economics*. The main common characteristics of models in this category are as follows: (i) there is equilibrium of demand and supply on all markets considered, (ii) this equilibrium is achieved essentially by price adjustments, and (iii) agents react exclusively to price signals.

These characteristics cover a wide range of models, from the partial equilibrium methods of Marshall to general intertemporal equilibrium in the Walras–Arrow–Debreu framework, including temporary equilibria as developed by Hicks.[1] Unfortunately, such phenomena as involuntary unemployment or, more generally, the underutilization of economic resources, which form the core of Keynesian macroeconomic theory, are by definition left out. It should therefore not come as a surprise that a significant body of literature has developed that implicitly or explicitly rejects some of the basic assumptions of equilibrium theory.

The Keynesian Puzzle

Even a quick examination of macroeconomic models in the Keynesian tradition shows us that they do indeed violate the main characteristics of equilibrium economics: (i) since the labor market shows some unemployment, at least one market is not in equilibrium, (ii) some adjustments are not brought about by price movements alone, e.g., the goods market is equilibrated through movements in the level of income, and, (iii) finally, agents do not react only to price signals, e.g., the Keynesian consumption function depends on the level of income.

These violations could be the unintended side effects of a particular formalization. But this is clearly not the case, as Keynes himself viewed them as essential elements in his attack against the then-dominant classical economics (Keynes 1937, p. 250):

> As I have said above, the initial novelty lies in my maintaining that it is not the rate of interest, but the level of incomes which ensures equality between savings and investment.

Unfortunately, for a long time macroeconomic theory did not go beyond adding the level of income as an endogenous variable, allowing in this way for possible unemployment. Concentration on the "equilibrium" of the goods and money markets, exemplified by the famous IS–LM model, further obscured the disequilibrium nature of the model. One had to wait for Clower (1965) and Leijonhufvud (1968)[2] to reinterpret Keynesian economics as economics of market disequilibrium and thereby open the way for more general theories.

The Economics of Market Disequilibrium

The purpose of this book is to develop a theory of disequilibrium states having these main characteristics: (i) some markets may not be in equilib-

---

[1] Walras (1874), Marshall (1890), Hicks (1939). Arrow and Debreu (1954), Debreu (1959), and Arrow and Hahn (1971).

[2] See also Hansen (1951), Patinkin (1956), and Hicks (1965), who presented a number of ideas in the same vein.

rium, (ii) adjustments can be made by quantities as well as by prices, and (iii) agents react to quantity signals as well as to price signals.

It is quite clear from the characterization given above of traditional microeconomic models and Keynesian macroeconomic models that such a theory will be a useful step toward their integration. It will, moreover, result in some generalization of both: of microeconomics by allowing the treatment of market disequilibrium states at the same disaggregated level and the enlargement of the "space" of signals to include quantity signals, and of macroeconomics by enabling us to consider many markets (not only the labor market) in disequilibrium.

The theory will allow us to describe not only the usual "competitive" system out of general equilibrium but also systems with imperfect competition or wage and price rigidities, which have become increasingly important phenomena in contemporary capitalist economies. It may also give us some insights into the working of economies where prices are fixed by central authorities, as in some socialist countries.

The Two Meanings of Equilibrium

Before going on to more specific issues, it may be useful to clear up a confusion that might arise about the word *equilibrium,* since two common but different meanings of this word are currently used in economics. The first refers to market equilibrium, i.e., the equality of supply and demand on markets. It was used by Marshall, Walras, and most subsequent authors in the neoclassical tradition, and it is this meaning of the word which we used above in talking about equilibrium and disequilibrium economics. The second meaning is borrowed from the physical sciences and describes a "state of rest" of a system. More precisely, an equilibrium is defined by Machlup (1958) as "a constellation of selected interrelated variables, so adjusted to one another that no inherent tendency to change prevails in the model which they constitute."

These two meanings have, unfortunately, often been confused, particularly in microeconomic theory, since in most models an equilibrium in the second sense would not have been considered attained unless demand and supply were equal on all markets considered. They must not be confused here, however, because we shall often encounter throughout the book, notably in Parts II and III, states that are equilibria according to the second meaning but where market disequilibrium in the first sense prevails. As these two meanings of *equilibrium* have a long tradition, we shall employ both, but in such a way that it will always be clear from the context which of the two meanings is used.

An Outline of the Book

This book is divided into three parts devoted, respectively, to the basic microeconomics of market disequilibrium, to the study of non-Walrasian equilibrium concepts, and to macroeconomic applications, notably the problems of unemployment and inflation. The exposition has deliberately been kept at a minimal level of technicality throughout. A number of additional elaborations are collected in 17 short appendices, either because their inclusion in the main text would have interrupted the continuity of the exposition or because they are more technical.

Part I deals with the microeconomics of market disequilibrium at the level of individual markets and agents. Chapter 1 briefly reviews Marshallian and Walrasian equilibrium theories and argues that they cannot be extended in a simple manner to cover situations of market disequilibrium. It then describes the institutional framework assumed in the subsequent analysis. Chapter 2 describes how exchange takes place on markets when supply and demand do not match, and how quantity signals are generated in the transaction process. Chapter 3 examines the formation of effective demands and supplies on a single market, generalizing the standard analysis to the case where quantity constraints are present. Chapter 4 does the same in a multimarket setting, with the integration of "spillover" effects. Finally, Chapter 5 studies the formation of prices.

Part II is devoted to the study of different non-Walrasian equilibrium concepts. These are, of course, equilibria in the second of the two senses discussed in the preceding section. Chapter 6 introduces the notation and institutional framework common to all these concepts. Chapter 7 studies fixprice equilibria. Chapter 8 analyzes explicitly the influence of expectations patterns—notably quantity expectations—on current equilibria. Chapter 9 introduces price flexibility by studying non-Walrasian equilibria where some prices are determined by the agents. Chapter 10 studies the efficiency properties of the various equilibria considered.

Part III presents some macroeconomic applications of the concepts studied in the first and second parts. Chapter 11 gives a synthetic account of alternative unemployment theories. Chapter 12 indicates the role of expectations in determining the nature of current unemployment. Both these chapters are treated in the framework of a short-period model with the wage and price levels given. Chapter 13 introduces price flexibility using the same basic model. The dynamic evolution of the corresponding equilibria is studied in Chapter 14 in order to construct a synthetic model of cost and demand inflation.

PART I

MICROECONOMICS

1

Market Equilibrium and Disequilibrium

1. The Market Equilibrium Paradigm

In market economies, most of the circulation and allocation of economic goods takes place through exchanges on markets. Moreover, most production decisions are directly or indirectly guided by these exchanges. It is thus a central task of economic theory to determine the level of prices and quantities exchanged. Traditionally economists have relied on models of *market equilibrium* to do this. The basic idea behind these models is that somehow (equilibrium) prices are sufficient market signals that correctly represent the scarcities of various economic goods. A typical model contains a set of demand and supply schedules that depend on price signals; the condition of equilibrium between supply and demand will determine the prices as well as the quantities exchanged on each market.

To be a little more precise, let us start, in the "partial equilibrium" tradition generally associated with the name of Marshall, by describing how a single market functions. In this tradition, goods are exchanged against money on separate markets. Let us consider one of them and let p be the monetary price on this market. There are demanders and suppliers, all indexed by $i = 1, \ldots, n$, who express demands or supplies as functions of price p, denoted by $d_i(p)$ and $s_i(p)$. These demand and supply functions are "notional" in the terminology of Clower (1965); that is, they are constructed under the assumption that the agents can purchase and sell as much as they want at the proposed price—hence the absence of any quantity signal. From these individual functions we derive aggregate de-

7

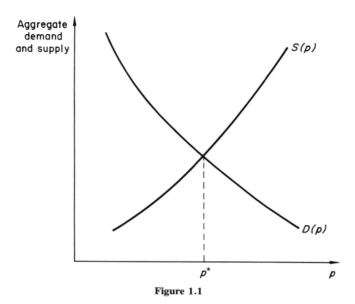

Figure 1.1

mand and supply curves

$$D(p) = \sum_{i=1}^{n} d_i(p), \qquad S(p) = \sum_{i=1}^{n} s_i(p).$$

The equilibrium price p^* is determined by the condition of equality between aggregate demand and supply (Fig. 1.1)

$$D(p^*) = S(p^*).$$

Transactions realized will be equal to demands and supplies at the equilibrium price, respectively, $d_i(p^*)$ and $s_i(p^*)$. At the equilibrium price each agent actually exchanges as much as he wants, thus justifying ex post his assumption that he will be able to do so.

2. The Relevance of the Equilibrium Paradigm

We now must ask ourselves whether the equilibrium paradigm is an adequate representation of real world markets. It is clear that the equilibrium assumption is very stringent and is satisfied by very few markets. Indeed, the paradigm applies, in its full rigor, only to such markets as auctions or security markets where a specialized agent, an "auctioneer," actually performs the task of finding the equilibrium price and where no trade takes place before it is found. But these markets are only a small fraction of existing markets.

Even though the equilibrium representation does not accurately portray the very short run functioning of markets, one might be satisfied with it as an adequate approximation of reality. Such may be the case for a few markets where competition is very intense—for example, markets for some agricultural products or raw materials, where prices are very flexible and respond with great speed to all variations in the state of supply and demand. However, nowadays even these markets are exceptions rather than the rule, and in many markets the "forces of supply and demand" are so hindered by other forces that the equilibrium representation is inappropriate even as an approximation. Reasons for this are numerous.

1. Some prices may be institutionally constrained. Governments may impose maximum prices (price controls) or minimum ones (guaranteed minimum prices for some agricultural commodities). Prices may simply be fixed by professional organizations or the government, as is the case with a number of services. Finally, in planned economies many prices are often fixed for quite long periods of time.

2. Imperfect competition may render price adjustments more sluggish. Product differentiation and sales promotion will partially replace price competition. The growing practice of cost-determined prices also falls under this heading.

3. Finally, the particular nature of some goods may make full adjustment to the conditions of supply and demand socially infeasible. Such is clearly the case for labor markets, where wages are influenced by other forces of a social nature.

All this clearly points to the need to study market economies that are out of equilibrium. This we shall do now, using the simple Marshallian framework outlined above.

3. Market Disequilibrium: A First Approach

Let us consider again the isolated market described above and assume that the price is not necessarily the equilibrium one. What transactions will be carried out in such a case? There is, unfortunately, very little in the literature about transactions realized by individual agents. At the ag-

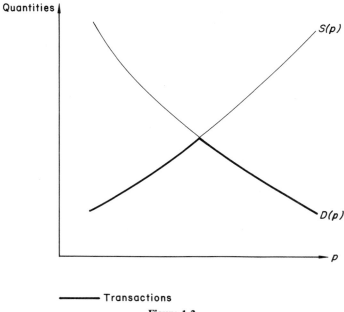

Figure 1.2

gregate level, however, there is by now a "traditional" answer which says that, in the absence of friction, agents on the short side of the market[1] will realize their desired transactions, and thus aggregate transactions will settle at the minimum of total demand and supply (Fig. 1.2). Indeed, this is the implicit assumption in most models that are Keynesian in inspiration. As noted by Clower (1960), it satisfies the assumptions of voluntary exchange (no one is forced to trade more than he wishes) and efficiency (neither side would benefit from any extra trade).

However, considering a market in isolation does not take us very far towards understanding macroeconomic models, since one of the main themes of Keynesian theory is the repercussion of disequilibria across markets. We thus must move to models that recognize the interdependence of all markets in the economy. As this has always been the central theme of Walrasian general equilibrium models, we turn to these models now.

---

[1] The "short" side of a market is that where the aggregate volume of desired transactions is smallest. It is thus the demand side if there is excess supply, the supply side if there is excess demand. The other side is the "long" side.

4. The Walrasian Paradigm: Equilibrium and Disequilibrium

The distinctive feature of Walrasian models, which cover both inter-temporal and temporary equilibrium settings, is that they explicitly consider the exchanges of all goods as mutually interdependent. The institutional framework is not a set of independently organized markets as in the Marshallian paradigm. Instead the agents exchange directly, through some implicit "clearinghouse," bundles of goods represented by vectors in a commodity space.

Let there be r commodities, indexed by $h = 1, \ldots, r$. The terms on which they can be exchanged for each other will be given by a price vector p, with components p_h, $h = 1, \ldots, r$. The exchanges desired by agent i, as a function of the price vector p, will be represented through *vector* demand and supply functions $d_i(p)$ and $s_i(p)$. Their components $d_{ih}(p)$ and $s_{ih}(p)$ represent the quantity of good h demanded or supplied, respectively, by agent i. One often works with the net excess demand function of agent i, that is, $d_{ih}(p) - s_{ih}(p)$. All these functions are, again, "notional," that is, constructed under the assumption that desired trades for all goods can actually be realized. By aggregation over the n traders we obtain the total demand and supply for each good h:

$$D_h(p) = \sum_{i=1}^{n} d_{ih}(p),$$

$$S_h(p) = \sum_{i=1}^{n} s_{ih}(p).$$

A *Walrasian equilibrium price vector* p^* is defined by the condition that aggregate demand equals aggregate supply for all goods, that is,

$$D_h(p^*) = S_h(p^*) \qquad \text{for all} \quad h.$$

The purchase or sale of good h realized by agent i at the price vector p^* will be $d_{ih}(p^*)$ or $s_{ih}(p^*)$.

Disequilibrium

Let us now assume that the price system is not an equilibrium one. What transactions will occur? Thus far we have provided no answer at the level of the individual agent, but we might be tempted to use at the aggregate level the "short-side rule" discussed in Section 3 for a single market and apply it to the vector demands and supplies, taking aggregate transactions for each good to be equal to the minimum of total supply and demand. Unfortunately, one can easily construct examples demonstrating that this would lead to inconsistent transactions violating either feasibility or the budget constraints of the agents.

Imagine, for example, a firm in a situation of excess demand for its inputs and outputs. Since there is excess demand on the input markets, the firm purchases fewer inputs than its Walrasian demand. However, since there is excess demand on the output markets and the firm is a seller, sales of outputs should be equal to the Walrasian supplies. The application of the "short-side rule" would thus call for producing the Walrasian outputs with fewer inputs than the Walrasian inputs—a technologically infeasible situation.

Analogously, imagine a household facing excess supply for the goods it purchases and the goods it sells. Under the short-side rule, its sales would be lower than its Walrasian supplies but its purchases would be equal to its Walrasian demands. As a result this household's transactions would violate the budget constraint.

The conclusion of such examples, which could be multiplied *ad infinitum,* is quite clear: the "short-side rule" does not work in a multimarket economy when one uses the traditional Walrasian demands and supplies. The consequences are obviously quite far-reaching, as we shall have to rework the whole theory of demand, supply, and market exchange. First, however, it is necessary to make clear the specific market structure in which we shall be working.

5. The Market Structure: Money versus Barter

A much neglected issue in most multimarket models of the whole economy is the problem of the actual institutions of exchange. If the economy is generally conceived of as a set of individual markets, it is by no means clear which markets are assumed to operate. Walras (1874) himself refers in his initial model of multimarket exchange to a barter organization with a market for each pair of goods. Others, on the contrary, assume that all exchanges are monetary.

Actually this problem is inconsequential in most of these models, since we are concerned only with the vector of net global exchanges for each agent. Circulation of goods is implicitly assumed to be carried out by some sort of centralized clearinghouse that sends goods directly from the original supplier to the ultimate demander. If, however, we want to study a really decentralized economy, possibly in disequilibrium situations, the actual organization of exchange will in fact matter very much. A given vector of net global exchanges will not be carried directly through the implicit clearinghouse but will have to be attained through sequences of partial exchanges on individual markets. These exchanges can be carried

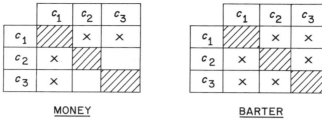

Figure 1.3

out in a barter setting, a pure monetary setting, or any intermediate arrangement. We shall now consider the question of which is the most appropriate framework for our analysis.

We must first define more precisely what we mean by a barter economy, a monetary economy, or other arrangements. We shall follow here the definition of Clower (1967), who gives as the basic concept the "exchange relation" of the economy, that is, the list of pairs of goods that can be exchanged directly, one for the other, on some markets. There will be a particular market for each of these pairs. The exchange relation can be represented by a "cross diagram," where the existence of a trading post for the exchange of two goods is indicated by a cross in the corresponding box. Figure 1.3 pictures the exchange relations that correspond to money and barter in an economy having three commodities labeled c_1, c_2, c_3. Boxes along the diagonal have been eliminated, as no market for a good against itself would exist.

The barter economy corresponds to a "maximal" exchange relation: each good can be exchanged against every other good. If there are r goods in the economy, there will thus be $r(r-1)/2$ markets. In the pure monetary economy, however, only one good—money—can be exchanged against all others. The nonmonetary goods can be exchanged only against money. The monetary economy thus has as many markets as nonmonetary goods. Between these two "extremes" there are, of course, numerous possible exchange relations, but for the sake of simplicity we shall concentrate mostly on money and barter.[2]

6. A Monetary Economy

We thus have to make a choice between these alternative frameworks of exchange, bearing in mind that we want a framework that bridges the

---

[2] Other exchange structures are defined in Clower (1967). A disequilibrium analysis is found in Benassy (1975a) and is sketched in part in Appendix N.

gap between microeconomic and macroeconomic models. From this viewpoint, and for obvious reasons of realism, monetary exchange clearly emerges as the most natural framework for our theorizing. Indeed, such a basic concept as the demand for a good makes sense only in a monetary economy, where this good is exchanged in only one market, against a monetary counterpart. In a barter economy, on the other hand, there is a specific demand for a good against every other good. Besides this representation problem, there are also difficulties with the functioning of a barter economy, related to the problem of the absence of double coincidence of wants. All these are briefly explored in Appendix A. So, we shall work henceforth almost exclusively with a monetary economy, where by legal rule or well-established habit only one good functions as a medium of exchange, and where nonmonetary goods can be exchanged only against this money good. Money will also be the numeraire and a store of value. Assume that r markets will be operated during the period of analysis considered. On each of these markets a nonmonetary good, indexed by $h = 1, \ldots, r$, is traded against money. We denote by p_h the money price of good h.

Each agent i visits the markets sequentially. On the market h, he may make a purchase $d_{ih} > 0$, paying $p_h d_{ih}$ units of money, or a sale $s_{ih} > 0$, receiving $p_h s_{ih}$ units of money. In all that follows, the symbols d_{ih} and s_{ih} represent the volume of the transaction (that is, purchase or sale) of good h against money. The elementary transaction consists of one unit of good h against p_h units of money. Accordingly, if we consider r markets, the net increase in the money holdings m_i of agent i associated with his transactions on the r markets will be

$$\Delta m_i = \sum_{h=1}^{r} p_h s_{ih} - \sum_{h=1}^{r} p_h d_{ih}.$$

7. Demands versus Transactions

Having clarified the market structure, we must now make an important distinction, which by nature is not made in equilibrium models, between *demands* and *transactions*. Transactions, that is, purchases and sales on a market, are the exchanges actually carried out on that market. They are thus subject to all traditional material and accounting identities. In particular, on each market transactions must balance as an identity. Demands and supplies, on the contrary, are signals transmitted by each agent to the market before exchange takes place and represent as a first approximation his desired trades. Of course, as we shall see, nothing ensures that the agents will be able to achieve these tentative trades.

In order to distinguish between these notions, we shall use different notations: d_{ih}^* and s_{ih}^* represent the actual purchase and sale of agent i on market h, $\tilde{d}_{ih}$ and $\tilde{s}_{ih}$, his demand and supply. We should stress immediately that $\tilde{d}_{ih}$ and $\tilde{s}_{ih}$ generally differ from the Walrasian demands and supplies, as we shall later see. With n agents in the economy, the identity of purchases and sales mentioned above is written

$$\sum_{i=1}^{n} d_{ih}^* \equiv \sum_{i=1}^{n} s_{ih}^*.$$

No such equality, however, necessarily holds for total demands and supplies, which may be different; for example, we may have

$$\sum_{i=1}^{n} \tilde{d}_{ih} \neq \sum_{i=1}^{n} \tilde{s}_{ih}.$$

Note, however, that for purchases to be equal to demands and sales equal to supplies for every agent, a necessary condition is that total demand equal total supply:

$$d_{ih}^* = \tilde{d}_{ih} \quad \text{and} \quad s_{ih}^* = \tilde{s}_{ih} \quad \text{for all} \ \ i \Rightarrow \sum_{i=1}^{n} \tilde{d}_{ih} = \sum_{i=1}^{n} \tilde{s}_{ih}.$$

The idea that any trader can trade as much as he wants is thus directly related to the assumption of market equilibrium.

8. Conclusions

The stage is now set for a study of economies in disequilibrium. The discussion in this chapter has shown us that to do this we must abandon totally the standard theory of prices, demands, and transactions since the assumption of market equilibrium intervenes at all crucial stages of the theory. First, the condition of equilibrium between supply and demand determines prices and transactions endogenously at the same time from the demand and supply functions. Second, the demand and supply functions themselves are determined under the assumption that transactions will be equal to demands and supplies—an assumption, as we have just seen, intimately connected with that concerning equilibrium.

Without the equilibrium assumption, the standard theory is unable to determine prices and transactions, and the choice-theoretic basis of traditional demand and supply functions collapses. We shall now sketch briefly the steps needed to rebuild the theory under more general assumptions. First, since total demands and supplies may not be equal, we shall have to determine how transactions are carried out in a market in disequilibrium and how quantity signals are generated in the process. Second, demands and supplies must be redefined to deal with possible quantity constraints Effective demands and supplies will thus be constructed by taking into account quantity signals as well as prices. Finally, we shall have to indicate how prices will be determined in the absence of their implicit determination through the equilibrium assumption.

All of these points will be investigated in the following chapters.

2

Disequilibrium Trading
and Quantity Signals

1. The Setting

As we noted in Chapter 1, the institutional setting assumed here is that of a system of independently organized and decentralized markets in each of which goods are exchanged for money. In this chapter we shall study the functioning of one of these markets for a specific good h. Since everything in what follows will pertain to this market, the corresponding subindex h will be dropped throughout the chapter in order to simplify notation. The time period considered is one in which the price is given, but not necessarily at its equilibrium value. Demands and supplies are expressed and transactions are carried out.

All traders (whether consumers, firms, or others) are indexed by $i = 1$, . . . , n. They present demands and supplies $\tilde{d}_i$ and $\tilde{s}_i$ on the market being considered. These may be pure flows (as a supply of labor) or may also include additions to or subtractions from a stock. We should emphasize immediately that $\tilde{d}_i$ and $\tilde{s}_i$ are not the notional demands and supplies found in equilibrium theory but are rather *effective demands and supplies*. (Their determination will be studied in later chapters.) *A priori,* there is no reason to assume that these demands and supplies balance, so that we may have

$$\tilde{D} = \sum_{i=1}^{n} \tilde{d}_i \neq \sum_{i=1}^{n} \tilde{s}_i = \tilde{S}.$$

From these inconsistent demands and supplies the market process generates a set of realized transactions—purchases d_i^* and sales s_i^*—which must balance as an identity in order to represent actual exchanges. That is,

$$D^* = \sum_{i=1}^{n} d_i^* = \sum_{i=1}^{n} s_i^* = S^*.$$

Clearly some demands and supplies will have to go unsatisfied in the exchange process; the precise determination of the transactions obviously depends on the particular organization of exchange on the market. With each market process we shall therefore associate a rationing scheme, which is the mathematical representation of the exchange process. The word *rationing* is introduced here as a reminder that purchases will differ from demands and sales from supplies, even though the presence of buffer stocks may prevent rationing in the usual sense from occurring. Before studying some properties of these rationing schemes, let us consider a few examples.

2. Rationing Schemes: Some Examples

Queueing and Priority Systems

In this case, demanders (or suppliers) are ranked in a predetermined order and are served according to this ranking. Assume, for example, that there are $n - 1$ demanders, ranked by $i = 1, \ldots, n - 1$, with i's demand $\tilde{d}_i$, facing one supplier who is indexed by n and supplies $\tilde{s}_n$. When demander i's turn arrives, the maximum he can get is what the agents before him (agents $j < i$) have left, that is,

$$\tilde{s}_n - \sum_{j<i} d_j^* = \max\left(0, \tilde{s}_n - \sum_{j<i} \tilde{d}_j\right),$$

and his realized purchase will simply be the minimum of this quantity and of his demand, that is,

$$d_i^* = \min\left[\tilde{d}_i, \max\left(0, \tilde{s}_n - \sum_{j<i} \tilde{d}_j\right)\right] \qquad (i = 1, \ldots, n - 1).$$

As for the supplier, he will trade the minimum of his supply and total demand:

$$s_n^* = \min\left(\tilde{s}_n, \sum_{j=1}^{n-1} \tilde{d}_j\right).$$

Proportional Rationing

In a proportional rationing scheme, agents on the short side of the market realize their demands or supplies; agents on the long side receive a level of transaction proportional to their demand or supply. The rationing coefficient is the same for all agents on the long side. The rule can thus be written

$$d_i^* = \tilde{d}_i \times \min[1, \tilde{S}/\tilde{D}],$$
$$s_i^* = \tilde{s}_i \times \min[1, \tilde{D}/\tilde{S}],$$

with

$$\tilde{D} = \sum_{j=1}^{n} \tilde{d}_j, \qquad \tilde{S} = \sum_{j=1}^{n} \tilde{s}_j.$$

The relation between the purchase d_i^* and demand $\tilde{d}_i$ of a specific agent i (the demands and supplies of the other agents being kept constant) has been plotted in Fig. 2.1.

3. Rationing Schemes: Some Properties

Having studied these examples, let us investigate two important properties that rationing schemes in general may possess.[1]

Voluntary Exchange

We shall say that there is *voluntary exchange* on market h if no agent is forced to purchase more than he demands or to sell more than he supplies. This is written

$$d_i^* \le \tilde{d}_i, \qquad s_i^* \le \tilde{s}_i \qquad \text{for all} \quad i.$$

Most markets in reality meet this condition, and although there are a few cases where involuntary exchange may occur (as on some labor markets), we shall assume voluntary exchange throughout the remainder of this book, except in Appendix F, where a simple exception is studied. Voluntary exchange can be illustrated by the usual picture of the single Marshallian market[2] (Fig. 2.2). Trades that satisfy voluntary exchange

---

[1] These properties have been stressed, to different extents, by Clower (1960, 1965), Hahn and Negishi (1962), Barro and Grossman (1971, 1976), Grossman (1971), and Howitt (1974). More formalized versions will be found in Chapter 6.

[2] Of course, it is not fully rigorous to use this representation, since demand and supply will depend upon many other signals besides the price on the market. It is used here, however, for its graphical convenience.

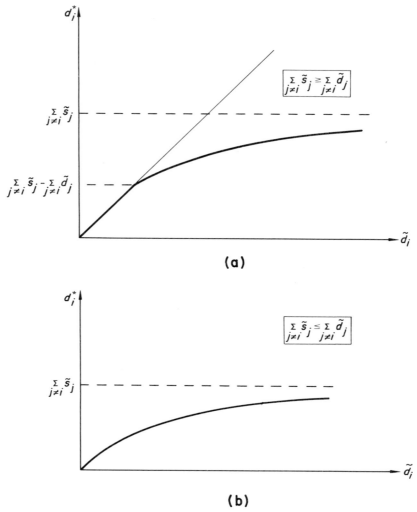

Figure 2.1

will yield a volume of transactions on or below the demand curve *and* the supply curve; that is, they will correspond to points on or below the heavy line in Fig. 2.2.

Market Efficiency

Clearly a number of trades that satisfy the voluntary exchange assumption are very unsatisfactory. For example, zero trade always satisfies vol-

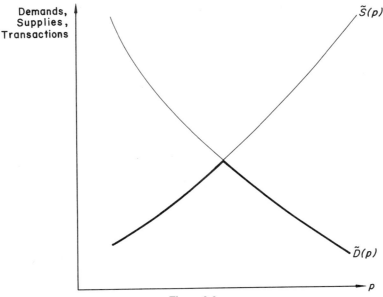

Figure 2.2

untary exchange. More generally, looking at Fig. 2.2 we see that any point that is strictly below the demand and supply curves corresponds to an inefficient trade, as at least one demander and one supplier would like to exchange more. The only "efficient" points are those that correspond to the minimum of supply and demand.

In light of this, we shall say that the rationing scheme is *market efficient*, or *frictionless*, if all mutually advantageous trades are carried out. Still assuming voluntary exchange, this implies that one will not find rationed demanders and rationed suppliers at the same time. Thus, all agents on the "short" side (that is, the suppliers if there is excess demand, the demanders if there is excess supply) will realize their demands and supplies:

$$\tilde{D} \geq \tilde{S} \Rightarrow s_i^* = \tilde{s}_i \qquad \text{for all} \quad i,$$
$$\tilde{D} \leq \tilde{S} \Rightarrow d_i^* = \tilde{d}_i \qquad \text{for all} \quad i.$$

The short-side rule is thus seen to be the consequence of both assumptions, voluntary exchange and market efficiency. As a direct corollary, total transactions will be the minimum of total demand and supply:

$$\sum_{i=1}^{n} d_i^* = \sum_{i=1}^{n} s_i^* = \min\left(\sum_{i=1}^{n} \tilde{d}_i, \sum_{i=1}^{n} \tilde{s}_i \right).$$

If we now ask ourselves about the empirical validity of the market efficiency assumption, we must note that for it to be valid in all circumstances, all demanders must in some way meet all suppliers. Such an assumption is quite acceptable if the market is "small" (as in the single queue of the above example) or centralized (as in the proportional rationing scheme). It becomes much less tenable if we consider a more extended or aggregated market functioning in a decentralized way, as the mutual search of buyers and sellers is costly and some buyers and sellers may not meet. Note, in particular, that the property of market efficiency is usually lost by aggregation (whereas voluntary exchange remains). An illustration is given in Fig. 2.3, which shows how the aggregation of two frictionless submarkets for the same physical good and at the same price, but perhaps at two different locations, yields an aggregated market that is not market efficient in some price range.

Indeed, let us consider two submarkets, indexed 1 and 2, with specific demand and supply functions. These markets are frictionless, so that transactions on each of these submarkets are given by

$$d_1^* = s_1^* = \min(\tilde{d}_1, \tilde{s}_1),$$
$$d_2^* = s_2^* = \min(\tilde{d}_2, \tilde{s}_2).$$

Now let us aggregate these two markets and define the aggregated demand and supply functions

$$\tilde{D}(p) = \tilde{d}_1(p) + \tilde{d}_2(p), \qquad \tilde{S}(p) = \tilde{s}_1(p) + \tilde{s}_2(p).$$

Similarly, transactions will be the sum of the transactions on the submarkets:

$$D^* = d_1^* + d_2^*, \qquad S^* = s_1^* + s_2^*.$$

We see immediately that in some price range the transactions will violate the market efficiency assumption. Specifically,

$$p_1^* < p < p_2^* \Rightarrow D^* = S^* < \min(\tilde{D}, \tilde{S}).$$

Indeed, in this price range there are both unsatisfied suppliers on the first submarket and unsatisfied demanders on the second submarket. More generally, we can conceive that in a market with many traders on each side and where it is costly to meet other traders, transactions may be lower than the minimum of total supply and demand, thus violating the market efficiency assumption. So, even though it will be useful in constructing simple examples or in obtaining some general efficiency results (as in Chapter 10), we shall not, without so stating, make the assumption of frictionless markets in this book.

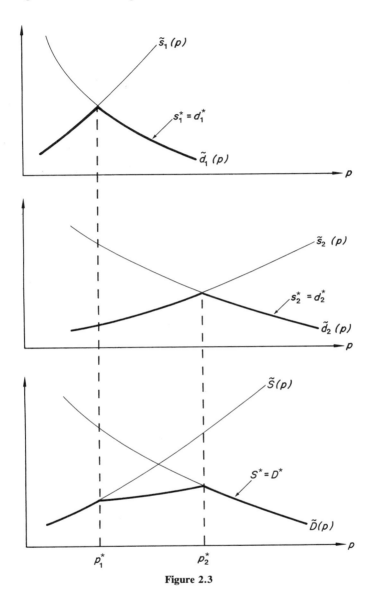

Figure 2.3

4. Manipulability

We shall introduce here a distinction that will prove important: that between *manipulable* and *nonmanipulable* rationing schemes. The difference is best seen graphically (Fig. 2.4). Here we have plotted as an example the purchase d_i^* of an agent against his demand $\tilde{d}_i$, the demands and supplies of the others being held constant.

In the manipulable case agent i can, even if rationed, continue to increase his transactions by quoting higher demands, thus somehow "manipulating" the outcome of the market rationing process. Clearly, the proportional rationing scheme seen above is manipulable (compare Fig. 2.1). In the nonmanipulable case, however, the agent faces a bound to his transaction which depends upon the demands and supplies of the other agents and which he cannot manipulate. We shall denote by $\bar{d}_i$ and $\bar{s}_i$ the bounds on purchase and sale, respectively. Accordingly, the rationing scheme can be written

$$d_i^* = \min(\tilde{d}_i, \bar{d}_i),$$
$$s_i^* = \min(\tilde{s}_i, \bar{s}_i).$$

The queueing system with given ordering, studied previously, is clearly nonmanipulable and can thus be written in the above form, with

$$\bar{d}_i = \max\left(0, \tilde{s}_n - \sum_{j<i} \tilde{d}_j\right), \qquad 1 \leq i \leq n - 1,$$
$$\bar{s}_n = \sum_{j=1}^{n-1} \tilde{d}_j.$$

5. Quantity Signals

We have just discussed how transactions can be carried out on a market where demands and supplies do not necessarily match. Another very important outcome of the market process is the formation of *quantity signals* in addition to the traditional price signals. These quantity signals will have a number of different forms, depending on the nature of the rationing scheme. We saw, for example, that in the case of proportional rationing the quantity signal was a rationing coefficient, the same for all agents, and was announced by the agent centralizing the demands and supplies.

If the rationing scheme is nonmanipulable—a category we shall study very often throughout this book—the quantity signal received always has the form of an upper bound on purchases or sales. These *perceived constraints* will be denoted by $\bar{d}_i$ and $\bar{s}_i$, respectively. In the previous section we gave an example of these perceived constraints in the case of a

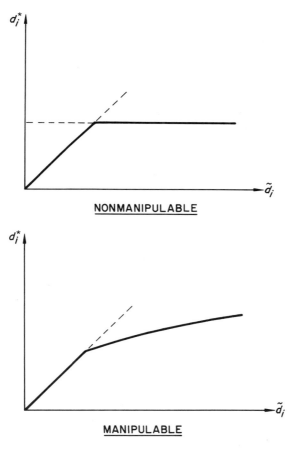

Figure 2.4

queueing system. We may make the general remark, valid for all nonmanipulable schemes, that whenever an agent is actually rationed the level of the perceived constraint is equal to the transaction realized, as the above formulas show.

Whatever the nature of the quantity signals received in past and current markets, it is reasonable to assume that they will generate expectations of quantity signals for future markets, and we must expect that past and expected quantity signals will have an effect on demands and supplies, just as price signals do. Before studying this effect in the next chapters, let us look at a few extensions of the rationing scheme.

6. Extensions of the Rationing Scheme

Manipulation through Transaction Costs

Up to now, we have assumed that the level of transactions was influenced by the agents' demands (and supplies) only. Correspondingly, manipulation was possible only through demand. However, in reality rationing schemes are influenced not only by the demands expressed but also by all sorts of "transactions costs" (understood here in a rather wide sense). Accordingly, the classification between manipulable and nonmanipulable rationing schemes becomes broader with the inclusion of transaction costs. Indeed, many rationing schemes in reality are nonmanipulable through demands but manipulable through transactions costs of some kind. Here are two simple examples.

• In all systems such as queues or priority systems, it is clear that one cannot manipulate through demand once the ranking is known. However, this ranking can be manipulated at a cost, such as by arriving earlier in a queue.

• In goods markets, the maximum sales that a firm can make (that is, the demand that is addressed to it) will generally not be influenced by the level of its supply, but rather by marketing expenses or price variations, both of which represent costs to the firm.

Stochastic Rationing Schemes

In reality most rationing schemes are deterministic once demands and supplies are known, and we shall therefore work only with deterministic schemes. However, we must mention for the sake of completeness the existence of stochastic rationing schemes. In such a case the transaction will not be given by a function; rather, it will have a probability density function, conditional upon all demands and supplies expressed. The corresponding random rationing schemes must be such that total sales equal total purchases with probability 1.

Stochastic schemes are quite rare in reality. They will typically be found when one has to divide "fairly" an insufficient quantity of some indivisible good. Consider, for example, an indivisible commodity that can be traded only in the amounts 0 or 1. Imagine that the supply of this commodity is n_s and the demand n_d (that is, n_d agents actually express a demand of size 1 and all others do not express any demand). If $n_d > n_s$, some demanders have to be rationed; specifically, n_s demanders will get one unit and $n_d - n_s$ will get nothing. If the choice of the rationed individuals is determined by a random drawing with equal probabilities, then for each of the n_d demanders the quantity he can trade will be

$$1 \quad \text{with probability} \quad n_s/n_d,$$
$$0 \quad \text{with probability} \quad 1 - n_s/n_d.$$

7. Conclusions

In this chapter we examined how trade would take place in a decentralized manner on markets without an auctioneer when the ruling price is not the equilibrium one. We saw that the trading process can be represented by a rationing scheme, which associates to a set of inconsistent demands and supplies a set of consistent transactions. We examined various possible characteristics of these rationing schemes—voluntary exchange, efficiency, manipulability—as well as extensions of the rationing schemes to cover situations involving transaction costs or uncertainty.

We saw also that, besides the formation of transactions, a second important outcome of the trading process is the generation of quantity signals, that inform each trader about his quantitative trade possibilities. In the next chapters we shall study the use of these quantity signals in the formation of effective demands and supplies and in the quotation of prices.

3

Effective Demand: A First Approach

1. The Problem

Throughout the preceding chapters, we worked with demands and supplies actually expressed on markets, that is, effective demands.[1] The time has come to study how these effective demands are determined in the presence of disequilibria. As indicated above, the traditional Walrasian, or "notional," demands will not be relevant here, as they are based fundamentally on the "equilibrium" assumption that transactions will be equal to demands on all markets. So we have to develop a new choice-theoretic framework for constructing these effective demands, taking into account quantity signals as well as price signals. As it turns out, quantity constraints on a market will affect effective demand on the same market and on other markets quite differently. Let us give a few intuitive arguments.

• Constraints on a market will modify the desired transactions on the other markets. For example, constraints on labor income will affect the effective demand for goods of households. Similarly, sales constraints will affect firms' effective demand for labor. These are the "spillover effects" traditionally associated with the idea of effective demand in Keynesian theory.

• But constraints on the *same* market will also modify effective demand. For example, an agent who expects in advance to be rationed may

[1] In what follows we shall often use, for short, the word *demand* in place of "demand and supply."

28

express a demand higher than his desired transaction if the rationing scheme is manipulable because this will increase the level of his realized transaction.

For simplicity of exposition, we shall treat the two types of effects separately. In this chapter we shall concentrate on the effect of quantity constraints on demand in the same market, since this can be treated in a single-market framework. In Chapter 4 we shall deal with spillover effects, which will require a multimarket approach.

2. The Setting

We shall consider here the market for a particular good (whose index will be omitted throughout the chapter) against money. Consider an agent i with an initial endowment of a good ω_i and of money $\bar{m}_i$. Let his preferences concerning final holdings of this good and money, x_i and m_i, be represented by a utility function $U_i(x_i, m_i)$.[2] Let p be the price on that market. Let us assume, as in Fig. 3.1, that the agent will always be a demander of the good. His final holdings of good and money will be, as a function of his purchase d_i on the market,

$$x_i = \omega_i + d_i,$$
$$m_i = \bar{m}_i - pd_i.$$

The optimal transaction for the agent, which we shall denote by $\hat{d}_i$, corresponds to the tangency point of the budget line and indifference curve (Fig. 3.1). To get an even simpler picture, however, we shall represent the preferences of the agent directly as a function of his trade d_i by defining

$$V_i(d_i) = U_i(\omega_i + d_i, \bar{m}_i - pd_i).$$

We shall assume that V_i is strictly concave. The optimal transaction $\hat{d}_i$ corresponds to the unconstrained maximum of V_i (Fig. 3.2).

In the absence of any constraint on the market, the agent would express a demand equal to this "target transaction" $\hat{d}_i$. We shall now see how the expectation of quantitative restrictions on the market will affect the effective demand $\bar{d}_i$ on this same market. In particular, we will be interested in comparing the effective demand with the target transaction $\hat{d}_i$.

---

[2] We thus assume that agents derive some indirect utility from money holdings, even if money has no intrinsic utility. Derivation of such indirect utility functions with money as a store of value is carried out in Chapter 8.

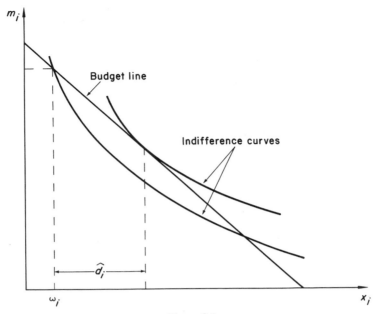

Figure 3.1

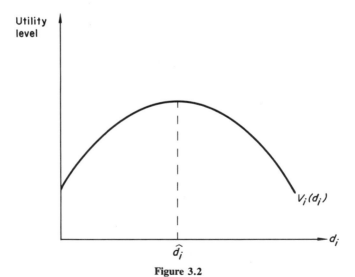

Figure 3.2

3. The Choice-Theoretic Basis:
The Perceived Rationing Scheme

The target demand $\hat{d}_i$ is "notional"; that is, it is constructed under the assumption that transaction will be equal to demand. Clearly we cannot maintain this assumption in our disequilibrium framework. However, a rational agent must still perceive some relation between transaction and demand in order to link his actions (the demands) and their consequences (the transactions). We shall call this relation the *perceived rationing scheme*, by an obvious analogy with the "true" relation, that is, the rationing scheme. It will give the transaction which the trader expects to carry on the market as a function of the demand he will express. If expectations are held with certainty, the perceived rationing scheme is a function, and we shall denote it by

$$d_i = \phi_i(\tilde{d}_i) \qquad \text{for a demander,}$$

or

$$s_i = \phi_i(\tilde{s}_i) \qquad \text{for a supplier.}$$

We shall generally assume that ϕ_i is a nondecreasing function and that the agent expects that the voluntary exchange assumption holds, that is,

$$\phi_i(\tilde{d}_i) \le \tilde{d}_i, \qquad \phi_i(\tilde{s}_i) \le \tilde{s}_i.$$

The perceived scheme may have different shapes depending on whether or not the original rationing scheme is manipulable (Fig. 3.3).

We should note that since the perceived rationing scheme depicts an *expected* relation between the transaction and the demand, it may be stochastic and thus be represented by a probability distribution on the transaction, conditional on the effective demand or supply expressed. Stochastic perceived rationing schemes are studied briefly in Appendix B. However, to simplify the exposition, we shall deal mostly with deterministic schemes in the rest of this chapter.

Effective Demand Determination

With a given perceived rationing scheme, effective demand will be given by the solution of the following program:

$$\text{Maximize} \quad V_i(d_i) \qquad \text{s.t.}$$

$$d_i = \phi_i(\tilde{d}_i).$$

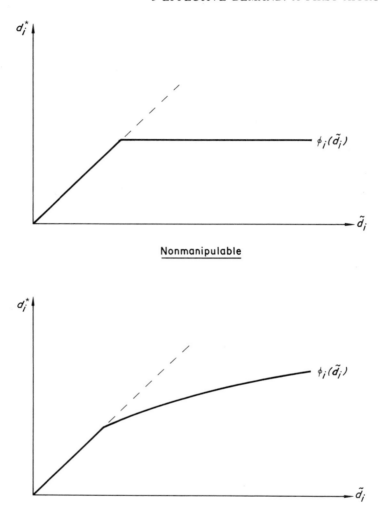

Figure 3.3

That is, the agent maximizes the utility of the transaction that he expects to result from his demand. Unfortunately, in spite of the apparent extreme simplicity of the method, its application poses a number of problems, which we shall now investigate.

4. The Nonmanipulable Case: A Problem
in Definition

We shall show here that in the absence of manipulation the agent will express his target transaction as effective demand:

$$\tilde{d}_i = \hat{d}_i.$$

However, to arrive at this result we must first solve a problem in definition that arises when the scheme is deterministic.

The Problem

A nonmanipulable perceived rationing scheme is written

$$\phi_i(\tilde{d}_i) = \min(\tilde{d}_i, \bar{d}_i^e),$$

where $\bar{d}_i^e$ is the *expected* bound on agent i's purchases. Effective demand is thus a solution in $\tilde{d}_i$ of

$$\text{Maximize} \quad V_i(d_i) \quad \text{s.t.}$$

$$d_i = \min(\tilde{d}_i, \bar{d}_i^e).$$

Looking at Fig. 3.2, we see that the solutions to this program will differ in nature, depending on the position of $\bar{d}_i^e$ with respect to $\hat{d}_i$:

• If $\bar{d}_i^e \geq \hat{d}_i$, the agent can realize his optimal transaction and will thus express it as his effective demand: $\tilde{d}_i = \hat{d}_i$.

• If $\bar{d}_i^e < \hat{d}_i$, the agent is constrained to trade less than he would like. The best transaction he can expect is $\bar{d}_i^e$. But this transaction will be obtained by expressing any demand between $\bar{d}_i^e$ and infinity. The program giving effective demand has an infinity of solutions, and there is a problem in definition.

A Solution

A number of considerations will lead us to choose $\hat{d}_i$ as effective demand. First, $\hat{d}_i$ is in the set of solutions to the above program *whatever the value* of $\bar{d}_i^e$, and it is the *only* demand to have this very strong property. Thus if we assume, as would be natural in any dynamic process, that the agent does not forecast with certainty the constraint he is going to face, he will be led to choose $\hat{d}_i$ as his effective demand, as this is the only demand that will guarantee him the best transaction possible against *any* constraint.

We may also assume that $\bar{d}_i^e$ is forecasted probabilistically and has a cumulative subjective probability distribution $\psi_i(\cdot)$. The agent will maximize the expected utility of his transaction with respect to this probability distribution. In Appendix B we show that if $\psi_i(\hat{d}_i) < 1$, that is, if the agent perceives some chance of being unconstrained, then $\hat{d}_i$ is the *only* solution to the expected utility maximization program, whatever the probability distribution: uncertainty about the quantity constraint he will face will make the agent express a well-defined effective demand equal to the target transaction $\hat{d}_i$.

5. Manipulability and Overbidding

If we now apply the methodology derived above to the manipulable case, we see that we will encounter a perverse phenomenon of overbidding that accompanies any expectation of rationing when the rationing scheme is manipulable. Each agent, if he wants to obtain a given transaction and expects to be on the long side, will express a demand higher than his desired transaction, and the more severe the rationing is expected to be, the higher will be the demand. This phenomenon is easily seen graphically in Fig. 3.4, where a target transaction $\hat{d}_i$ and the corresponding effective demand have been plotted.

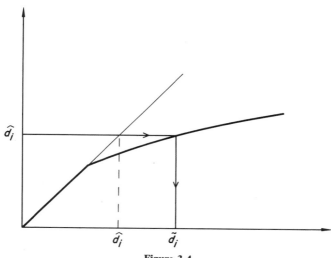

Figure 3.4

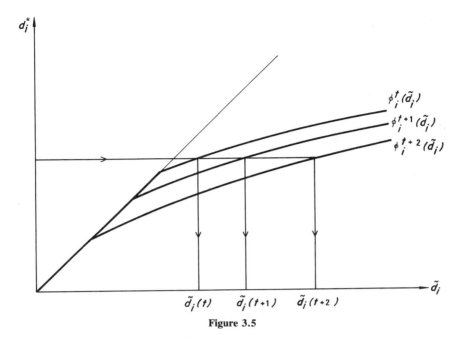

Figure 3.5

This overbidding process would reach some limit if the perceived rationing schemes were themselves stable. But if there are many constrained agents overbidding in the way we just described, the result will be a displacement of the perceived rationing scheme of the kind pictured in Fig. 3.5. The same level of demand will yield a decreasing amount of transaction, or, accordingly, it will be necessary to express ever-increasing demands to obtain the same transaction level ex ante.

An Example

Consider a market operated under proportional rationing, with one supplier and two demanders. At each step they express, respectively, a supply $\tilde{s}(t)$ and demands $\tilde{d}_1(t)$, $\tilde{d}_2(t)$. The rationing scheme is thus

$$d_i^*(t) = \tilde{d}_i(t) \times \min\left[1, \frac{\tilde{s}(t)}{\tilde{d}_1(t) + \tilde{d}_2(t)}\right], \qquad i = 1, 2,$$

$$s^*(t) = \min[\tilde{s}(t), \tilde{d}_1(t) + \tilde{d}_2(t)].$$

Assume that each trader knows the rationing rule and the demands and supplies of the others after they have been expressed. Moreover, he expects these to remain the same from period $t - 1$ to period t. The perceived rationing scheme at time t is thus for, say, the first demander

$$\phi_1^t(\tilde{d}_1) = \tilde{d}_1 \times \min\left[1, \frac{\tilde{s}(t-1)}{\tilde{d}_1 + \tilde{d}_2(t-1)}\right].$$

Now each trader has a "target transaction" resulting from unconstrained utility maximization, which is assumed to be the same in all periods. These target transactions are denoted by $\hat{d}_1$, $\hat{d}_2$, and $\hat{s}$. We shall assume that the supplier could serve each demander individually, but not both, that is,

$$\hat{d}_1 < \hat{s}, \qquad \hat{d}_2 < \hat{s}, \qquad \hat{s} < \hat{d}_1 + \hat{d}_2.$$

The supplier will not be constrained and thus will express his target transaction as effective supply:

$$\tilde{s}(t) = \hat{s}.$$

The demanders, however, will be rationed, and their effective demands will be given by

$$\phi_1^t(\tilde{d}_1(t)) = \hat{d}_1,$$
$$\phi_2^t(\tilde{d}_2(t)) = \hat{d}_2.$$

These equations yield

$$\tilde{d}_1(t) = \tilde{d}_2(t-1) \times \frac{\hat{d}_1}{\hat{s} - \hat{d}_1},$$

$$\tilde{d}_2(t) = \tilde{d}_1(t-1) \times \frac{\hat{d}_2}{\hat{s} - \hat{d}_2}.$$

Combining them, we obtain

$$\tilde{d}_1(t) = \tilde{d}_1(t-2) \times \frac{\hat{d}_1}{\hat{s} - \hat{d}_1} \times \frac{\hat{d}_2}{\hat{s} - \hat{d}_2},$$

a divergent sequence since $\hat{d}_1 + \hat{d}_2 > \hat{s}$. Of course, this phenomenon of "explosive overbidding" occurs because manipulation through demand does not entail any cost in this framework. If manipulation is costly, however, it is likely that there will be limits to its amount, as we shall see later. In any case, it is clear that a manipulable rationing scheme will lead to totally distorted and unreliable demands as soon as the expectation of rationing develops.

6. Estimation of the Perceived Rationing Scheme

Up to now, we have worked with a given perceived rationing scheme, whether deterministic or probabilistic. We shall now say a few words about its estimation. The estimation problem arises because, even though the agents generally know the form of the true rationing scheme, they do not know the demands and supplies that the other agents will express. Instead, each agent must estimate the perceived rationing scheme using the quantity signals he received previously in the same market. We shall see, by studying a few examples, how such an estimation can be made and the problem it poses, notably in the manipulable case.

Let us start with nonmanipulable schemes, where the estimation problem is easier. Indeed, if we assume the point of view of agent i, the true rationing scheme is fully defined by the maximum bound on his trades ($\bar{d}_i$ or $\bar{s}_i$). Since the agent knows this constraint after each trading round, the estimation problem reduces to forecasting the expected constraint in a period t, $\bar{d}_i^e(t)$ or $\bar{s}_i^e(t)$, from all previous information. That information includes, notably, the value of the same constraint in previous periods, $\bar{d}_i(\tau)$ or $\bar{s}_i(\tau)$ for $\tau < t$. For example, a "myopic" estimation will take the expected constraint in period t to be the same as the perceived constraint in the preceding period:

$$\bar{d}_i^e(t) = \bar{d}_i(t-1), \qquad \bar{s}_i^e(t) = \bar{s}_i(t-1).$$

In the manipulable case, things are more complex, since even if each agent assumes that the others will express the same demands and supplies as in the previous period, a multiplicity of rationing schemes may be consistent with the signals received by an agent. We shall now study a simple example of this phenomenon.

An Example

Let us consider again the proportional rationing scheme of the example in the previous section. For the demanders, it is written

$$d_i^*(t) = \tilde{d}_i(t) \times \min\left[1, \frac{\tilde{s}(t)}{\tilde{d}_1(t) + \tilde{d}_2(t)}\right], \qquad i = 1, 2.$$

Assume that all agents receive the same information after expressing their demands and supplies, that is, the rationing coefficient μ,

$$\mu(t) = \frac{\tilde{s}(t)}{\tilde{d}_1(t) + \tilde{d}_2(t)},$$

and that this is the only information they receive. Consider now demander

1 and assume that he believes that the other agents will express the same demand and supply in period t as in period $t - 1$ (myopic expectations). If he knew $\tilde{d}_2(t - 1)$ and $\tilde{s}(t - 1)$, his perceived rationing scheme in t would be, as we saw in Section 5,

$$\phi_1^t(\tilde{d}_1) = \tilde{d}_1 \times \min\left[1, \frac{\tilde{s}(t - 1)}{\tilde{d}_1 + \tilde{d}_2(t - 1)}\right].$$

However, all agent 1 knows is

$$\mu(t - 1) = \frac{\tilde{s}(t - 1)}{\tilde{d}_1(t - 1) + \tilde{d}_2(t - 1)},$$

and he must make guesses about $\tilde{s}(t - 1)$ and $\tilde{d}_2(t - 1)$. Let us thus take $\delta = \tilde{d}_2(t - 1)$ as a parameter. From the definition of $\mu(t - 1)$, we compute

$$\tilde{s}(t - 1) = \mu(t - 1)[\delta + \tilde{d}_1(t - 1)],$$

and the perceived rationing scheme in period t will be written

$$\phi_1^t(\tilde{d}_1) = \tilde{d}_1 \times \min\left[1, \frac{\mu(t - 1)[\delta + \tilde{d}_1(t - 1)]}{\delta + \tilde{d}_1}\right].$$

This yields a whole family of perceived rationing schemes indexed by the parameter δ (Fig. 3.6). They are all consistent with the experience in

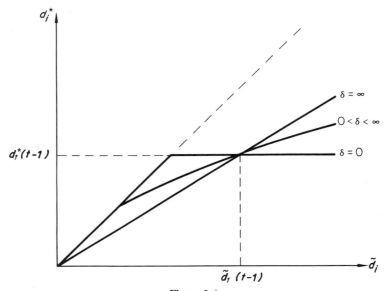

Figure 3.6

period $t - 1$, since they "go through" the point of coordinates $\tilde{d}_1(t - 1)$ and $d_1^*(t - 1)$. Indeed, we can easily check that

$$\phi_1^t(\tilde{d}_1(t - 1)) = \tilde{d}_1(t - 1) \times \min[1, \mu(t - 1)] = d_1^*(t - 1).$$

7. Extensions

The Extent of Manipulation

The preceding sections have shown us that whereas nonmanipulable rationing schemes lead agents to correctly reveal their desired transactions to the market, manipulability would lead, in the case of repeated rationing, to an explosive process of overbidding, which makes it a rather impractical object of study. This insight clearly induces us to enquire about the empirical extent of the different types of rationing schemes and to see whether this has some relation to the properties.

Actually we find that manipulable schemes, of which the most commonly found is the proportional rationing scheme, are generally used in cases where the market is assumed ex ante to clear and where only occasional disequilibria occur (for example, bonds and equities markets). In such a case, since expectations of rationing do not have time to develop, the ex ante perceived curve is the 45° line (at least up to the level of desired transaction) and the agents will express their "true" demand.

Consequently, in the rest of this book we shall mostly use rationing schemes that are nonmanipulable. Accordingly, quantity signals will take the form of maximum bounds on purchases and sales.

Manipulation through Transaction Costs

Although rationing schemes that are manipulable through demand are not encountered very often in reality, there is, as we mentioned in Chapter 2, the important category of schemes that are manipulable through transaction costs. In such cases, agents will not present inflated demands to the market, but there may still be a phenomenon of increasing manipulation, in the sense that the agents will tend over time to increase the amount of resources devoted to manipulating the rationing scheme. However, the fact that such costs enter negatively into the objective function prevents this phenomenon from being indefinitely divergent in this case. For example, if queueing is the allocation mechanism, agents will devote more and more time to arriving earlier in the queue. But this process will have a limit since the time that each agent can use to manipulate is bounded. In all such cases, one must expect the resulting allocations to be fairly inefficient because of the amount of resources devoted purely to manipulation.

8. Conclusions

In this chapter we treated the determination of effective demands and supplies as the choice of an optimal action aimed at yielding the best possible transaction in the presence of possible quantity rationing. This led us to develop the concept of a perceived rationing scheme that relates demands or supplies to the expected resulting transaction. We were then able to compare the effective demands and supplies obtained ($\bar{d_i}$ or $\bar{s_i}$) to those that would have been expressed ($\hat{d_i}$ or $\hat{s_i}$) had the market been expected to clear. We saw that we had to distinguish between manipulable and nonmanipulable rationing schemes and that the former gave rise to a perverse phenomenon of overbidding.

Besides being optimal actions from an individual agent's point of view, demands and supplies are also a "signal" to the market and to the other agents. They have often been interpreted as providing an indication, or even a measure, of disequilibrium on markets. The results in this chapter demonstrate that caution is required in using the effective demand signals for such measures. Indeed, we saw that, in the case of manipulation, overbidding would lead to inflated demands or supplies on the rationed side. Conversely, Appendix B shows us that in the presence of fixed transaction costs, the expectation of quantity constraints may lead an agent to express no demand or supply at all.

We saw, however, that in the nonmanipulable case without transaction costs (which is what we shall study mainly in what follows), the agent would express his target transaction ($\hat{d_i}$ or $\hat{s_i}$) as effective demand, thus ignoring the quantity constraint on the market considered. We shall pursue the inquiry further in the next chapter and shall see that even in this case the effective demand will generally be influenced by quantity signals on *other* markets. Such "spillover" effects will make effective demands and supplies different from the Walrasian ones.

4

Effective Demand and Spillover Effects

1. The Problem and Setting

Having described the effects of quantity signals on a single market, we shall now study the problem of their influence across markets, the so-called spillover effects. The existence of such effects is intuitively quite evident: an involuntarily unemployed worker will not maintain his Walrasian consumption demand, nor will a firm that is experiencing sales difficulties continue to employ the Walrasian profit-maximizing quantity of labor.

These ideas are clearly an integral part of Keynesian theory, where consumption is a function of realized income and employment is determined by sales on the goods market, but they are inconsistent with traditional microeconomic theory. We shall show in this chapter how introducing quantity signals into a multimarket scheme of effective demand formation will allow us to make sense of these spillover effects.

The Setting

Our framework for investigating the problem of effective demand is that of a decentralized monetary economy where markets are independently operated and are visited sequentially by the agents, who express their effective demands and supplies market by market. In this setting, the natural way to pose the problem is as a sequential dynamic programming problem (Bellman 1957): each agent has to make a sequence of decisions (the effective demands) in order to maximize the expected utility of the re-

41

sulting sequence of transactions. At each step, effective demand and expected transaction are related through a perceived rationing scheme.

After seeing in Chapter 3 the difficulties encountered in treating only one market, we can expect that a general treatment would be quite cumbersome. Since manipulation was shown to yield quite unreliable results, we shall restrict ourselves in this chapter to nonmanipulable schemes without transaction costs. Accordingly, the quantity signals considered will have the form of expected maximum bounds on trades. We shall first investigate the case where these expected constraints are deterministic and then study an example with stochastic constraints. In what follows we shall assume all prices given, as price determination will not be treated until the next chapter.

2. Deterministic Constraints: A Definition and Examples

Each agent coming to a particular market has already realized transactions on past markets and expects some constraints on current and future markets. If the expected constraints are deterministic, we can use the following definition of effective demand: it is the trade that maximizes the decision criterion of the agent, subject to the usual budget or technological constraints and also taking into account the given past transactions and the expected constraints on future markets.[1] The expected constraint on the current market is thus disregarded. Using an argument similar to that in Chapter 3, Section 4, it can be shown that this effective demand yields the best expected transaction for all values of the current expected constraint. We shall now look at two examples of the application of this definition, which will allow us to derive a consumption and employment function.

Past Transactions: The Consumption Function

A good example of an effective demand function that takes into account realized transactions is the Keynesian consumption function, which incorporates the quantity of labor households *actually* sell, not the quantity they offer to sell (Clower 1965). To illustrate how this modifies the Walrasian consumption function, let us take the example of a household with an endowment of labor l_0 and of money $\bar{m}$, and a utility function

---

[1] A more formalized definition using the notation of Part II is found in Appendix D.

$$U(c, l, m/p) = \alpha_1 \operatorname{Log} c + \alpha_2 \operatorname{Log}(m/p) + \alpha_3 \operatorname{Log}(l_0 - l),$$

where c is consumption, l, the sale of labor, m, final money balances, and p, the price of goods. Let w be the wage rate. The household's budget constraint is

$$pc + m = wl + \bar{m}.$$

The Walrasian consumption demand c^d and labor supply l^s are obtained by maximizing the utility function, subject to the budget constraint. Assuming that w is high enough for the labor supply to be positive, this yields

$$l^s = l_0 - \frac{\alpha_3}{\alpha_1 + \alpha_2 + \alpha_3} \frac{\bar{m} + wl_0}{w},$$

$$c^d = \frac{\alpha_1}{\alpha_1 + \alpha_2 + \alpha_3} \frac{\bar{m} + wl_0}{p}.$$

We may remark that these are functions only of price p, wage w, and initial endowments $\bar{m}$ and l_0. Now, let us say that the consumer visits the goods market after the labor market. His sale on the labor market l^* is now for him a given quantity that may differ from his Walrasian labor supply l^s. His preferred consumption will be given by the program

Maximize $\quad \alpha_1 \operatorname{Log} c + \alpha_2 \operatorname{Log}(m/p) + \alpha_3 \operatorname{Log}(l_0 - l) \quad$ s.t.

$$pc + m = wl + \bar{m},$$
$$l = l^*,$$

whose solution is

$$\tilde{c} = \frac{\alpha_1}{\alpha_1 + \alpha_2} \frac{\bar{m} + wl^*}{p},$$

In this solution we recognize a Keynesian-type consumption function, since $\tilde{c}$ now depends on the *realized* income of the household wl^*. Note that if $l^* = l^s$, then $\tilde{c} = c^d$: the Walrasian situation is thus a particular case, that corresponds to a situation in which labor sales equal the Walrasian labor supply. Figure 4.1 plots consumption demand versus real income wl^*/p. The propensity to consume out of real income is constant and is equal to $\alpha_1/(\alpha_1 + \alpha_2)$. We have stopped the curve at the Walrasian point, since under voluntary exchange the household's actual sales of labor will never go beyond the Walrasian supply in this example.

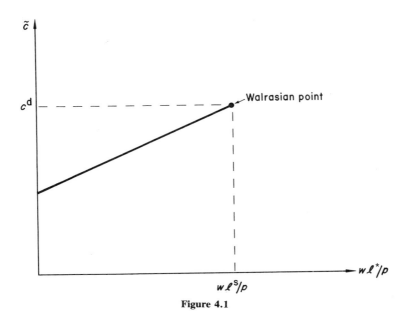

Figure 4.1

Future Constraints: The Employment Function

The effect of future constraints on effective demand can be well illustrated by studying the example of the employment function of the firm (Patinkin 1956, Barro and Grossman 1971).

Consider a firm with a production function $q = F(l)$. Let p and w be price and wage, respectively, and s the sales of the firm. The firm tries to maximize its profits $ps - wl$. Its Walrasian demand for labor l^d is the solution in l of the program

$$\text{Maximize} \quad ps - wl \quad \text{s.t.}$$

$$s \le q = F(l),$$

yielding $l^d = F'^{-1}(w/p)$.

Now assume that the firm forecasts a maximum level of sales $\bar{s}^e$. The program yielding the effective demand for labor must take into account this future constraint by adding to the above program the inequality $s \le \bar{s}^e$. The effective demand for labor $\tilde{l}$ is thus the solution in l of the program

$$\text{Maximize} \quad ps - wl \quad \text{s.t.}$$

$$s \le q = F(l),$$
$$s \le \bar{s}^e,$$

whose solution is

$$\tilde{l} = \min[F'^{-1}(w/p), F^{-1}(\bar{s}^e)].$$

There are thus two possible cases:

1. If the constraint $s \leq \bar{s}^e$ is not operative, the solution is the Walrasian employment demand function

$$\tilde{l} = F'^{-1}(w/p).$$

2. If, however, the constraint is operative, the optimal quantity of labor is determined by the output the firm expects to be able to sell, which corresponds to the "Keynesian" employment function

$$\tilde{l} = F^{-1}(\bar{s}^e).$$

3. Effective Demand with Stochastic Constraints

In Section 2 we assumed that expected future constraints are known with certainty. It is more realistic, however, to assume some uncertainty in expectations. We shall therefore study as an illustration the labor demand and output supply policies of a firm faced with uncertain demand for its product. An inevitable complication of the model is the introduction of inventories, as the possibility of storing unsold goods will be a key element in the firm's production plan. The resulting model will thus bear a strong resemblance to previous models in the inventory-theoretic literature.[2]

The Model

Let us consider a firm operating in a sequence of periods, indexed by t. Suppose it has a simple linear production function

$$q_t = l_t/\lambda,$$

where λ is a technical coefficient. In each period t the firm visits successively the labor and output markets. On the labor market, the wage is w and the firm presents a demand $\tilde{l}_t$. On the goods market, the price is p and the firm has a supply $\tilde{s}_t$. We shall study here how the firm makes its two basic decisions, $\tilde{l}_t$ and $\tilde{s}_t$.

We assume that the firm is always unconstrained on the labor market, so that labor purchase l_t will be equal to $\tilde{l}_t$. Thus production will be given by

$$q_t = l_t/\lambda = \tilde{l}_t/\lambda.$$

[2] See, notably, Arrow et al. (1958) and Bellman (1957).

Let I_t be the inventories at the outset of period t. The supply of output must be smaller than the sum of inventories and production:

$$\tilde{s}_t \le q_t + I_t.$$

Let ξ_t be the demand addressed to the firm. Sales s_t will be the minimum of supply and demand:

$$s_t = \min(\tilde{s}_t, \xi_t).$$

If some unsold goods are left, they are stored and depreciate at a given rate

$$I_{t+1} = \gamma(I_t + q_t - s_t), \qquad 0 \le \gamma \le 1.$$

Expected demands ξ_t are assumed to be independently distributed random variables with a common cumulative probability distribution $\psi(\xi_t)$. The decision problem of the firm is to choose the strategy $(\tilde{l}_t, \tilde{s}_t)$ that maximizes the sum of expected discounted profits:

$$\text{Maximize} \quad E\left(\sum_{t=0}^{\infty} \delta^t(ps_t - wl_t)\right), \qquad 0 \le \delta \le 1.$$

The Optimal Strategy

First, we can remark that the optimal supply strategy is

$$\tilde{s}_t = q_t + I_t.$$

Indeed, because the price is the same in subsequent periods and discount and depreciation are present, no speculative inventory will be held, and all available goods will be put for sale. Accordingly, sales in period t will be given by

$$s_t = \min(q_t + I_t, \xi_t).$$

Since $\tilde{l}_t = \lambda q_t$ and $\tilde{s}_t = q_t + I_t$, the firm's strategy will be fully determined by its production decisions, which can be shown to be (Appendix C)

$$q_t = \begin{cases} \hat{I} - I_t & \text{if} \quad I_t \le \hat{I}, \\ 0 & \text{if} \quad I_t \ge \hat{I}, \end{cases}$$

where the constant $\hat{I}$ is determined by

$$\psi(\hat{I}) = \frac{p - \lambda w}{p - \gamma\delta\lambda w}.$$

The firm thus has a "target supply" $\hat{I}$. Its strategy is to choose the levels of employment and production so as to make the total level of goods available before sale, that is, $q_t + I_t$, equal to $\hat{I}$. An intuitive way to characterize this target supply is to compute the ex ante probability of demand rationing associated with the target supply. This probability is simply equal to the probability that demand exceeds $\hat{I}$, that is,

$$\text{Prob}(\xi_t > \hat{I}) = 1 - \psi(\hat{I}) = \frac{\lambda w(1 - \gamma\delta)}{p - \lambda w\gamma\delta}.$$

Note that the firm chooses a lower probability, and thus a higher target supply, when γ, δ, or $p/\lambda w$ increases, that is, (i) if there is less depreciation, (ii) if there is less discounting, or (iii) if the ratio of price to production cost increases. All these results conform naturally to our intuition.

4. Stocks and Flows

The preceding section has drawn our attention to the importance of stocks and inventories in forming effective demands and supplies in a multiperiod system. We shall now study a few cases where stocks intervene specifically in our theory—cases which the preceding example has highlighted.

Stocks, Uncertainty, and Rationing

We saw above that, in the presence of uncertainties on trade possibilities, the firms might choose to hold inventories as "buffer stocks" against these uncertainties. In our example the producer faced with uncertain demand holds inventories of output. If these inventories are sufficiently large, random changes in demand are absorbed into stock variations. Rationing in the usual sense of the word occurs less frequently than in a stockless economy: in the example above the probability of demand being rationed was equal to $\lambda w(1 - \gamma\delta)/(p - w\gamma\delta)$. This probability decreases as γ (the "storability" of the good) increases.

Stocks and Spillover Effects

In a "pure-flow" model, the signals that influence effective demands are the expected constraints (themselves functions of past perceived constraints). In a stock-flow model, transactions, whether rationed or not, result in stock variations, and the level of stocks plays a role as a quantity signal. Stocks influence effective demands and supplies, as well as expected constraints, and thereby play a role in spillover effects.

To illustrate the role of stock and flow effects in these spillovers, let us consider the example of a firm that is experiencing a decline in its sales.

This firm may decide to reduce production and employment because it expects lower sales (the *flow* effect). But if the good is storable, the firm may also want to reduce production and employment in order to reduce the involuntary buildup of inventories (the *stock* effect). We may remark that in our example of the firm faced with uncertain demand (Section 3), only the stock effect was at work, since expected sales had an invariant probability distribution.

5. Spillover and Multiplier Effects

We have seen how quantity constraints on one market influence effective demands and supplies on the other markets. Via these spillover effects, an "initial" disturbance can be transmitted from market to market. A particularly interesting case occurs if the initial disturbance, after having been transmitted to other markets, returns to the initial market with the same sign, causing another round of changes (multiplication). A typical example of this phenomenon is described in the traditional Keynesian multiplier situation. Here an initial "shock" on the demand side (for example, an "autonomous" decrease in the demand for goods) leads to a reduction in employment via a decrease in the effective demand for labor. This in turn leads, via the consumption function, to an additional decrease in the demand for goods, which again launches reductions in employment and in transactions on the goods market. The initial shock has thus been "multiplied" through the spillover effects. Note that this phenomenon of "demand multiplier" occurs with excess supply on the two markets considered.

Generalizing this situation to a more disaggregated level, we can define *multiplier chains* along which a similar phenomenon may occur. Specifically, we define a *demand multiplier chain* as a set of k traders (i_1, . . . , i_k) and k goods (h_1, . . . , h_k) whose markets are all in excess supply such that

i_1 is $\begin{cases} \text{constrained in his supply of } h_1, \\ \text{unconstrained in his demand for } h_2. \end{cases}$

i_2 is $\begin{cases} \text{constrained in his supply of } h_2, \\ \text{unconstrained in his demand for } h_3. \end{cases}$

. . .

i_k is $\begin{cases} \text{constrained in his supply of } h_k, \\ \text{unconstrained in his demand for } h_1. \end{cases}$

In this case, an initial disturbance on the demand side of one of the k

markets is transmitted with the same sign to all markets in the chain[3] and returns ultimately to the initial market, launching a new wave of disturbances and thus yielding a multiplier effect. Generally, many different chains of this type may exist if there is excess supply on many markets. Demand multiplier effects may be observed especially in the case of general excess supply.

Symmetrically to this case, one may define *supply multiplier chains,* with all goods in the chain in excess demand and all traders' demands constrained. In such chains, shocks on the supply side of one market in the chain will be transmitted to the other markets with the same sign and will thereby give rise to multiplier effects.

6. Conclusions

In this chapter, we extended the analysis of the determination of effective demands to a multimarket framework. We showed how effective demands are influenced by quantity signals as well as by price signals, placing particular stress on spillover effects across markets, that is, on how quantity constraints on one market modify effective demands and supplies on the other markets. In particular, by employing a simple definition of effective demand with deterministic constraints, we were able to formalize the traditional Keynesian consumption and employment functions. The employment function was then extended, together with the firm's supply behavior, to a case with stochastic constraints. This led us to emphasize the particularly important role played by inventories in our theory: inventories are both quantity signals that give rise to spillover effects and buffer stocks that allow reduction of the probability of rationing in the face of random demand. Finally, we saw how the combination of spillover effects on many markets could give rise to multiplier effects very much akin to those of Keynesian theory, provided the excess demands on the markets concerned had the appropriate signs.

Of course, the introduction of quantity signals modifies not only the determination of demands and supplies but also the process of price determination. To this we turn in Chapter 5.

---

[3] We thus assume here that an involuntary reduction in sales of one good leads to a reduction in the effective demand for other goods. Although theoretically the opposite result is also possible, we shall take this assumption to be a description of the normal case.

5

Price Making

1. Price Setting in a Decentralized Economy

Conventional price theory relies basically on two elements. First, all agents take the price as a given parameter and assume that they can exchange whatever they want at this price. Second, the price itself is determined by the equality of supply and demand. Since it is assumed that no trade takes place until this equilibrium price has been found, the first assumption is verified ex post for all agents, making the theory self-consistent. As already noted, the theory applies in reality only to the few markets in which some agent institutionally acts as an auctioneer. For most truly decentralized markets, however, there is no such auctioneer: some of the traders themselves quote prices, and transactions are carried out before an equilibrium has been reached. We thus must develop a theory of the price-making process for such decentralized markets.

As we shall see, quantity signals are bound to play an important role in this process, even if the market considered is very "competitive." Indeed, it is the inability to sell as much as they want that leads suppliers to propose, or to accept from other agents, a lower price, and it is the inability to buy as much as they want that leads demanders to propose, or to accept, a higher price. As a result of this introduction of quantity signals into the price-making process, the theory will bear, at least formally, some resemblance, as Arrow (1959) has noted, to the traditional theories of monopolistic competition in the short run (Chamberlin 1933, Robinson 1933). This will be so even if the market is "atomistic": as we showed in

Chapter 1, the absence of quantity signals is characteristic only of equilibrium, not of the competitive structure of the market.

Besides the "auctioneer" type, one can generally observe in reality two types of decentralized price-making arrangements: (i) one side of the market (most often the sellers) quotes the prices and the other side consists of price takers, or (ii) prices result from bilateral bargaining between demanders and suppliers after an initial quotation from one or both sides. In what follows, we shall deliberately not study the second arrangement, which would immediately involve us in some unsolved problems in game theory, and shall thus concentrate on the first arrangement.

2. Price and Quantity Perceptions of Price Makers

Definition of a Market

Our representation of a market will thus have one side, (demanders or suppliers) consisting of price takers and the other side of price makers. In this setting, we immediately encounter a difficulty in the definition of a "good" or a "market." Indeed, as soon as there are many price makers on a market, there is no reason why they should quote the same prices, even if the goods they sell are physically identical. However, to be consistent with what has preceded, our theory must consider a good or a market as having only one price at a time.

We are thus naturally led in what follows to characterize a good not only by its physical and temporal characteristics but also by the agent who sets its price. With markets redefined in this way, each price maker is alone on his side of the market, and he thus appears formally as a monopolist. However, this does not imply anything as to his degree of monopoly power, since there may be competitors' markets where other agents sell or buy goods that are identical, or close substitutes.

Quantity Signals

In traditional equilibrium price theory, the perception of every agent is that the price is parametric and that any quantity he wants can be traded at that price. We shall now see that this perception about prices and quantities must be very substantially modified for price makers.

First, we saw in previous chapters that the assumption of unlimited trading at market price had to be given up. Indeed, each agent, whether a price taker or a price maker, perceives *after* trading a quantity constraint giving the maximum level of purchases and sales he could have realized. To be precise we denoted these perceived constraints (again omitting the market's index) by

$\bar{d}_i$: maximum possible purchase of agent i,

$\bar{s}_i$: maximum possible sale of agent i.

By our definition of a market, each price maker is the only one on his side (that is, he is the only seller or buyer of the good he prices). Thus, if i is a price maker, $\bar{d}_i$ will be equal to the total supply of the other agents on the market and $\bar{s}_i$ will be equal to the total demand of the other agents.

If we now consider a market *before* the price has been announced, the assumption of a parametric price does not make any sense for price makers, since they determine the price. Moreover, price makers perceive that their price decision will influence the demand or supply they will face. They will thus use the price to "manipulate" their quantity constraints on the markets they control. Let us now make this more formal through the concepts of perceived demand and supply curves.

Perceived Demand and Supply Curves

Assume first that agent i is a seller and call p_i the price he controls. Obviously there is a relation between the maximum quantity he expects to be able to sell, $\bar{s}_i^e$ (that is, the total demand he expects from the other agents), and the price p_i. The relation between the expected constraint and the price is the perceived demand curve (Bushaw and Clower 1957). Of course, it would be totally unrealistic to assume, as is too often done, that the agent knows the "true" demand curve. The perceived demand curve is an estimate of the "true" curve, which depends on a set of parameters θ_i (thus θ_i is usually a vector). These parameters themselves will be estimated using all observations available to the price maker, in a way we shall see below. The perceived demand curve is thus denoted by

$$\bar{s}_i^e = \bar{S}_i(p_i, \theta_i).$$

The function $\bar{S}_i$ is assumed to be nonincreasing in p_i. Note that the perceived *demand* curve is denoted by $\bar{S}_i$, because the demand of the other agents represents a constraint on the *sales* of the price maker.

Similarly, if the agent who controls the price is a buyer, he will have a perceived supply curve that relates the maximum quantity he expects to be able to buy, $\bar{d}_i^e$ (that is, the total supply he expects from the other agents), to the price p_i he sets. We shall denote this curve by

$$\bar{d}_i^e = \bar{D}_i(p_i, \theta_i).$$

The function $\bar{D}_i$ will be assumed to be nondecreasing in p_i. Again the perceived *supply* curve is denoted by $\bar{D}_i$, as the supply of the other agents represents a constraint on the *purchases* of the price maker.

3. Perceived Demand Curve and the Nature of Competition

From an economic and empirical point of view, we are very interested in the shape and slope of the perceived demand or supply curve. It is obvious that this depends crucially on the nature of competition prevailing for the good considered. We shall now briefly investigate this relationship, taking the case of a seller. (The case of a demander would be treated analogously.)

In general, a price maker i has competitors, that is, other agents selling goods that are physically identical to, or close substitutes for, the good sold by agent i. The "original" perceived demand curve should be a function of p_i, but also of prices p_j, where $j \in J$ is the index of agent i's competitors. Now, since what we are ultimately interested in is the effects of p_i on the demand for the good, we must determine how competitors' prices p_j are affected by the level of p_i. For that we use a *reaction function* (compare, for example, Friedman 1968)

$$p_j = \rho_j(p_i), \qquad j \in J,$$

which gives the expected price of competitor j as a function of agent i's own price choice. By inserting the values of p_j given by these reaction functions into the expression for the "original" curve, we obtain a perceived demand curve that is a function of p_i only. This way of constructing the curve shows us most clearly that the parameters of $\bar{S}_i$ and, notably, its elasticity depend crucially on the price reactions of the other agents, that is, on the nature of competition prevailing in the market considered. This we shall now illustrate by a simple example.

An Example

Assume that the expected demand (and actually its logarithm) has been estimated under the following loglinear form:

$$-a \, \mathrm{Log} \, p_i + \sum_{j \in J} b_j \, \mathrm{Log} \, p_j + c,$$

with $a - \Sigma_{j \in J} b_j > 0$.

We may consider as examples three particular cases of competitive structures:

- If agent i is a price leader, all other agents are assumed to fix the same price as i: $p_j = p_i$ for all $j \in J$. In this case, the elasticity of the perceived demand curve with respect to p_i will be $-a + \Sigma_j b_j$, which may be relatively low in absolute value.
- If a situation of monopolistic competition in the sense of Chamberlin (1933) prevails, competitors are assumed by agent i not to move their prices in response to changes in p_i. The elasticity of the perceived demand curve is then $-a$, which is higher in absolute value than in the previous case.
- If we have a situation of oligopolistic interdependence in the sense of Sweezy (1939), the reaction functions are the following: competitors match price decreases but do not move their prices in case of an increase. In such a case, the perceived demand curve has a *kink:* the elasticity is $-a$ for price increases, $-a + \Sigma_j b_j$ for price decreases.

4. Price Making

Let us assume for the moment that the parameters θ_i of the perceived demand curve are known. Then the choice of the price p_i will go along traditional lines; that is, the agent will maximize a criterion, subject to the usual constraints plus the additional constraint that sales should be smaller than the quantity given by the perceived demand curve.

For example, assume that a price-making firm i has a cost function $C_i(q_i)$, q_i being the level of output. The firm will choose its price so as to maximize profits, subject to the maximum expected sales given by the perceived demand curve $\bar{S}_i(p_i, \theta_i)$. Price p_i will be the solution of the program

$$\text{Maximize} \quad p_i s_i - C_i(q_i) \quad \text{s.t.}$$

$$s_i \leq q_i,$$
$$s_i \leq \bar{S}_i(p_i, \theta_i).$$

We may first remark that the price maker will always choose his price p_i and planned sales s_i so as to be "on" the perceived demand curve, that is, so as to satisfy the expected demand. Indeed, suppose on the contrary that the constraint is not effective, that is,

$$s_i < \bar{S}_i(p_i, \theta_i).$$

Then it is easy to see that the firm could increase its price and maintain the same sales without violating the constraint of the perceived demand curve, thus increasing its profit.

The price chosen will satisfy the usual condition that marginal cost equal marginal expected revenue. Note that the price so obtained will be a function of the parameters θ_i of the perceived demand curve. We shall now turn to the problem of estimating θ_i.

5. Estimation of the Perceived Demand Curve

The problem we shall address here is, how to estimate the parameters θ_i so as to make the perceived demand curve $\bar{S}_i(p_i, \theta_i)$ consistent with the signals the agent receives.

A First Approach

The signals received by the agent ex post include at least the observed price $\bar{p}_i$ and the perceived constraint $\bar{s}_i$ on the market. Now, it is quite natural to assume that these correspond to a point on the "true" demand curve, in which case the perceived demand curve, estimated ex post, should go through this point. This property of consistency with observations, first proposed by Bushaw and Clower (1957), will be denoted mathematically by

$$\bar{s}_i = \bar{S}_i(\bar{p}_i, \bar{\theta}_i),$$

where $\bar{\theta}_i$ is the estimated parameter. We can remark that usually this condition does not fully determine the parameters of the curve $\bar{S}_i$. Indeed, even though the position of the perceived demand curve is determined at the point observed, the elasticity, among other parameters, is not, so that even ex post a wide variety of perceived demand curves is consistent with the price and quantity constraint observed in a single period (Fig. 5.1).

Estimation and Time

When deriving the above consistency condition, we proceeded as though the price maker somehow knew the price and the perceived constraint of the current period before he had to construct the perceived demand curve of the same period. This is an acceptable procedure if we are interested in estimating the curve ex post or are studying an equilibrium concept where expected and realized values of the current variables are the same. (Such a concept of non-Walrasian equilibrium with price makers will be studied in Chapter 9.)

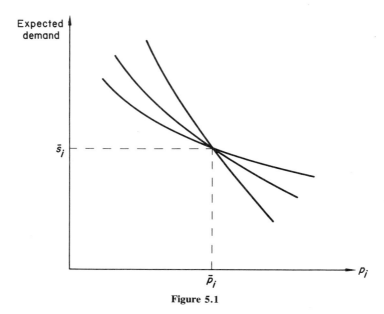

Figure 5.1

However, this consistency condition cannot be used as such if we want to describe a truly dynamic process of price making where expected and realized values of prices and quantities cannot be assumed *a priori* to be the same, even in the "short period." Indeed, in such a dynamic framework, things happen in the following sequence: the price maker estimates the perceived demand curve for the current period, then decides on his price, and only then observes his perceived constraint. This means that the current price and perceived constraint do not belong to the set of observations available for constructing the current perceived demand curve. So, the parameters of the current and future perceived demand curves will be estimated from the set of previous observations. This includes, notably, the stream of previous prices and perceived constraints, that is, if we consider a period t,

$$\{p_i(t-1), \bar{s}_i(t-1), p_i(t-2), \bar{s}_i(t-2), \ldots . p_i(t-T), \bar{s}_i(t-T), \ldots \}.$$

In such a dynamic framework, we may expect the estimation of the perceived demand curve to involve a good deal of uncertainty. In our framework this would mean that parameters would not be forecasted deterministically but rather would have a probability distribution, depending on all previous observations. Appendix C sketches an example of price determination with such stochastic perceived demand curves.

6. Conclusions

In this chapter we studied price determination in decentralized economies in which agents on one side of the market (buyers or sellers) quote the price. We saw that instead of considering a parametric price as in traditional theory, each price maker had to evaluate the effect of his price decision on his sales (or purchases) via a perceived demand (or supply) curve. Once this curve is known, the theory of price determination is very similar to the traditional theory of price making under monopolistic competition.

We saw, however, that a price maker faces uncertainty in estimating the parameters of the perceived demand and supply curves—their slope and position, for example. This is due to the fact that the "true" parameters of the demand curve depend on both the behavior of demanders and the price strategies of the price maker's competitors. The price maker has only imperfect information about these two elements—hence the uncertainty in the estimation process. As a result, the outcome of the price-making process gives rise to many more possibilities than the traditional determination through the equality between demand and supply. Much work is still needed to construct models of interaction between price making and the learning process of price makers. In any case, a most likely outcome is the realization, at least in the short run, of prices that are not those corresponding to a full Walrasian general equilibrium. In order to evaluate the consequences of such non-Walrasian prices at the level of the whole economy, we shall now study, in Part II, a number of non-Walrasian equilibrium concepts.

PART II

NON-WALRASIAN EQUILIBRIUM CONCEPTS

6

The General Framework

1. Introduction

In Part I we studied the microeconomic theory of individual agents and markets and showed how quantity signals, in addition to price signals, would be generated on markets that were out of equilibrium. We then saw how agents would take these signals into account in expressing their demands and supplies and eventually in making price decisions. On this basis it would be possible in principle to construct dynamic models of the whole economy by having the set of agents interacting in this way in a sequence of markets. However, the models obtained would be fairly cumbersome, as one would have to specify such things as the order in which agents visit markets, or short-run expectations formation, and our knowledge of such factors is not strong enough for the results to be at all robust.

Therefore, in Part II we shall follow another strategy, pioneered by Keynes (1936) himself, and study a number of *non-Walrasian equilibrium concepts*. These concepts will be non-Walrasian in that quantity signals will play as much of a role in the adjustments as price signals, while prices themselves, when they are flexible, will not necessarily adjust so as to equate supply and demand. Discrepancies between supply and demand will thus generally be present, at least on some markets. However, our concepts will involve equilibria in the second of the two senses indicated in the introduction to this book, that is, states where the price and quantity actions of the agents have been mutually adjusted.

The Structure of Non-Walrasian Equilibria

To be a little more precise, we shall construct different concepts of short-run equilibrium concerned with the equilibrium values of prices and quantities in a current period. A certain number of markets will be assumed to be operating during this current period. We shall say that there is equilibrium when the actions of all agents have adjusted to each other on these current markets. This does not preclude the future plans of the agents from being totally inconsistent, and thus the equilibria we shall study will be temporary equilibria.

We may remark that this structure of temporary non-Walrasian equilibrium corresponds exactly to the usual notion of Keynesian equilibrium. Indeed, in such an equilibrium the consumption, employment, and production plans of households, firms, and government have adjusted to each other on the current markets via income movements. However, their future plans are independent of each other and are usually inconsistent.

All the concepts studied will be applied to an exchange economy. They would clearly be generalizable to an economy with production (and Parts II and III do contain illustrations that describe productive activities). However, the exposition would have been burdened by the traditional problem of the objective function of the firm, which we did not want to tackle here.

Another simplifying assumption we shall use is that agents act simultaneously on all markets in the current period, whereas in reality agents visit markets sequentially. This assumption is absolutely standard in all multimarket equilibrium models and it will simplify the exposition, as we shall not have to formalize the ordering of the markets.

Before studying specific concepts in the next chapters, we shall outline their common "institutional" framework, that is, the structure of market organization.

2. A Monetary Economy

In the chapters that follow, we shall work in a monetary exchange economy.[1] There will be in the current period r markets, where money will be exchanged against r nonmonetary goods, assumed nonstorable. Money itself will be storable and will have simultaneously the functions of numeraire, medium of exchange, and store of value.

The agents in the economy will be n traders, indexed by $i = 1, \ldots, n$. At the outset of the period, trader i has an initial quantity of money $\bar{m}_i \geq 0$

---

[1] Non-Walrasian equilibrium concepts for a barter economy are sketched in Appendix N.

and an initial endowment of goods represented by a vector $\omega_i \in R_+^r$, with components $\omega_{ih} \geq 0$. After trading he will hold a quantity of money $m_i \geq 0$ and a final quantity of goods represented by a vector $x_i \in R_+^r$, with components $x_{ih} \geq 0$. This last vector will usually be called briefly the *consumption vector*, since the goods are nonstorable.

Let p_h be the monetary price of good h. We shall call z_{ih} the volume of agent i's net transaction of good h against money, the elementary transaction being the exchange of one unit of good h against p_h units of money. With the usual sign convention, z_{ih} is positive in the case of a purchase, negative for a sale; in terms of the notation in Chapter 1, $z_{ih} = d_{ih} - s_{ih}$. We shall call $z_i \in R^r$ the vector of these net transactions for agent i and $p \in R_+^r$ the vector of prices. The final holdings of goods and money, x_i and m_i, are related to these through the following relations:

$$x_i = \omega_i + z_i,$$
$$m_i = \bar{m}_i - pz_i.$$

Note that the second equation, describing the evolution of money holdings, replaces the traditional budget constraint.

3. Walrasian Equilibrium

We briefly describe here the Walrasian demands and equilibrium in this monetary economy in order to contrast them with the concepts that will follow. Assume that agent i ranks his consumption vector and money holdings according to a utility function $U_i(x_i, m_i)$.[2] Then his vector net demand function $z_i(p)$ is given by the solution in z_i of the following program:

Maximize $U_i(x_i, m_i)$ s.t.

$$x_i = \omega_i + z_i \geq 0,$$
$$m_i = \bar{m}_i - pz_i \geq 0.$$

We may remark that we have no demand for money, since there is no such thing as a market for money. The short-run Walrasian equilibrium prices are then given by the condition that net demands are zero on all markets:

$$\sum_{i=1}^{n} z_{ih}(p) = 0, \qquad h = 1, \ldots, r.$$

[2] m_i enters the utility function U_i as a store of value, in a manner that will be derived rigorously in Chapter 8.

4. Demands, Transactions,
and Rationing Schemes

Outside of Walrasian equilibria, we must distinguish carefully, as we have said, between demands and transactions. The net transaction of agent i on market h will be denoted by z_{ih}^* and his net effective demand by $\tilde{z}_{ih}$. Net transactions must balance as an identity on each market, that is,

$$\sum_{i=1}^{n} z_{ih}^* = 0 \qquad \text{for all} \quad h.$$

Effective demands, however, being only tentative trades, need not balance on a market, so that we may have

$$\sum_{i=1}^{n} \tilde{z}_{ih} \neq 0.$$

Each market has a particular organization through which possibly inconsistent demands and supplies are converted into consistent transactions. This organization can be represented by a rationing scheme, that is, a set of n functions relating the transaction of each of the n agents to the effective demands of all agents on the market considered. We shall now denote them by

$$z_{ih}^* = F_{ih}(\tilde{z}_{1h}, \dots, \tilde{z}_{nh}), \qquad i = 1, \dots, n.$$

The particular form of the rationing functions F_{ih} depends on the actual exchange process on market h; we saw a few examples in Chapter 2. The functions F_{ih} must have the fundamental property

$$\sum_{i=1}^{n} F_{ih}(\tilde{z}_{1h}, \dots, \tilde{z}_{nh}) = 0 \qquad \text{for all} \quad \tilde{z}_{1h}, \dots, \tilde{z}_{nh}.$$

In what follows, it will often be more convenient to rewrite these functions in the form

$$z_{ih}^* = F_{ih}(\tilde{z}_{ih}, \tilde{Z}_{ih}),$$

with

$$\tilde{Z}_{ih} = \{\tilde{z}_{1h}, \dots, \tilde{z}_{i-1,h}, \tilde{z}_{i+1,h}, \dots, \tilde{z}_{nh}\}.$$

$\tilde{Z}_{ih}$ is simply the set of all effective demands on market h, except agent i's. When we want a more compact notation, we shall represent all functions F_{ih} concerning an agent i as a vector function:

$$z_i^* = F_i(\tilde{z}_i, \tilde{Z}_i),$$

where z_i^* is the vector of transactions of agent i, $\tilde{z}_i$ his vector of effective demands, and $\tilde{Z}_i$ the set of all effective demand vectors except agent i's.

The representation of trading activities having been made precise, we shall now turn to a discussion of the properties of rationing schemes.

5. Some Properties of Rationing Schemes

We shall generally assume that the rationing function F_{ih} is continuous in its arguments and nondecreasing in $\tilde{z}_{ih}$. Besides this, it may also have the properties of voluntary exchange and efficiency, which we studied briefly in Chapter 2 and will restate now in terms of net demands and transactions.

Voluntary Exchange

We shall say that there is voluntary exchange if no agent is forced to trade more than he wants or to change the sign of his trade, which will be written

$$|z_{ih}^*| \leq |\tilde{z}_{ih}| \qquad \text{and} \qquad z_{ih}^* \cdot \tilde{z}_{ih} \geq 0 \qquad \text{for all} \quad i.$$

As we have indicated, we shall make this assumption throughout this book.[3] The property of voluntary exchange can be illustrated in an Edgeworth box diagram (Fig. 6.1) representing two agents A and B exchanging a good against money on a particular market. Quantities of the good are measured along the horizontal axis and quantities of money along the vertical axis. Point O represents the initial allocation; DC the budget line for the given price. Any point along DC represents a trade satisfying the budget constraint for both agents.

We saw in Chapter 3 that on a single market agents would express their unconstrained transactions as their effective demands. Thus point A corresponds to the net demand of trader A, point B to the net demand of trader B. In this figure, all trades that satisfy the assumption of voluntary exchange will be represented by points on the segment OA, such as E, for example.

Market Efficiency

The other property we want to emphasize is that of "efficiency." A rationing scheme will be efficient, or frictionless, if no mutually advantageous trade can be carried out from the transaction attained (and here we shall take an advantageous trade for an agent to be one that gets him closer to his net demand on that market). Looking again at Fig. 6.1, we see that the transaction represented by point E would not correspond to a

---

[3] See, however, Appendix F, where we treat a case of involuntary exchange.

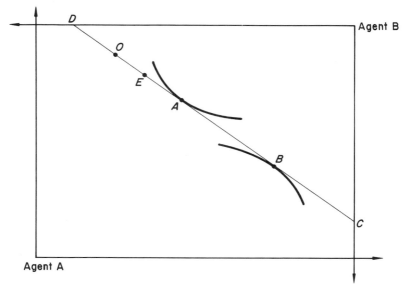

Figure 6.1

frictionless scheme because both traders would gain in exchanging more. However, all points on the segment AB would correspond to a frictionless scheme. Formally, a rationing scheme will be frictionless if and only if the discrepancy between net demand and transaction has the same sign for all agents,[4] that is,

$$(\tilde{z}_{ih} - z_{ih}^*)(\tilde{z}_{jh} - z_{jh}^*) \geq 0 \qquad \text{for all pairs} \quad i, j.$$

Indeed, if there were a pair i, j such that, for example, $\tilde{z}_{ih} - z_{ih}^* > 0$ and $\tilde{z}_{jh} - z_{jh}^* < 0$, agent j could sell some good h to agent i and both would get closer to their demands. It is easy to check that an equivalent set of conditions for a frictionless market is the following: if there is aggregate excess demand for a good h, no agent can have an unsatisfied supply of h; if there is an aggregate excess supply of h, no agent can have an unsatisfied demand for h. That is,

$$\sum_{j=1}^{n} \tilde{z}_{jh} \geq 0 \Rightarrow z_{ih}^* \leq \tilde{z}_{ih} \qquad \text{for all} \quad i,$$

$$\sum_{j=1}^{n} \tilde{z}_{jh} \leq 0 \Rightarrow z_{ih}^* \geq \tilde{z}_{ih} \qquad \text{for all} \quad i.$$

---

[4] This condition is very close to that used by Hahn and Negishi (1962) in their study of nontâtonnement processes.

We may note that together these imply

$$\sum_{j=1}^{n} \tilde{z}_{jh} = 0 \Rightarrow z_{ih}^{*} = \tilde{z}_{ih} \qquad \text{for all} \quad i.$$

The Short-Side Rule

Combining the two properties of voluntary exchange and market efficiency, we immediately obtain the "short-side rule," according to which agents on the short side will realize their effective demands:

$$\left(\sum_{j=1}^{n} \tilde{z}_{jh} \right) \cdot \tilde{z}_{ih} \leq 0 \Rightarrow z_{ih}^{*} = \tilde{z}_{ih}.$$

This assumption is certainly very convenient when constructing pedagogical models, and we shall thus use it a number of times in our applications. However, we saw in Chapter 2 that frictionless markets could not be assumed in general. The short-side rule assumption will thus not be made in our general study unless specifically indicated.

6. Manipulability

We have stressed the importance of the difference between manipulable and nonmanipulable rationing schemes. This difference is seen clearly in Fig. 6.2, where we have plotted the relation between the net transaction of an agent z_{ih}^{*} and his demand $\tilde{z}_{ih}$, the demands of the others, $\tilde{Z}_{ih}$, being held constant.

Intuitively, a scheme is nonmanipulable if each trader faces in his trades upper and lower bounds that he cannot manipulate. A scheme is manipulable if a trader can, even if he is rationed, increase his transaction by increasing his demand. Let us define mathematically the upper and lower bounds of the net demands that agent i can succeed in fulfilling on market h as a function of the net demands expressed by other individuals on the market, $\tilde{Z}_{ih}$ (cf. Fig. 6.2):

$$\bar{G}_{ih}(\tilde{Z}_{ih}) = \max\{\tilde{z}_{ih} \,|\, F_{ih}(\tilde{z}_{ih}, \tilde{Z}_{ih}) = \tilde{z}_{ih}\},$$
$$\underline{G}_{ih}(\tilde{Z}_{ih}) = \min\{\tilde{z}_{ih} \,|\, F_{ih}(\tilde{z}_{ih}, \tilde{Z}_{ih}) = \tilde{z}_{ih}\}.$$

Because of voluntary exchange, $F_{ih}(0, \tilde{Z}_{ih}) = 0$, and thus we have

$$\bar{G}_{ih}(\tilde{Z}_{ih}) \geq 0, \qquad \underline{G}_{ih}(\tilde{Z}_{ih}) \leq 0.$$

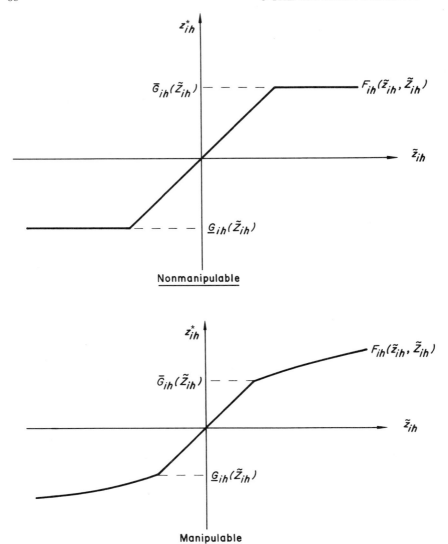

Figure 6.2

The rationing scheme on market h is *nonmanipulable* if we can write for all $i = 1, \ldots, n$

$$F_{ih}(\tilde{z}_{ih}, \tilde{Z}_{ih}) = \begin{cases} \min[\tilde{z}_{ih}, \bar{G}_{ih}(\tilde{Z}_{ih})] & \text{if } \tilde{z}_{ih} \geq 0, \\ \max[\tilde{z}_{ih}, \underline{G}_{ih}(\tilde{Z}_{ih})] & \text{if } \tilde{z}_{ih} \leq 0, \end{cases}$$

or, more compactly,[5]

$$F_{ih}(\bar{z}_{ih}, \tilde{Z}_{ih}) = \min\{\bar{G}_{ih}(\tilde{Z}_{ih}), \max[\underline{G}_{ih}(\tilde{Z}_{ih}), \bar{z}_{ih}]\}.$$

Otherwise the scheme is *manipulable*.

7. Perceived Constraints

In Chapter 3 we saw that the overbidding phenomenon associated with manipulation would generally lead to divergent demands, making any equilibrium analysis quite problematic. Therefore in what follows we shall be concerned mostly with nonmanipulable schemes.[6] These can be written

$$z_{ih}^* = \begin{cases} \min(\tilde{z}_{ih}, \bar{z}_{ih}) & \text{if } \tilde{z}_{ih} \geq 0, \\ \max(\tilde{z}_{ih}, \underline{z}_{ih}) & \text{if } \tilde{z}_{ih} \leq 0, \end{cases}$$

or, more compactly,

$$z_{ih}^* = \min[\bar{z}_{ih}, \max(\underline{z}_{ih}, \tilde{z}_{ih})],$$

where $\bar{z}_{ih}$ and $\underline{z}_{ih}$, the *perceived constraints* of agent i, are functions of the demands of the other agents:

$$\bar{z}_{ih} = \bar{G}_{ih}(\tilde{Z}_{ih}) \geq 0, \qquad \underline{z}_{ih} = \underline{G}_{ih}(\tilde{Z}_{ih}) \leq 0.[7]$$

Note that in the nonmanipulable case the functions $\bar{G}_{ih}(\tilde{Z}_{ih})$ and $\underline{G}_{ih}(\tilde{Z}_{ih})$ are continuous in their arguments if and only if the rationing function $F_{ih}(\bar{z}_{ih}, \tilde{Z}_{ih})$ is continuous in its arguments, since they are related by

$$F_{ih}(\bar{z}_{ih}, \tilde{Z}_{ih}) = \min\{\bar{G}_{ih}(\tilde{Z}_{ih}), \max[\underline{G}_{ih}(\tilde{Z}_{ih}), \bar{z}_{ih}]\}.$$

To shorten notation, in the remainder of Part II we shall work sometimes with the vectors of perceived constraints for an agent, $\bar{z}_i$ and $\underline{z}_i$, which will

---

[5] Under the assumption of voluntary exchange, which we make throughout the following chapters, the two ways of expressing nonmanipulability are equivalent, since $\bar{G}_{ih} \geq 0$ and $\underline{G}_{ih} \leq 0$. In the case in which involuntary exchange may be present, only the second expression can be used.

[6] See, however, Appendix I, where we extend a few concepts to the case in which manipulability may be present.

[7] We may thus remark that we take agent i's perceived constraints as being equal to the "objective" bounds on his trades, as defined in the previous section. A more general but more complicated formulation that allows for different perceptions in some cases is studied in Appendix J. It does not change the results obtained in the next chapters in any substantial way, however.

be denoted functionally by

$$\bar{z}_i = \bar{G}_i(\tilde{Z}_i), \qquad \underline{z}_i = \underline{G}_i(\tilde{Z}_i).$$

8. Conclusions

In this chapter we described the general framework in which we shall investigate the different concepts of non-Walrasian equilibrium. All of these will be concepts of temporary equilibrium that deal with how price and quantity variables adjust to each other on current markets, with given patterns of expectations about future variables for each agent. For obvious reasons of realism, the trading post structure was chosen to be a monetary one, with a market for the exchange of each nonmonetary good against money. All current markets were assumed to operate simultaneously.

On each market, the trading process was represented by a rationing scheme. We studied these, together with their possible properties, in a more formal way than in Chapter 2. We also described the structure of the quantity signals received by the agents in the trading process, focusing on the case of perceived constraints, which corresponds to nonmanipulable rationing schemes.

We are now ready to study various concepts of non-Walrasian equilibrium that differ in the degree of price flexibility assumed and that will be designated by the generic name K-equilibria. We shall start with a simple polar case, that of fixprice equilibria.

7

Fixprice Equilibria

1. Why Study Fixprice Equilibria?

We shall show in this chapter how quantity adjustments can lead to an economic equilibrium when prices are rigid.[1] The implicit assumption behind such an equilibrium is a complete inversion of the traditional relative speeds of adjustment between prices and quantities: quantities adjust before any movement in prices occurs, whereas in traditional models nothing happens until prices have fully adjusted. Of course, in reality markets display different degrees of imperfect price flexibility, and the assumption of total price rigidity has no more claim to realism than does the polar assumption of total price flexibility. The study of fixprice models will nonetheless be extremely rewarding for a number of reasons:

• First, some countries, notably socialist countries, do indeed have prices that are fixed by central decisions for a fairly long period of time. The model thus applies directly to these countries.
• Second, it is certainly the tradition of Keynesian theory and of many macroeconomic models to assume that quantities (that is, income in most Keynesian models) react faster than prices. This assumption is based on the observed sluggishness of some prices and wages—in particular, their

[1] Alternative formalizations of fixprice equilibria have been given, notably in the seminal paper by Drèze (1975). See also Younès (1975), Böhm and Levine (1979), and Heller and Starr (1979).

downward rigidity. Accordingly, fixprice models can be thought of as modeling the very short run.

• Finally, at a theoretical level, the study of fixprice equilibria will be a useful preliminary to the study of other non-Walrasian equilibrium concepts that include more price flexibility: we shall show that fixprice equilibria exist for all positive prices under fairly standard assumptions. These equilibria will thus form a very wide class, with a number of other equilibrium concepts as particular cases, as we shall see in subsequent chapters. It is therefore particularly important to make clear the structure of these fixprice equilibria—a task to which we shall now turn.

2. The Setting

Markets and Agents

We shall consider here a simple monetary exchange economy with r markets indexed by $h = 1, \ldots, r$. On each market the money price p_h is given. We shall denote by $p \in R_+^r$ the vector of these prices.

The agents are traders, indexed by $i = 1, \ldots, n$. Agent i has an initial endowment of goods $\omega_i \in R_+^r$ and money $\bar{m}_i \geq 0$. His utility function depends on his final holdings of goods x_i and of money m_i. This function will be denoted by $U_i(x_i, m_i)$. U_i may be interpreted as an indirect utility function, where the utility of money derives from its role as a store of value in a way that will be described in detail in Chapter 8. We shall assume throughout this chapter that U_i is continuous and concave in its arguments, with strict concavity in x_i. x_i and m_i are related to the basic trades z_i through the relations

$$x_i = \omega_i + z_i,$$
$$m_i = \bar{m}_i - pz_i.$$

Trading Processes

On each market exchange is organized in a specific way. The trading process on market h will be represented by a rationing scheme

$$z_{ih}^* = F_{ih}(\tilde{z}_{ih}, \tilde{Z}_{ih}), \qquad i = 1, \ldots, n.$$

We saw in Chapter 3 that we could not expect a reasonable equilibrium to obtain if these schemes were manipulable, as the rationed traders would overbid in a divergent fashion. We shall thus assume from the start that these schemes are nonmanipulable. Accordingly, each agent receives quantity signals $\bar{z}_{ih}$ and $\underline{z}_{ih}$, the perceived constraints, which are upper and lower bounds on his trades. These constraints are functions of the demands emitted by other agents on the market, and we denote them by

$$\bar{z}_{ih} = \bar{G}_{ih}(\tilde{Z}_{ih}),$$
$$\underline{z}_{ih} = \underline{G}_{ih}(\tilde{Z}_{ih}).$$

As we said in the previous chapter, we shall generally denote the rationing schemes and perceived constraints in a more compact way as vector functions:

$$z_i^* = F_i(\tilde{z}_i, \tilde{Z}_i),$$
$$\bar{z}_i = \bar{G}_i(\tilde{Z}_i),$$
$$\underline{z}_i = \underline{G}_i(\tilde{Z}_i).$$

Quantity Interrelations

The fixprice equilibrium concept will involve for each trader three types of quantities: effective demand vectors $(\tilde{z}_i)$, perceived constraints $(\bar{z}_i, \underline{z}_i)$, and transactions (z_i^*). Their equilibrium values may be thought of as the outcome of some process of "quantity tâtonnement," working simultaneously on all markets, which will be sketched below. We have already seen how transactions and perceived constraints were derived from effective demands:

$$z_i^* = F_i(\tilde{z}_i, \tilde{Z}_i),$$
$$\bar{z}_i = \bar{G}_i(\tilde{Z}_i),$$
$$\underline{z}_i = \underline{G}_i(\tilde{Z}_i).$$

It remains for us to study the determination of effective demands themselves, a task to which we now turn.

3. Effective Demands

We shall now see how a trader facing a price system p and quantity constraints $\underline{z}_i$ and $\bar{z}_i$ will express his demands. The framework here is different from that studied in Chapter 4; instead of trading sequentially, each agent, owing to the simultaneous nature of the adjustment process, has to announce a *vector* of effective demands. The general method will be the same, however, and we shall look for effective demands that yield the best possible transactions under the given constraints.

Optimal Transactions

With quantity signals $\tilde{z}_i$ and $\underline{z}_i$, trader i knows that his attainable transactions on each market will be limited to an interval

$$\underline{z}_{ih} \leq z_{ih} \leq \tilde{z}_{ih}.$$

Accordingly, the best transaction vector that agent i can attain, which we shall denote by $\zeta_i^*(p, \tilde{z}_i, \underline{z}_i)$, will be the solution in z_i of the program

Maximize $U_i(x_i, m_i)$ s.t.

$$\begin{aligned}
&x_i = \omega_i + z_i \geq 0, \\
&m_i = \bar{m}_i - pz_i \geq 0, \\
&\underline{z}_{ih} \leq z_{ih} \leq \tilde{z}_{ih}, \qquad h = 1, \ldots, r.
\end{aligned} \tag{A}$$

Note that since we assumed U_i strictly concave in x_i, there is a unique solution vector, and thus ζ_i^* is a function.

Effective Demands as Optimal Actions

In our system, however, agents do not choose their transactions directly. These are the consequences of the demands expressed by all traders. We thus want to determine an effective demand vector $\tilde{z}_i$ that will lead to the optimal transaction vector $\zeta_i^*(p, \tilde{z}_i, \underline{z}_i)$. If agent i expresses a demand $\tilde{z}_{ih}$ on market h, the resulting transaction will be

$$z_{ih}^* = \begin{cases} \min(\tilde{z}_{ih}, \tilde{z}_{ih}), & \tilde{z}_{ih} \geq 0, \\ \max(\tilde{z}_{ih}, \underline{z}_{ih}), & \tilde{z}_{ih} \leq 0, \end{cases}$$

or

$$z_{ih}^* = \min[\tilde{z}_{ih}, \max(\tilde{z}_{ih}, \underline{z}_{ih})].$$

So the effective demand vector that yields the best possible transactions is a solution in $\tilde{z}_i$ of the program

Maximize $U_i(x_i, m_i)$ s.t.

$$\begin{aligned}
&x_i = \omega_i + z_i \geq 0, \\
&m_i = \bar{m}_i - pz_i \geq 0, \\
&z_{ih} = \min[\tilde{z}_{ih}, \max(\tilde{z}_{ih}, \underline{z}_{ih})], \qquad h = 1, \ldots, r.
\end{aligned} \tag{B}$$

We shall call $\Delta_i(p, \tilde{z}_i, \underline{z}_i)$ the set of solution vectors $\tilde{z}_i$ to the above program. Unfortunately, this set may contain more than one element, even when the utility function is strictly concave and the optimal transaction ζ_i^*

unique. Indeed, the set Δ_i consists of all vectors leading to the optimal transaction ζ_i^*, that is, of all vectors $\tilde{z}_i$ such that

$$\min[\tilde{z}_i, \max(\tilde{z}_i, \underline{z}_i)] = \zeta_i^*(p, \bar{z}_i, \underline{z}_i).$$

We remark that ζ_i^* belongs to Δ_i, but many other vectors generally do. In what follows, rather than working with an effective demand correspondence, we shall make a selection in the solution set and define an effective demand function, which will be easier to handle.[2]

An Effective Demand Function

Confronted with the similar problem of multivaluedness of effective demand in Chapter 3, we saw that the problem could be solved by ignoring the quantity constraint on the market considered. As we shall see, this method will also work here and, following the same idea, we shall define effective demand on market h as the utility-maximizing trade, taking into account quantity constraints on the other markets.

Formally, the effective demand function on market h, which we shall denote functionally by $\tilde{\zeta}_{ih}(p, \bar{z}_i, \underline{z}_i)$, will be the solution in z_{ih} of the program

$$\text{Maximize} \quad U_i(x_i, m_i) \quad \text{s.t.}$$

$$\begin{aligned}
x_i &= \omega_i + z_i \geq 0, \\
m_i &= \bar{m}_i - p z_i \geq 0, \\
\underline{z}_{ik} &\leq z_{ik} \leq \bar{z}_{ik}, \qquad k \neq h.
\end{aligned} \qquad \text{(C)}$$

We remark that this effective demand function integrates the spillover effects from all other markets. Repeating the above operation for all markets, we obtain a vector of effective demands, denoted by $\tilde{\zeta}_i(p, \bar{z}_i, \underline{z}_i)$. Of course, one must verify that this effective demand function belongs to the correspondence Δ_i, which is done by the following proposition.

Proposition 7.1 *Assume that U_i is strictly concave in x_i; then*

$$\tilde{\zeta}_i(p, \bar{z}_i, \underline{z}_i) \in \Delta_i(p, \bar{z}_i, \underline{z}_i).$$

Proof The proof is found in Appendix E, where we prove the equivalent statement that $\tilde{\zeta}_i$ leads to the optimal transaction ζ_i^*, that is,

$$\min\{\bar{z}_i, \max[\underline{z}_i, \tilde{\zeta}_i(p, \bar{z}_i, \underline{z}_i)]\} = \zeta_i^*(p, \bar{z}_i, \underline{z}_i).$$

---

[2] Appendix G develops the concept of fixprice equilibrium using an effective demand correspondence.

Effective Demand as
Revealing Constrained Agents

For reasons that will become clear subsequently, we would like effective demand to "reveal" an agent's being quantity constrained, in the sense that effective demand by agent i on market h should be different from the associated transaction ζ_{ih}^* whenever the agent is constrained on market h. To be precise, we shall say that agent i is constrained on market h if his maximum expected utility (as given by programs (A) or (B) above) would be increased by suppressing all constraints on market h ($\bar{z}_{ih}$ and $\underline{z}_{ih}$).

We can further specialize the definition by making precise which constraint is binding. Thus we shall say that $\bar{z}_{ih}$ is binding if i can be made better off by deleting the constraint $\bar{z}_{ih}$. Symmetrically, $\underline{z}_{ih}$ is binding if i can be made better off by deleting the constraint $\underline{z}_{ih}$. Intuitively, we see that agent i would like to purchase more when $\bar{z}_{ih}$ is binding and to sell more when $\underline{z}_{ih}$ is binding. Now our effective demand function will reveal an agent's being constrained in the sense that

$$\bar{z}_{ih} \quad \text{is binding} \iff \tilde{\zeta}_{ih}(p, \bar{z}_i, \underline{z}_i) > \bar{z}_{ih} = \zeta_{ih}^*(p, \bar{z}_i, \underline{z}_i),$$
$$\underline{z}_{ih} \quad \text{is binding} \iff \tilde{\zeta}_{ih}(p, \bar{z}_i, \underline{z}_i) < \underline{z}_{ih} = \zeta_{ih}^*(p, \bar{z}_i, \underline{z}_i).$$

The importance of this property will be seen in Section 5. We are now ready to proceed to the definition of a fixprice equilibrium.

4. Fixprice Equilibrium: Definition
and Example

The data in our framework are a set of prices p and the rationing schemes on all markets. We can now give the following definition:

Definition *A fixprice equilibrium, or K-equilibrium, associated with a price system p and a set of rationing schemes represented by F_i, $i = 1, \ldots, n$,[3] is a set of effective demand vectors $\tilde{z}_i$, transactions z_i^*, and quantity constraints $\bar{z}_i$, $\underline{z}_i$ such that*

$$\tilde{z}_i = \tilde{\zeta}_i(p, \bar{z}_i, \underline{z}_i) \qquad \text{for all} \quad i, \tag{1}$$

$$z_i^* = F_i(\tilde{z}_i, \tilde{Z}_i) \qquad \text{for all} \quad i, \tag{2}$$

$$\bar{z}_i = \bar{G}_i(\tilde{Z}_i) \qquad \text{for all} \quad i,$$
$$\underline{z}_i = \underline{G}_i(\tilde{Z}_i) \qquad \text{for all} \quad i. \tag{3}$$

---

[3] Functions $\bar{G}_i$ and $\underline{G}_i$ are determined from the F_i, as seen in Chapter 6.

The intuitive idea behind our equilibrium concept is that the quantity constraints from which agents construct their effective demands are the ones that will actually be generated by the trading process. All agents thus have a correct perception of quantity signals at equilibrium.

A K-equilibrium may be viewed intuitively as a fixed point of the following tâtonnement process in quantities: Assume that all agents have expressed effective demands on all markets $\tilde{z}_i, i = 1, \ldots, n$. From these we obtain the perceived constraints, given by the formulas

$$\bar{z}_i = \bar{G}_i(\tilde{Z}_i), \qquad \underline{z}_i = \underline{G}_i(\tilde{Z}_i).$$

On the basis of these perceived constraints, the agents will determine a new set of effective demands $\tilde{\zeta}_i(p, \bar{z}_i, \underline{z}_i), i = 1, \ldots, n$, and so on. A K-equilibrium is reached when these new effective demands are the same as the former ones.

An Example

Let us take the traditional Edgeworth box example (Fig. 7.1), representing a single market where agents A and B exchange a good (measured horizontally) against money (measured vertically). Point O corresponds

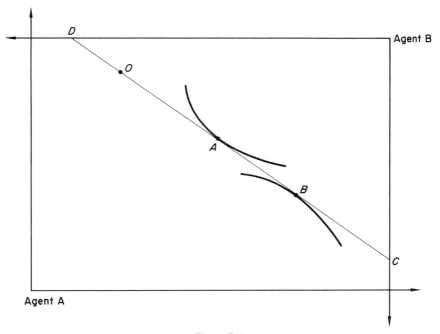

Figure 7.1

to the initial endowments; points A and B are the tangency points of the indifference curves with the price line.

Measuring trades along the line OC, we see that A will demand a quantity OA and that B will supply a quantity OB. They will exchange the minimum of these, that is, OA, leaving B rationed and A unrationed. Correspondingly, B will perceive a binding constraint OA, A a nonbinding constraint OB.

5. Properties of Fixprice Equilibria

A fixprice equilibrium yields a set of transactions z_i^* for each agent. Being determined through rationing schemes, these transactions are by construction consistent on each market, that is,

$$\sum_{i=1}^{n} z_{ih}^* = 0, \qquad h = 1, \ldots, r.$$

We shall see that they have, in addition, a number of efficiency properties that derive more or less directly from the way we constructed effective demands. We shall study these properties now.

Individual Rationality and the Nash Property

A first natural property to ask for is that the transactions should be the best, taking into account all signals received by the agent; that is, transactions should be equal to the optimal vector $\zeta_i^*(p, \bar{z}_i, \underline{z}_i)$. Since effective demands were constructed so as to yield the optimal transactions, we must expect such a property to hold trivially. Indeed:

Proposition 7.2 *At a K-equilibrium, we have*

$$z_i^* = \zeta_i^*(p, \bar{z}_i, \underline{z}_i).$$

Proof This follows directly from Proposition 7.1 above, where we proved that

$$\zeta_i^*(p, \bar{z}_i, \underline{z}_i) = \min\{\bar{z}_i, \max[\underline{z}_i, \tilde{\zeta}_i(p, \bar{z}_i, \underline{z}_i)]\},$$

and from the fact that

$$z_i^* = \min[\bar{z}_i, \max(\underline{z}_i, \tilde{z}_i)]. \qquad\qquad \text{Q.E.D.}$$

If we next consider the property of individual rationality from the point of view of effective demands, we see that K-equilibria are Nash equilibria in the effective demands.[4] Indeed, we constructed the effective demands so that they would be the utility-maximizing ones, given the signals received $(p, \bar{z}_i, \underline{z}_i)$. The perceived constraints $\bar{z}_i$ and $\underline{z}_i$ are themselves functions of the other agents' effective demands $\tilde{Z}_i$, and the effective demands have the Nash property.

Market-by-Market Efficiency

The properties just described are not strong enough, however, since, for example, a state where each agent expresses a zero effective demand and where thus no trade occurs is a Nash equilibrium in effective demands and is individually rational. One wants some additional conditions that eliminate such trivial equilibria, and such a condition has been proposed by Drèze (1975). Accordingly, we shall say that an equilibrium is *D-efficient* on market h if there are not constrained demanders and constrained sellers simultaneously on this market. The intuitive idea behind this is that a constrained demander and a constrained seller would manage to meet and trade until at least one of them is no longer constrained. Thus, the idea of a frictionless market is implicit in this formulation. We shall show that in K-equilibria the property of D-efficiency indeed prevails on all frictionless markets.

Proposition 7.3 *If the rationing scheme on market h is frictionless, then the K-equilibrium allocation is D-efficient on market h.*

Proof Since the rationing scheme is frictionless, at least for traders on the short side $z_{ih}^{*} = \tilde{z}_{ih}$. But since the effective demand function has the property of revealing binding constraints, this means that traders on the short side are unconstrained. Q.E.D.

This and the preceding proposition allow us to compare our concept of K-equilibrium with another concept of fixprice equilibrium developed by Drèze (1975).[5] A Drèze equilibrium is defined as a set of transactions and quantity constraints (analogous to the z_i^{*} and $\bar{z}_i$, $\underline{z}_i$, respectively) that fulfills the following properties: (i) transactions balance on each market, (ii) transactions are the utility-maximizing ones, taking all constraints into account, and (iii) one does not find rationed demanders and rationed suppliers simultaneously on any market. Propositions 7.2 and 7.3 show that if

---

[4] A Nash equilibrium is an equilibrium at which each agent's actions are best, taking the actions of the others as given. Such a concept was used in fixprice theory by Böhm and Levine (1979) and by Heller and Starr (1979).

[5] See also Grandmont and Laroque (1976) for an extension of this concept. Note that the original concept by Drèze allows, in addition, prices to be flexible within given bounds.

rationing schemes on *all* markets are frictionless, K-equilibria as defined above are also Drèze equilibria.

Our concept of K-equilibrium, however, is also valid for rationing schemes that are not frictionless. In that case the criterion of D-efficiency is not adequate, and more complex properties have to be used (Appendix H). We shall now show that these properties of market-by-market efficiency are related directly to the assumption that effective demands "reveal" the binding constraints.

The Importance of Revealing Binding Constraints

In defining effective demand, we insisted on the need for any binding constraint to be signaled by an effective demand of larger magnitude. We did this because, otherwise, very unsatisfactory equilibria might occur as a result of the failure of advantageous trade possibilities to be communicated between the demand and supply sides of each market.

To show this, imagine that we waive the "constraint revelation" condition and replace our effective demand function $\tilde{\zeta}_i$ with one that is still individually rational but that does not reveal when a constraint is binding, for example, $\zeta_i^*(p, \bar{z}_i, \underline{z}_i)$. In the original definition of fixprice equilibrium, condition (1) would be replaced by

$$\tilde{z}_i = \zeta_i^*(p, \bar{z}_i, \underline{z}_i). \tag{1'}$$

Note that the resulting equilibria would still be Nash equilibria. However, most of them would be very unsatisfactory. For example, the zero-trade point would be an equilibrium under this definition. The problem is well illustrated by the Edgeworth box example in Fig. 7.2.

Consider a point E between O and A, and assume that the two traders emit a demand and supply, respectively, both equal to OE. Consequently they transact an amount OE, both also perceiving a constraint equal to OE. The reader can verify that this is an equilibrium within the new definition. It has an unfortunate property: both traders would be better off by trading more, since both of them feel binding constraints, but since neither signals to the other his desire to trade more, both remain "stuck" at this too low level of trade.

In order for an acceptable equilibrium to be reached, all desires for additional trades must somehow be signaled to the other side. Here signaling takes place via effective demands and supplies. Thus, whenever an agent faces a binding constraint on a market, his effective demand and supply must exceed his expected transaction.[6] We saw above that our effective

---

[6] Actually, only one party to a mutually advantageous trade need signal his desire for further trade.

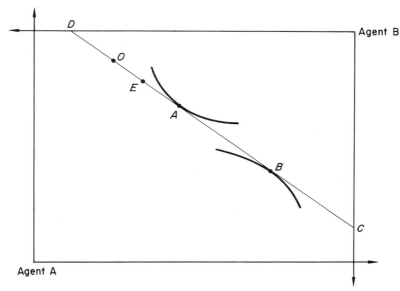

Figure 7.2

demand function satisfied this requirement, hence the market-by-market efficiency properties of K-equilibria.

6. An Existence Theorem

We suggested above that fixprice equilibria form a very wide class. Indeed, we shall now show that for every set of positive prices and every set of rationing schemes F_{ih}, $i = 1, \ldots, n$, $h = 1, \ldots, r$ (which we shall denote simply by F), fixprice equilibria exist under very mild and standard assumptions. More precisely, we shall prove the following theorem.

Theorem 7.1 *Let us assume:*

(a) $p \gg 0$.
(b) *All functions* $U_i(x_i, m_i)$ *are continuous and concave in their arguments, with strict concavity in* x_i.
(c) *All rationing schemes are continuous and nonmanipulable.*

Then a K-equilibrium corresponding to p and F exists.

Proof Consider the following mapping:

$$\{\bar{z}_i, z_i^*, \tilde{z}_i, \underline{z}_i \,|\, i = 1, \ldots, n\} \to \{\tilde{\zeta}_i, F_i, \bar{G}_i, \underline{G}_i \,|\, i = 1, \ldots, n\};$$

that is, from an initial set of effective demands $\tilde{z}_i$, transactions z_i^*, and perceived constraints $\bar{z}_i$ and $\underline{z}_i$ for all agents $i = 1, \ldots, n$, we derive a new set of effective demands $\zeta_i(p, \bar{z}_i, \underline{z}_i)$, transactions $F_i(\tilde{z}_i, \tilde{Z}_i)$, and perceived constraints $\bar{G}_i(\tilde{Z}_i)$ and $\underline{G}_i(\tilde{Z}_i)$. This mapping is a function, because of the strict concavity of U_i in x_i, and is continuous, as may easily be checked. Effective demands are bounded:

$$-\omega_{ih} \le \tilde{z}_{ih} \le (p\omega_i + \bar{m}_i)/p_h,$$

and so are transactions and perceived constraints. The restriction of the mapping to the corresponding compact set is a continuous function from a compact convex set into itself. By Brouwer's theorem, it thus has a fixed point, which yields the equilibrium effective demands, transactions, and perceived constraints as they satisfy, by construction, conditions (1–3) of equilibrium.   Q.E D.

7. Conclusions

In this chapter we studied the concept of fixprice equilibrium and some of its properties. Two building blocks, the processes of transaction and quantity signal formation, had already been defined in Chapter 6. We have now defined an effective demand vector function, which has the notable property of yielding the best transaction vector for any set of prices and quantity constraints.

In a fixprice equilibrium, each agent has a correct perception of the quantity constraints he faces. As a result, the transactions he realizes are the best possible, given these constraints. Also, from the way the effective demand function was constructed, whenever an agent is constrained on a market, his effective demand exceeds his transaction. Finally, we showed that at a fixprice equilibrium it is impossible for agents to obtain further gains from trade on a single market, given the transaction structure. (The possibility of advantageous trades that involve more than one market will be examined in Chapter 10.)

Turning to the problem of existence, we saw that fixprice equilibria existed for all positive prices and all continuous nonmanipulable rationing schemes under very standard assumptions on the objective functions. This therefore defines a very wide class of equilibria and will give us a useful starting point for the study of other non-Walrasian equilibrium concepts, where more price flexibility is allowed (Chapter 9). Before that, we shall clarify an important point that was dealt with only implicitly in this chapter: the role of expectations in the formation of current equilibrium.

8

Expectations and Temporary Fixprice Equilibria

1. Introduction

In Chapter 7 we studied the nature of the quantity adjustments that would take place in a given period, the "short period," in a manner analogous to the simple Keynesian multiplier models, where only current variables are taken into account. However, the period considered is not isolated in time; it has a past and a future, and we shall now see how these influence current trading.

The legacy of the past comprises stocks of accumulated physical and financial assets. The future is represented by expectations about trading opportunities, themselves functions of past observations. These expectations are very important elements in Keynesian macroeconomic theory, where they are embedded, at least implicitly, in the schedule of the marginal efficiency of capital and the demand function for money.

A key to the integration of expectations into the theory is to show how they affect the valuation of current stocks, since stocks are the physical link between successive periods, and their valuation will transform expectations about future trading into desires to exchange current goods. (An example of this is the Keynesian marginal efficiency of capital schedule, through which expectations about the future state of demand lead to current investment demand.) In the following sections we shall study how the valuation of stocks depends on expected trading opportunities and how these influence the current equilibrium. This will be done first by means of a very simple example, then in the framework of a general two-period exchange economy. To simplify the exposition, we shall take money as the only store of value, but the method would be valid for other stocks as well.

2. An Example

We shall show here how expectations about future prices and quantity constraints influence the valuation of a household's money holdings. In particular, we shall see that money will be more "valuable" to an agent expecting to be unemployed than to an agent expecting to be employed. Conversely, the expectation of constraints on purchases will reduce the value of savings. We shall now make all these interdependences precise by introducing a formal model.

Utility and Expectations

The household that we are considering makes plans covering two periods, current and future. Variables in the future period will have a superindex e (denoting "expected"). The household's endowments of labor are l_0 and l_0^e in the current and future periods, respectively. It has a utility function over current and future consumption $W(c, c^e)$, which we assume increasing in c and c^e. Let p and w be the current price and wage. We assume that the household expects for the future period a price p^e, wage w^e, and quantity constraints $\bar{l}^e$ and $\bar{c}^e$ on the labor and goods markets, respectively.

The Indirect Utility of Money

Assuming that the household has transferred a quantity of money m to the second period, let us determine the level of consumption this will allow. Consumption in the second period c^e is given by the following program, where c is given:

$$\text{Maximize} \quad W(c, c^e) \qquad \text{s.t.}$$

$$p^e c^e \leq w^e l^e + m,$$
$$l^e \leq l_0^e,$$
$$l^e \leq \bar{l}^e,$$
$$c^e \leq \bar{c}^e.$$

Since the utility function is increasing in c^e, the optimal consumption in the second period will be the maximum attainable, that is,

$$c^e = \min\{\bar{c}^e, [m + w^e \min(\bar{l}^e, l_0^e)]/p^e\},$$

and the corresponding expected utility U^e will be defined by

$$U^e(c, m) = W(c, \min\{\bar{c}^e, [m + w^e \min(\bar{l}^e, l_0^e)]/p^e\}).$$

This function depends on current consumption c and money holdings m, but also on price and quantity expectations p^e, w^e, $\bar{c}^e$, $\bar{l}^e$. Notice that the indirect utility of money will decrease if the expected constraint on the goods market $\bar{c}^e$ becomes more severe. The marginal indirect utility of money will even become zero for

$$[m + w^e \min(\bar{l}^e, l_0^e)]/p^e \geq \bar{c}^e.$$

Conversely, and provided we assume decreasing marginal utility of second-period consumption, expectations of increased labor rationing in the future will increase the marginal indirect utility of money.

3. The General Model

We now return to the general exchange economy considered in Chapters 6 and 7. A problem left unsolved there was why money, which we assume to have no intrinsic utility, entered the utility function of traders together with current consumption x_i. We shall now assume explicitly that each agent derives utility directly only from his intertemporal stream of consumptions. The "utility" of money will derive from the utility of future trades made possible by the money holdings; accordingly we shall construct the utility function via a multiperiod optimization program taking expectations about future prices and quantities into account. Our construction will thus provide a formalization of the role of money as a store of value in situations where markets do not clear. The current equilibrium will have the character of a temporary equilibrium, since it depends on future expectations.

Markets and Agents

We will consider a monetary exchange economy with n traders and r current markets, as in the previous chapters. Each trader has a two-period horizon and plans for the current and future periods.[1] Variables for the future period will be indexed by e (indicating "expected").

---

[1] The method that, for expositional simplicity, we present here for two periods could easily be extended to any greater finite number. We may also note that, even if all traders considered here plan only for a finite number of periods, economic activity does not necessarily stop after these periods. As in models with "generations" (Samuelson, 1958), other traders may arise later whose horizon will extend further.

Trader i has vectors of endowments ω_i and ω_i^e in the first and second periods, respectively. His consumption vectors are denoted by x_i and x_i^e. They are related to his trades z_i and z_i^e by the following relations:

$$x_i = \omega_i + z_i \geq 0,$$
$$x_i^e = \omega_i^e + z_i^e \geq 0.$$

At the outset of the first period, the agent has an initial quantity of money $\bar{m}_i$. He transfers to the second period a quantity m_i given by

$$m_i = \bar{m}_i - pz_i \geq 0.$$

Planned transactions in the second period will have to satisfy

$$p^e z_i^e \leq m_i.$$

We assume that each agent has a utility function over his current and future consumptions $W_i(x_i, x_i^e)$, which is continuous and strictly concave in its arguments.

Expectations

As we indicated above, a most important element in the valuation of money (and of stocks in general) is the set of expectations formed by agents about future trading opportunities. For a price taker,[2] expected trading opportunities in the second period will be fully described by the vectors of expected prices and quantity constraints, which we shall denote by[3]

$$\sigma_i^e = \{p^e, \bar{z}_i^e, \underline{z}_i^e\}.$$

These expectations are based on the available information, that is, the stream of past and present price–quantity signals. Since everything that has happened before the current period is past and assumed given, we shall make explicit in the formalization only the dependence of σ_i^e on current signals $\sigma_i = \{p, \bar{z}_i, \underline{z}_i\}$. Accordingly we shall represent expectations by a function

$$\sigma_i^e = \psi_i(\sigma_i).$$

If expectations are stochastic, this function will be replaced with a conditional probability distribution, as we shall see later.

---

[2] The formalization for a price maker is more complex and is treated in Appendix K, which should be read preferably after Chapter 9.

[3] To simplify notation, we do not stress the dependence of the expected price p^e on the agent.

4. The Indirect Utility of Money

Let us assume that agent i has consumed x_i in the first period and carried a quantity of money m_i to the second period. Given his expectations $(p^e, \bar{z}_i^e, \underline{z}_i^e)$, his trade and consumption vectors in the second period will be those maximizing his utility, subject to the budget constraint and all quantity signals; that is, they are the solution of the following program (where x_i and m_i are given):

$$\text{Maximize} \quad W_i(x_i, x_i^e) \qquad \text{s.t.}$$

$$x_i^e = \omega_i^e + z_i^e \geq 0,$$
$$p^e z_i^e \leq m_i,$$
$$\underline{z}_i^e \leq z_i^e \leq \bar{z}_i^e.$$

In order to stress the functional dependence, we write the vector solution x_i^e of this program as

$$\mathcal{X}_i^e(x_i, m_i, p^e, \bar{z}_i^e, \underline{z}_i^e) = \mathcal{X}_i^e(x_i, m_i, \sigma_i^e).$$

We can now express the level of utility, as expected from the first period, through the function U_i^e defined by

$$U_i^e(x_i, m_i, \sigma_i^e) = W_i(x_i, \mathcal{X}_i^e(x_i, m_i, \sigma_i^e)),$$

and, using the expression for σ_i^e given above, we obtain the indirect utility function U_i as

$$U_i(x_i, m_i, \sigma_i) = U_i^e(x_i, m_i, \psi_i(\sigma_i)).$$

The indirect utility function has money as an argument, together with first-period consumption x_i. It also depends on the current signals σ_i, through their influence on expected prices and quantity constraints.

Stochastic Expectations

When expectations are stochastic, the method is similar. For each value of first-period variables (x_i and m_i) and second-period expectations (σ_i^e), we can compute the expected level of utility, given that optimal actions are taken in the second period, that is, $U_i^e(x_i, m_i, \sigma_i^e)$. Expectations about σ_i^e are defined by a cumulative probability distribution on σ_i^e, conditional upon σ_i, that is,

$$\varphi_i(\sigma_i^e \mid \sigma_i).$$

We obtain the indirect utility function U_i as the expectation of U_i^e with respect to the probability distribution on σ_i^e, that is,

$$U_i(x_i, m_i, \sigma_i) = \int U_i^e(x_i, m_i, \sigma_i^e) \, d\varphi_i(\sigma_i^e \,|\, \sigma_i).$$

5. Effective Demand and Temporary Fixprice Equilibrium

Effective Demand

Given the indirect utility function just derived, we now define effective demand and equilibrium in the same way as in Chapter 7. Effective demand on market h, $\tilde{\zeta}_{ih}(p, \bar{z}_i, \underline{z}_i)$, will be the solution in z_{ih} of the following program:

$$\text{Maximize} \quad U_i(x_i, m_i, \sigma_i) \quad \text{s.t.}$$

$$x_i = \omega_i + z_i \geq 0,$$
$$m_i = \bar{m}_i - pz_i \geq 0,$$
$$\underline{z}_{ik} \leq z_{ik} \leq \bar{z}_{ik}, \qquad k \neq h.$$

Note that the spillover effects are enriched by the introduction of expectations, since not only current but also expected constraints will influence effective demands.

Temporary Fixprice Equilibrium

In the same way as in Chapter 7, we define a temporary fixprice equilibrium for a given set of prices p and rationing schemes F_i as a set of effective demand vectors $\tilde{z}_i$, transactions z_i^*, and quantity constraints $\bar{z}_i$ and $\underline{z}_i$ such that

$$\tilde{z}_i = \tilde{\zeta}_i(p, \bar{z}_i, \underline{z}_i) \forall\, i, \tag{1}$$

$$z_i^* = F_i(\tilde{z}_i, \tilde{Z}_i) \quad \forall\, i, \tag{2}$$

$$\bar{z}_i = \bar{G}_i(\tilde{Z}_i) \quad \forall\, i,$$
$$\underline{z}_i = \underline{G}_i(\tilde{Z}_i) \quad \forall\, i. \tag{3}$$

6. Existence Theorems

We shall see here that temporary fixprice equilibria exist under quite standard conditions. We present two existence theorems. The first states existence conditions on the indirect utility functions; the second links existence to the "basic" properties of the original utility functions W_i and the expectations patterns ψ_i.

Theorem 8.1 *Assume:*

(a) $p \gg 0$.

(b) $U_i(x_i, m_i, \sigma_i)$ *is continuous in all its arguments, concave in x_i, m_i, with strict concavity in x_i.*

Then a temporary fixprice equilibrium exists.

Proof The proof is identical to that in Chapter 7. The only difference is the inclusion of σ_i in the utility function U_i, but, owing to assumption (b) above, this does not change the continuity properties of the effective demand function $\tilde{\zeta_i}$. Q.E.D.

We shall now give a set of sufficient existence conditions for the original utility functions W_i and expectations patterns ψ_i in the deterministic case.

Theorem 8.2 *Assume:*

(a) $p \gg 0$.

(b) $W_i(x_i, x_i^e)$ *is continuous and strictly concave in its arguments.*

(c) $\psi_i(\sigma_i)$ *is continuous. Moreover, the expected price vector is strictly positive for $p \gg 0$.*

Then a temporary fixprice equilibrium exists.

Proof We need to prove only that properties (b) and (c) are sufficient to ensure that the indirect utility function U_i possesses the properties given in Theorem 8.1, which can then be applied directly. Proving concavity is easy but tedious and is left to the reader. In order to prove continuity, let us define $\gamma_i(m_i, \sigma_i^e)$ as the set of x_i^e that satisfies the following inequalities:

$$x_i^e = \omega_i^e + z_i^e \geq 0,$$
$$p^e z_i^e \leq m_i,$$
$$\underline{z}_i^e \leq z_i^e \leq \bar{z}_i^e.$$

From Section 4 above, we see that the function $U_i^e(x_i, m_i, \sigma_i^e)$ may be defined as

$$U_i^e(x_i, m_i, \sigma_i^e) = \max\{W_i(x_i, x_i^e) \mid x_i^e \in \gamma_i(m_i, \sigma_i^e)\}.$$

With the vector of second-period prices p^e strictly positive, the set $\gamma_i(m_i, \sigma_i^e)$ depends continuously on its arguments. Thus, by the theorem of the maximum, U_i^e is continuous in its arguments. Now, remember that U_i is defined by

$$U_i(x_i, m_i, \sigma_i) = U_i^e(x_i, m_i, \psi_i(\sigma_i)).$$

Since U_i^e is continuous, and ψ_i is a continuous function, U_i is continuous in x_i, m_i, and σ_i.   Q.E.D.

7. Conclusions

This chapter has made clear how expectations about future trade possibilities influence current K-equilibria. We started with an intertemporal problem in which the intertemporal valuation function depended only on sequences of transactions. Then, by means of recursive dynamic programming, we converted this function into a one-period indirect valuation function, having as arguments only current transactions but dependent on the state of expectations. This conversion was achieved mainly via the indirect valuation of stocks. As an example, we saw that a store of value such as money becomes more valuable to a consumer the more he expects to be rationed on future labor markets, and less valuable the more he expects to be rationed on future goods markets.

As a result of this explicit introduction of expectations, we shall find that the size, and even the sign, of excess demands and supplies on all markets for a given set of prices depends very much on expectations. We shall see a macroeconomic example of this in Chapter 12.

The existence results in this chapter showed us that the explicit introduction of expectations did not require a strengthening of the assumptions for the existence proofs, since all that was needed was continuity of expectations. *A contrario,* Grandmont (1974) has shown that the conditions with respect to the expectations patterns for the existence of a temporary Walrasian equilibrium are fairly restrictive. Thus, even in cases where a temporary Walrasian equilibrium does not exist, a temporary fixprice equilibrium generally exists for *all* positive prices. As a consequence it will be possible, by introducing some degree of price rigidity, to study cases where a Walrasian analysis would have been empty owing to the lack of equilibrium.

Of course, the case studied in this chapter, with full price rigidity, was an extreme one, and we shall now study non-Walrasian equilibrium concepts involving some price flexibility.

9

Temporary Equilibria
with Price Makers

1. Introduction

The fixprice models of the previous chapters are obviously only a first step, and we shall now study models in which at least some prices are flexible. In Chapter 5 we saw that assuming prices are set by agents internal to the system leads to models reminiscent of the imperfect competition literature. We shall now extend the analysis there to a multimarket framework.

One of the first attempts toward a treatment of monopolistic competition in a general equilibrium setting was made by Triffin (1940). Then the seminal paper by Negishi (1961) gave an existence proof for a general equilibrium with monopolistic competition, and this was followed by other contributions in the same direction (Arrow and Hahn 1971, Negishi 1972). Here we shall make a synthesis between this line of work and the developments seen above by describing the concept of a K-equilibrium with price makers and giving conditions for its existence. The general idea relating this concept to those of the previous chapters is that price makers change their prices so as to "manipulate" the quantity constraints they face (that is, so as to increase or decrease their possible sales or purchases). An equilibrium is reached when all price makers are satisfied with the price–quantity combination they have obtained and thus no one desires to change his prices.

The results we shall present extend previous analyses in the literature in two directions. First, in previous models *all* markets, whether perfectly or imperfectly competitive, were cleared. In reality, prices on different markets react with different speeds of adjustment, and thus it may be important to investigate cases where some prices are rigid and others adjust during the period considered. One may think, for example, of some Keynesian models where the wage is given but the price of goods is flexible. Accordingly, we shall construct a multimarket model where some prices are fixed and others adjust in a framework of monopolistic competition. This will cover a wide range of different models, from the pure fixprice model to the general equilibrium of monopolistic competition. Specific applications of this general model to the problems of unemployment and inflation will be made in Chapters 13 and 14.

Second, we want to emphasize a point that is central to Keynesian theory but that has been neglected in the monopolistic competition literature: the importance of expectations in the formation of current equilibrium (which, like those studied in the previous chapters, is a temporary equilibrium). We shall see, in particular, that an equilibrium may not exist in the current period, owing to the nature of the expectations pattern.

2. The Setting

The economy considered will again be a simple monetary exchange economy with r markets and n traders. Each trader i ranks his actions according to an indirect utility function $U_i(x_i, m_i, \sigma_i)$. This function integrates the effects of expected future trades via the quantity of money m_i and the price–quantity signals σ_i, as explained in Chapter 8.[1]

As indicated, we assume that prices are either given *a priori* (as may be the case for previously bargained prices, for example) or determined by one of the agents in the economy. We call H_0 the set of goods whose price is fixed, H_i the set of goods whose price is controlled by agent i. Goods are distinguished both by their physical characteristics and by the agent who sets their price, so that

$$H_i \cap H_j = \{\varnothing\}, \qquad i \neq j.$$

We denote by $p_i \in R_+^{H_i}$ the vector of prices controlled by agent i.

Perceived Constraints of Price Makers

As do all agents, every price maker will receive quantity signals on each market, $\bar{z}_{ih}$ and $\underline{z}_{ih}$. By our definition of markets, a price maker i is the

---

[1] The analysis in the previous chapter is actually applicable only to price takers. The derivation of an indirect utility for price makers is found in Appendix K.

only seller (or buyer) of the goods whose price he controls ($h \in H_i$). Thus on these markets his perceived constraint on purchases $\bar{z}_{ih}$ will be the sum of the effective supplies of the other agents; his perceived constraint on sales $\underline{z}_{ih}$ will be the sum of the effective demands of the other agents:

$$\bar{z}_{ih} = -\sum_{j \neq i} \min(0, \tilde{z}_{jh}), \quad h \in H_i,$$

$$\underline{z}_{ih} = -\sum_{j \neq i} \max(0, \tilde{z}_{jh}), \quad h \in H_i.$$

Perceived Demand and Supply Curves

Every price maker has, for each of the products he controls, a perceived demand or supply curve that shows how he can "manipulate" the quantity constraints he faces by changing his prices. These perceived curves are estimates of the "true" curves and depend on a vector of parameters θ_i. These parameters themselves are estimated using the stream of past and current price–quantity signals, as we shall see below.

The *perceived demand curve* for good h links the maximum sales that agent i expects to be able to carry out to the prices he sets. It is denoted by

$$\underline{Z}_{ih}(p_i, \theta_i),$$

which is assumed to be nondecreasing in p_h. As we explained in Chapter 5, the perceived demand curve is denoted as a constraint on sales because the total demand of the other agents represents the maximum quantity the price maker can sell. Similarly, the *perceived supply curve* for good h relates the maximum purchases agent i expects to be able to carry out to the prices quoted. It is denoted by

$$\bar{Z}_{ih}(p_i, \theta_i),$$

which is assumed to be nondecreasing in p_h. Note that we allow interdependence between the goods controlled by a price maker, since every curve is a function of the full vector p_i of prices announced by agent i. Such an interdependence may arise, for example, if the agent practices product differentiation.

3. Price Making

As we saw in Chapter 5, the price-making process consists of two sub-processes: the estimation of the perceived demand curves and the price decision itself. We shall briefly describe these two processes here and continue in the next section with a description of the equilibrium notion.

Estimation of the Perceived Demand Curves

As we indicated in the previous section, the parameters θ_i of the perceived demand curves are obtained by an estimation procedure that makes use of the stream of past and current price–quantity signals. Since the past is given, we shall make only the dependence on current signals σ_i explicit, and thus write

$$\theta_i = \theta_i(\sigma_i).$$

Many estimation procedures can be conceived, depending on the parametrization of the perceived demand curves, and we shall thus not study them in more detail. However, since we shall deal with an equilibrium concept for the current period, the estimation procedure must be such that the perceived demand and supply curves are consistent with the *current* observations. This implies that, whatever the estimation procedure, the functions $\bar{Z}_{ih}(p_i, \theta_i(\sigma_i))$ and $\underline{Z}_{ih}(p_i, \theta_i(\sigma_i))$ must satisfy the following consistency conditions: if a specific signal $\sigma_i = \{\bar{p}, \bar{z}_i, \underline{z}_i\}$ is currently observed, we have

$$\bar{Z}_{ih}(p_i, \theta_i(\bar{p}, \bar{z}_i, \underline{z}_i)) = \bar{z}_{ih} \qquad \text{for} \quad p_i = \bar{p}_i,$$
$$\underline{Z}_{ih}(p_i, \theta_i(\bar{p}, \bar{z}_i, \underline{z}_i)) = \underline{z}_{ih} \qquad \text{for} \quad p_i = \bar{p}_i;$$

that is, the perceived curves "go through" the observed point.

The Price Decision

Once the perceived demand and supply curves are estimated, a price maker will choose a price vector so as to maximize his utility, subject to the trades that he perceives as possible. Assume that he receives price and quantity signals $\sigma_i = \{\bar{p}, \bar{z}_i, \underline{z}_i\}$. He will choose his vector of prices p_i so as to

$$\text{Maximize} \quad U_i(x_i, m_i, \sigma_i) \qquad \text{s.t.}$$

$$x_i = \omega_i + z_i \geq 0,$$
$$m_i = \bar{m}_i - p z_i \geq 0,$$
$$p_h = \bar{p}_h, \qquad \underline{z}_{ih} \leq z_{ih} \leq \bar{z}_{ih}, \qquad\qquad h \notin H_i,$$
$$\underline{Z}_{ih}(p_i, \theta_i(\sigma_i)) \leq z_{ih} \leq \bar{Z}_{ih}(p_i, \theta_i(\sigma_i)), \qquad h \in H_i.[2]$$

We denote the optimal price vector functionally as $\mathcal{P}_i^*(\sigma_i)$.

---

[2] Actually, on a specific market $h \in H_i$, only one of the two curves $\bar{Z}_{ih}$ or $\underline{Z}_{ih}$ will be used, as the price maker is on a given side of the market.

A Remark

We should note at this point that the above formulation of the pricing mechanism and the ensuing definition of a K-equilibrium with price makers in the next section implicitly combine in an instantaneous interaction two processes that (as indicated in Chapter 5) take place sequentially in reality, namely, the estimation of the parameters of the perceived demand and supply curves and the price decision itself.

We may remark that, as a result of this implicit instantaneous interaction, the vector of prices p_i controlled by price maker i, which is determined by the function $\mathscr{P}_i^*$, is also, via σ_i, an argument of this function as an information variable. Similarly, the constraints perceived by agent i on the markets he controls (that is, $\bar{z}_{ih}$ and $\underline{z}_{ih}$, $h \in H_i$) are also arguments of the function $\mathscr{P}_i^*$, even though, as we noted in Part I (see notably Chapter 5, Section 5), perceived constraints become known to traders *after* the price has been announced.

These ambiguous features — which are found, implicitly or explicitly, in all the literature on equilibria with monopolistic competition — are due to the instantaneous interaction process that is inherent in the use of an equilibrium concept in this framework. In Appendix L we describe a pseudo-dynamic process, a tâtonnement in prices and quantities, that allows for the sequentiality of the estimation and price decision procedures and admits as a fixed point the K-equilibria with price makers that we shall describe now.

4. Equilibrium: Definition and Characterization

Intuitively, one can define a *K-equilibrium with price makers* as a K-equilibrium such that no price maker has any incentive to change his prices. We shall now make this precise.

Definition *A K-equilibrium with price makers is defined by a vector p^*, net trades z_i^*, effective demands $\tilde{z}_i$, and quantity constraints $\bar{z}_i$ and $\underline{z}_i$ such that*

$$(z_i^*), (\tilde{z}_i), (\bar{z}_i, \underline{z}_i) \text{ is a K-equilibrium with respect to } p^*, \tag{1}$$

$$p_i^* = \mathscr{P}_i^*(p^*, \bar{z}_i, \underline{z}_i) \quad \text{for all } i. \tag{2}$$

We may remark that the equilibrium will depend on the prices of goods $h \in H_0$, that is, the rigidly given prices. At a K-equilibrium with price makers, one can show that each agent's transactions, and his prices if he is a price maker, will be the utility-maximizing ones, taking into account all constraints on trades. Thus z_i^* and p_i^* will be the solution in z_i and p_i of the following program:

$$\text{Maximize} \quad U_i(x_i, m_i, \sigma_i) \quad \text{s.t.}$$

$$x_i = \omega_i + z_i \geq 0,$$
$$m_i = \bar{m}_i - pz_i \geq 0,$$
$$p_h = p_h^*, \qquad \underline{z}_{ih} \leq z_{ih} \leq \bar{z}_{ih}, \qquad\qquad h \notin H_i,$$
$$\underline{Z}_{ih}(p_i, \theta_i(\sigma_i)) \leq z_{ih} \leq \bar{Z}_{in}(p_i, \theta_i(\sigma_i)), \quad h \in H_i.$$

A Property of Equilibrium: Demand and Supply Satisfaction

In a fixprice equilibrium, one does not know *a priori* which side of the market is constrained and which is not. However, in the literature on monopolistic competition it is traditionally assumed that price makers satisfy the demands (or supplies) of the other agents, a property that we showed in Chapter 5 to hold for the single-market case. We shall now show that this property carries over to the multimarket framework, provided we make some reasonable assumptions about perceived demand and supply curves.

To do that, let us partition the set of goods controlled by price maker i into two subsets: those supplied by i and those demanded by i. We shall assume that within each of these two subsets the goods are perceived by i as gross substitutes for each other (which may be due, for example, to product differentiation) but that there is no perceived influence of prices across the two subsets. This simple assumption is sufficient to ensure that price makers satisfy the supplies and demands of other agents at the equilibrium. This we shall now make precise through the following propositions.

Proposition 9.1 *Consider a good $h \in H_i$ supplied by price maker i, and assume*

$$\frac{\partial \underline{Z}_{ik}}{\partial p_h} \leq 0, \qquad k \in H_i, \quad k \neq h, \tag{a}$$

$$\frac{\partial \bar{Z}_{ik}}{\partial p_h} = 0, \qquad k \in H_i, \quad k \neq h. \tag{b}$$

Then agent i will choose the price vector so as to be "on" the perceived demand curve on market h, that is,

$$z_{ih}^* = \underline{Z}_{ih}(p_i^*, \theta_i).$$

Proof Assume instead that agent i chooses a price–quantity plan such that on market h he does not serve all the demand, that is,

$$z_{ih}^* > \underline{Z}_{ih}(p_i^*, \theta_i).$$

Then he can increase the price p_h slightly without violating the constraint on market h. From our assumptions, the constraints on the other markets will be released or maintained at the same level. Thus when p_h is raised slightly, the initial plan in transactions can be maintained; this procedure increases agent i's final holdings of money, and thus his utility. So, the initial plan was not optimal.   Q.E. D.

An analogous proposition can be proved for the goods demanded by the price maker

Proposition 9.2 *Consider a good $h \in H_i$ demanded by price maker i, and assume*

$$\frac{\partial \overline{Z}_{ik}}{\partial p_h} \leq 0, \qquad k \in H_i, \quad k \neq h, \tag{a}$$

$$\frac{\partial \underline{Z}_{ik}}{\partial p_h} = 0, \qquad k \in H_i, \quad k \neq h. \tag{b}$$

Then the price-making agent i will choose the price vector so as to be "on" the perceived supply curve on market h, that is,

$$z_{ih}^* = \overline{Z}_{ih}(p_i^*, \theta_i).$$

As a corollary of these propositions, whenever the above conditions are met on a market h, all non-price-setting agents see their effective demands and supplies satisfied on that market.

5. The Existence of an Equilibrium

The existence proof of a K-equilibrium with price makers is equivalent to the existence proof of a K-equilibrium satisfying

$$p_i^* = \mathscr{P}_i^*(p^*, \bar{z}_i, \underline{z}_i) \qquad \forall i.$$

In the following theorem we state a number of sufficient assumptions for existence.

Theorem 9.1 *Assume:*

(a) *All given prices are positive:*

$$p_h > 0, \qquad h \in H_0.$$

(b) $U_i(x_i, m_i, \sigma_i)$ *is continuous in its arguments, concave in* x_i, m_i, *with strict concavity in* x_i.

(c) $\mathscr{P}_i^*(\sigma_i)$ *is a continuous function in its arguments.*

(d) $\mathscr{P}_i^*$ *is bounded in the sense that one can find* $p_i^{\min} > 0$ *and* $p_i^{\max} > 0$ *such that*

$$p_i^{\min} \leq p_i \leq p_i^{\max} \; \forall \; i \Rightarrow p_i^{\min} \leq \mathscr{P}_i^*(p, \bar{z}_i, \underline{z}_i) \leq p_i^{\max} \; \forall \; i,$$

where the $\bar{z}_i$ *and* $\underline{z}_i$ *are those associated with a K-equilibrium for* p. *Then a K-equilibrium with price makers exists.*

Proof   Consider the following mapping:

$$\{\tilde{z}_i, z_i^*, \bar{z}_i, \underline{z}_i, p_i | i = 1, \dots, n\} \rightarrow \{\tilde{\zeta}_i, F_i, \bar{G}_i, \underline{G}_i, p_i' | i = 1, \dots, n\};$$

that is, from an initial set of effective demands $\tilde{z}_i$, transactions z_i^*, perceived constraints $\bar{z}_i$ and $\underline{z}_i$, and controlled prices p_i for all agents $i = 1, \dots, n$, we derive a new set of effective demands $\tilde{\zeta}_i(p, \bar{z}_i, \underline{z}_i)$, transactions $F_i(\tilde{z}_i, \tilde{Z}_i)$, perceived constraints $\bar{G}_i(\tilde{Z}_i)$ and $\underline{G}_i(\tilde{Z}_i)$, and prices p_i', with

$$p_i' = \min\{p_i^{\max}, \max[p_i^{\min}, \mathscr{P}_i^*(p, \bar{z}_i, \underline{z}_i)]\}.$$

Let us first restrict this mapping to prices p_i such that $p_i^{\min} \leq p_i \leq p_i^{\max}$ for all i. The restricted mapping is a continuous function from a compact convex set into itself. By Brouwer's theorem it thus has a fixed point. By construction, this fixed point yields a K-equilibrium such that

$$p_i^* = \min\{p_i^{\max}, \max[p_i^{\min}, \mathscr{P}_i^*(p^*, \bar{z}_i, \underline{z}_i)]\},$$

but then, since we are in a K-equilibrium, boundedness assumption (d) of Theorem 9.1 ensures that

$$p_i^{\max} \leq \mathscr{P}_i^*(p^*, \bar{z}_i, \underline{z}_i) \leq p_i^{\max} \qquad \forall \; i,$$

and consequently that

$$p_i^* = \mathscr{P}_i^*(p^*, \bar{z}_i, \underline{z}_i) \qquad \forall \; i. \qquad\qquad \text{Q.E.D.}$$

Comments on the Assumptions

The assumptions given here are fairly standard except for assumption (d) on boundedness, which is somewhat *ad hoc*. We now examine some instances in which it may be violated.

Our first case corresponds to badly behaved price functions $\mathscr{P}_i^*$, that is, functions that may take unbounded values for bounded arguments. Such would be the case, for example, if an agent has a family of isoelastic perceived demand curves, with the elasticity smaller than 1 in absolute value.

Then the optimal price is infinite, whatever the signal observed. But such a case is obviously unrealistic.

We shall now turn to an example in which existence is jeopardized even if the price function $\mathscr{P}_i^*$ is bounded for bounded arguments.

6. The Role of Expectations

We shall construct here a simple example of nonexistence of an equilibrium where boundedness assumption (d) of Theorem 9.1 is not satisfied, however well behaved the price function, because of a particular expectations pattern.

Let us consider a simple economy with two traders, a household and a firm, and two current markets, for labor and for goods. Quantities traded on these markets are, respectively, l and y. The wage w is given; the price p is chosen by the firm.

The firm has a short-run production function $F(l)$ and maximizes current profits $py - wl$. All profits are distributed to the household, whose real income is thus equal to y.

The horizon of the household extends to two periods. It has an endowment of labor l_0 in the two periods, an initial endowment of money $\bar{m}$, and a utility function with current and future consumptions c and c^e as arguments:

$$\alpha \operatorname{Log} c + (1 - \alpha) \operatorname{Log} c^e.$$

The consumption demand of the household will be the solution in c of the following program:

$$\text{Maximize} \quad \alpha \operatorname{Log} c + (1 - \alpha) \operatorname{Log} c^e \quad \text{s.t.}$$

$$pc + p^e c^e \leq py + p^e y^e + \bar{m},$$
$$pc \leq py + \bar{m},$$

where p^e and y^e are the expected price and real income for the future period. If we assume that the household expects the same income and price in the future period as in the current one, that is, $y^e = y$ and $p^e = p$, we obtain

$$\tilde{c} = \min[\alpha(\bar{m}/p + 2y), \bar{m}/p + y].$$

We see that for $\alpha \geq \frac{1}{2}$ the demand for consumption is always greater than y, which means that *all* K-equilibria will be characterized by excess demand on the goods market. However, in an equilibrium where the firm chooses the price, the demand for goods is satisfied. Therefore no equilibrium exists, even though assumptions (a–c) of Theorem 9.1 are satisfied.

7. Conclusions

In this chapter we defined and studied a concept of non-Walrasian equilibrium involving both quantity and price adjustments. The prices associated with a subset of goods (this subset may be empty) are fixed, but all other prices are determined by agents internal to the system. Each price maker evaluates the repercussions of his price decisions via a set of perceived demand and supply curves. His price decision will be a function of all the price and quantity signals he receives. In a K-equilibrium with price makers each agent has the best price–quantity combination he can attain. We found that under fairly mild assumptions each price maker will satisfy the demands or supplies of the other agents on the markets he controls.

The concept of a K-equilibrium with price makers covers a very wide range of equilibria. Indeed, one can choose not only which goods have their prices fixed but also which agent determines the price for each of the remaining goods. At one extreme of this range of equilibria one obtains the fixprice model, at the other extreme the equilibria of monopolistic competition that have been studied in the literature.

We gave a number of sufficient conditions for the existence of K-equilibria with price makers. These conditions need not always be satisfied, however, and we presented an example where an equilibrium does not exist owing to a particular expectations pattern. In such cases of nonexistence, we are not left as helpless as Walrasian theory was. Indeed, the nonexistence of an equilibrium just implies that too many prices were assumed flexible for the model to be operational. The results of the previous chapter suggest that by reducing the number of flexible prices sufficiently one will obtain an equilibrium that can be shown to exist. One may then study the dynamic evolution of such equilibria when prices move.

We now have at our disposal concepts that give a very rich structure of equilibria, ranging from complete price inflexibility to complete price flexibility. We may remark that even in the case of full price flexibility the price system obtained will usually be different from a Walrasian price system, unless all perceived demand curves are infinitely elastic in the relevant range. A fortiori, if some prices are predetermined, we must expect the price system to be non-Walrasian. We shall now turn to a very important issue, the efficiency properties of the corresponding equilibria.

10

Efficiency

1. The Problem

It has been argued by a number of authors (Clower 1965, Leijonhufvud 1968) that in a depression a peculiar kind of inefficiency develops because potential trades that would make everybody better off are not carried out. This inefficiency is in striking contrast with the usual efficiency results obtained in Walrasian equilibrium theory. Indeed, a general Walrasian equilibrium can be shown to be Pareto-optimal under quite weak conditions (Debreu 1959), which means that all potential gains from trade have been exhausted.

We shall now investigate the possibility that potential trades that would be profitable to everybody (we shall call them Pareto-improving trades) remain unrealized in fixprice equilibria. Fixprice equilibria are examined because they form the widest class of non-Walrasian equilibria studied so far. *A fortiori,* the results will be applicable to the other non-Walrasian equilibrium concepts, since they are particular cases of fixprice equilibria.

In this framework, the following types of results will be obtained: First, we shall see that unachieved Pareto-improving trades may exist even if each market is itself organized efficiently. The possibility of such trades depends on the pattern of excess demands and supplies in the economy. We shall characterize the inefficient patterns and see, in particular, that "multiplier" equilibria usually lead to inefficiencies.

The second type of results pertains to the role of expectations — notably, quantity expectations — in generating inefficiencies. In particular, we shall see that discrepancies between the future plans of firms and of consumers may cause the economy to settle at an inefficient multiplier state, even in the case where the current price vector is equal to that which would prevail in an intertemporal Walrasian equilibrium under perfect foresight.

Before demonstrating these results, we shall first define an efficiency criterion adapted to our fixprice framework.

2. The Criterion

The traditional criterion of Pareto efficiency is inappropriate in this framework of fixed prices, and we shall instead adopt a criterion of efficiency that is conditional on the presence of given prices[1]. We shall say that an allocation is p-efficient if, at the given set of prices, no chain of trades involving pairs of goods can strictly improve the utility of all the agents involved in these additional trades.

The reason for restricting trades to pairs of goods is that only this type of trade can reasonably be organized in a complex economy, at least through traditional market procedures. Moreover, this will allow comparison with a "trading post" barter economy, such as the one considered by Walras (1874), where all such pairwise trades are allowed.[2] That the trades must be carried out at given prices is inherent in the fixprice nature of the model.

We shall now state the criterion and the definition of Pareto-improving trades formally. To this end, we shall first make precise the conditions under which an agent would gain in an exchange involving a pair of goods. Let us consider an agent i who has quantities x_{ih} and x_{ik} of the goods h and k, respectively. Let U_i be his utility function and define the relation $\mathcal{R}_i$ by

$$h(\mathcal{R}_i)k \Leftrightarrow \begin{cases} \dfrac{1}{p_h}\dfrac{\partial U_i}{\partial x_{ih}} - \dfrac{1}{p_k}\dfrac{\partial U_i}{\partial x_{ik}} > 0 \\ x_{ik} > 0. \end{cases}$$

$h(\mathcal{R}_i)k$ means that i has a positive quantity of good k and would like to supply good k against good h at the going set of prices p. We can now define Pareto-improving trades and p-efficiency as follows:

---

[1] The criterion, in a slightly simpler form, is due to Arrow and Hahn (1971, Chapter 13). It was used in a fixprice setting by Younès (1975).

[2] Such a trading post barter economy is sketched in Appendix A. An analysis of efficiency for non-Walrasian prices is carried out briefly in Appendix N.

Definition *A Pareto-improving chain is a chain of exchanges involving pairs of goods and improving the utility of all traders involved; that is, it is a set of goods* $h_i, \ldots, h_k$ *and traders* $i_1, \ldots, i_k$ *such that*

$$h_1(\mathscr{R}_{i_1})h_2, \ h_2(\mathscr{R}_{i_2})h_3, \ \ldots, \ h_k(\mathscr{R}_{i_k})h_1.$$

An allocation is p-*efficient if no Pareto-improving chain exists at the set of prices p.*

Note that we consider not only bilateral exchanges involving just two traders but also indirect chains of trades involving more than two agents. This is because in a microeconomic model, owing to the absence of double coincidence of wants, Pareto-improving trades are usually the result of indirect multilateral exchanges.

In the simple case where all agents have positive quantities of each good, an allocation is p-efficient if and only if for all pairs (h, k) the quantities

$$\frac{1}{p_h} \frac{\partial U_i}{\partial x_{ih}} - \frac{1}{p_k} \frac{\partial U_i}{\partial x_{ik}}$$

have the same sign for all agents i. (This is the criterion given in Arrow and Hahn, 1971.)

3. The Efficiency Results

We shall assume here that all markets have frictionless rationing schemes. In this way we avoid the trivial situations where Pareto-improving trades could be carried out on a single market.[3] However, we shall see that, even with frictionless markets, K-equilibria are not necessarily efficient with respect to our criterion and that there may exist Pareto-improving chains. These chains, however, can only involve goods whose excess demands have the same sign, as in the traditional Keynesian depression case. In particular, we prove the following theorem.

Theorem 10.1 *If all markets are frictionless, all goods* $h_1, \ldots, h_k$ *in a Pareto-improving chain are simultaneously in excess demand or simultaneously in excess supply.*

Proof We know that at a fixprice equilibrium the final allocation x_i^* and

---

[3] This corresponds to the property, proved in Chapter 7, that a K-equilibrium allocation is D-efficient on a frictionless market.

transaction vector z_i^* are the solution of the following program:

$$\text{Maximize} \quad U_i(x_i, m_i, \sigma_i) \qquad \text{s.t.}$$

$$x_i = \omega_i + z_i \geq 0,$$
$$m_i = \bar{m}_i - pz_i \geq 0,$$
$$\underline{z}_{ih} \leq z_{ih} \leq \bar{z}_{ih}, \qquad h = 1, \ldots, r.$$

The Kuhn–Tucker conditions for this program are

$$\frac{\partial U_i}{\partial x_{ih}} \leq \epsilon_{ih}, \qquad \text{with equality if} \quad x_{ih} > 0,$$

$$\frac{\partial U_i}{\partial m_i} \leq \epsilon_{im}, \qquad \text{with equality if} \quad m_i > 0,$$

$$\epsilon_{ih} = \epsilon_{im} \, p_h + \delta_{ih}.$$

ϵ_{ih} and ϵ_{im} are nonnegative real numbers that may be interpreted as the exchange values of good h and money, respectively. δ_{ih} is an index of rationing on market h.

- $\delta_{ih} > 0$ if i is constrained in his demand of h $(0 \leq z_{ih}^* < \bar{z}_{ih})$.
- $\delta_{ih} < 0$ if i is constrained in his supply of h $(0 \geq z_{ih}^* > \bar{z}_{ih})$.
- $\delta_{ih} = 0$ if i is not constrained on market h $(z_{ih}^* = \bar{z}_{ih})$.

The assumption of frictionless rationing schemes implies that the δ_{ih} have the same sign for all agents on a market h, since only one side is constrained. (By convention we take $\delta_{im} = 0$, where m is the subindex referring to money.) We shall see that this property allows us to derive the above theorem.

Let us first consider the simple case where all final allocations are strictly positive. Then

$$\frac{1}{p_h} \frac{\partial U_i}{\partial x_{ih}} - \frac{1}{p_k} \frac{\partial U_i}{\partial x_{ik}} = \frac{\delta_{ih}}{p_h} - \frac{\delta_{ik}}{p_k}$$

The sign property on the δ's implies that the quantity $\delta_{ih}/p_h - \delta_{ik}/p_k$ has the same sign for all agents for the following pairs of goods: (i) pairs in which one good is money, (ii) pairs in which one good is in equilibrium, and (iii) pairs in which one good is in excess demand, the other in excess supply. Consequently, Pareto-improving exchanges cannot involve one of the above pairs. They can thus involve only pairs of goods where both goods are in excess demand or both are in excess supply.

Turning now to the general case, we shall first prove that if a Pareto-improving chain starts with a good in excess demand, there can only be goods in excess demand in this chain. Indeed, if this were not the case, we should have at some point in the chain

$$h(\mathcal{R}_i) \; k,$$

where good k is in excess demand (and thus $\delta_{ik} > 0$) and good h is either in excess supply or in equilibrium (and thus $\delta_{ih} \leq 0$). But if we use the definition of $\mathcal{R}_i$ in Section 2 and the above Kuhn–Tucker conditions, we find that

$$h(\mathcal{R}_i) \; k \Rightarrow \delta_{ih}/p_h - \delta_{ik}/p_k > 0,$$

which is impossible if $\delta_{ik} > 0$ and $\delta_{ih} \leq 0$. There is a contradiction, and thus all goods in the chain must be in excess demand. A similar method of proof can be used to show that if a Pareto-improving chain starts with a good in excess supply, all goods in the chain must be in excess supply, and that no chain can start with a good in equilibrium, or with money. These results put together prove the theorem. Q.E.D.

4. Inefficiencies and Multiplier Effects

The preceding theorem shows us that if we consider sets of goods all of which are in excess demand or all of which are in excess supply, there will be some likelihood that Pareto-improving exchanges exist. In such a case the K-equilibrium is inefficient. We shall now present a few cases where such inefficiencies may occur.

Inefficiency and Rationing Schemes

Inefficiency may originate from the fact that the rationing schemes are not coordinated across markets, so that some redistribution of rationed goods among rationed traders might be profitable to everybody. For example, imagine two goods h and k, both in excess demand, and two agents i and j who are both demanders of these two goods. The final allocation may be such that

$$\frac{1}{p_h} \frac{\partial U_i}{\partial x_{ih}} > \frac{1}{p_k} \frac{\partial U_i}{\partial x_{ik}} \geq \frac{\partial U_i}{\partial m_i},$$

$$\frac{1}{p_k} \frac{\partial U_j}{\partial x_{jk}} > \frac{1}{p_h} \frac{\partial U_j}{\partial x_{jh}} \geq \frac{\partial U_j}{\partial m_j}.$$

In this case both agents would gain by directly reexchanging h and k, even though neither of them would want to sell either of the goods for money.

Multiplier Chains

A particularly interesting situation arises if, in a Pareto-improving chain, each trader buys one of the two goods he would like to exchange in the chain and sells the other (in which case he is constrained in only one of them). If, for example, the goods $h_1, \ldots, h_k$ in the chain are all in excess supply, the following situation prevails:

i_1 is $\begin{cases} \text{constrained in his supply of good } h_1, \\ \text{unconstrained in his demand for good } h_2. \end{cases}$

i_2 is $\begin{cases} \text{constrained in his supply of good } h_2, \\ \text{unconstrained in his demand for good } h_3. \end{cases}$

. . .

i_k is $\begin{cases} \text{constrained in his supply of good } h_k, \\ \text{unconstrained in his demand for good } h_1. \end{cases}$

The corresponding allocation is clearly inefficient. We may remark that this situation corresponds to a demand multiplier chain, as we saw in Chapter 4, Section 5. Demand multiplier chains will be observed particularly in the case of generalized excess supply. The best-known example of these inefficient states is the deflationary Keynesian case: an increase in employment would increase both firms' profits and individuals' utilities, but unfortunately the market does not provide any signal of the existence of such a profitable trade. (This particular example will be studied more precisely in Chapter 11.)

An analogous case occurs when all markets in a Pareto-improving chain are in excess demand. In such a case we have an inefficient supply multiplier state.

5. An Example of Multiplier Inefficiency

We shall give here a very simplified example that is designed to show numerically the inefficiency property of "multiplier equilibria" and the nature of the trades that might reestablish efficiency.

The Economy

Consider a simple monetary economy with two markets, 1 and 2, and two agents, A and B. Both agents have the same utility functions

$$U_A = \text{Log } x_{A1} + \text{Log } x_{A2} + \text{Log } m_A,$$
$$U_B = \text{Log } x_{B1} + \text{Log } x_{B2} + \text{Log } m_B,$$

but different initial endowments

$$\omega_A = (2, 0), \quad \bar{m}_A = 1,$$
$$\omega_B = (0, 2), \quad \bar{m}_B = 1.$$

Prices are denoted by p_1, p_2. Depending on the values of p_1, p_2, we can distinguish four regions (Fig. 10.1), separated by the lines $p_1 = 1$, $p_2 = 1$, according to the signs of the aggregate effective demands. (Note that these regions differ from those that would be given by Walrasian demands.)

From the results above, we know that the fixprice equilibrium allocation will be p-efficient in regions β and δ, since the aggregate effective demands are of opposite sign. On the other hand, "multiplier" effects will occur in regions α and γ. As an illustration, we shall show what happens in region α (general excess supply).

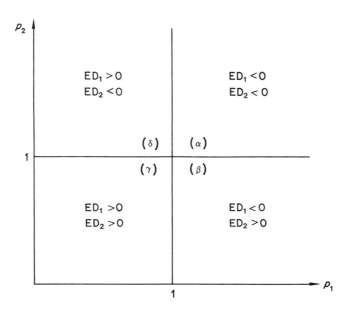

ED$_1$: Aggregate excess demand of good 1

ED$_2$: Aggregate excess demand of good 2

Figure 10.1

Computation of Equilibrium Transactions (Region α)

With excess supply on both markets, transactions are determined by the demand side, that is,

$$\tilde{z}_{A2} = z^*_{A2} = -z^*_{B2}, \tag{1}$$

$$\tilde{z}_{B1} = z^*_{B1} = -z^*_{A1}. \tag{2}$$

Agent A's effective demand for good 2, $\tilde{z}_{A2}$, is given by

Maximize $\text{Log}(2 + z_{A1}) + \text{Log } z_{A2} + \text{Log } m_A$ s.t.

$m_A = 1 - p_1 z_{A1} - p_2 z_{A2},$
$z_{A1} \geq \underline{z}_{A1}.$

Since A's supply of good 1 is constrained, the last constraint is binding, hence

$$p_2 \tilde{z}_{A2} = \tfrac{1}{2}(1 - p_1 \underline{z}_{A1}) = \tfrac{1}{2}(1 - p_1 z^*_{A1}). \tag{3}$$

We see that A's propensity to consume out of money holdings and sales of good 1 is $\tfrac{1}{2}$. Similarly, B is constrained in his sales of good 2, and his demand for good 1 is

$$p_1 \tilde{z}_{B1} = \tfrac{1}{2}(1 - p_2 \underline{z}_{B2}) = \tfrac{1}{2}(1 - p_2 z^*_{B2}). \tag{4}$$

Solving the above system of equations (1–4), we obtain the realized transactions

$$-z^*_{A1} = z^*_{B1} = 1/p_1,$$
$$-z^*_{B2} = z^*_{A2} = 1/p_2,$$

from which we see that the monetary value of transactions is equal to 1 for each of the two goods. Final holdings are

$$x_A = (2 - 1/p_1, 1/p_2), \qquad m_A = 1,$$
$$x_B = (1/p_1, 2 - 1/p_2), \qquad m_B = 1.$$

Inefficiency

Since both aggregate excess demands are negative in the interior of region α, according to the analysis of the previous section we would expect Pareto-improving trades involving goods 1 and 2 to exist. That this is actually the case is easy to check by computing the propensities to exchange good 1 against good 2 at the K-equilibrium:

$$\frac{1}{p_2}\frac{\partial U_A}{\partial x_{A2}} - \frac{1}{p_1}\frac{\partial U_A}{\partial x_{A1}} = \frac{2(p_1 - 1)}{2p_1 - 1} > 0,$$

$$\frac{1}{p_1}\frac{\partial U_B}{\partial x_{B1}} - \frac{1}{p_2}\frac{\partial U_B}{\partial x_{B2}} = \frac{2(p_2 - 1)}{2p_2 - 1} > 0.$$

We see that A and B would both gain in exchanging good 1 against good 2 directly. However, in a monetary structure where a third good plays the role of money, there is no way they can communicate to each other these desires for trade.

A Barter Exchange[4]

Let us now assume that the market for good 1 against good 2 is open. We shall see that this is enough to restore efficiency. Indeed, in this very simplified example we shall show that it is enough for agents A and B to trade on the market of good 1 against good 2 to reach a p-efficient state in region α. Let us call λ the volume of trade on this market, expressed in terms of money (as a numeraire). The final holdings are, as a function of λ,

$$x_{A1} = 2 - \lambda/p_1, \qquad x_{A2} = \lambda/p_2, \qquad m_A = \bar{m}_A = 1,$$
$$x_{B1} = \lambda/p_1, \qquad x_{B2} = 2 - \lambda/p_2, \qquad m_B = \bar{m}_B = 1.$$

The desired volume of trade for agent A, $\tilde{\lambda}_A$, will be given by solving

$$\text{Maximize} \quad \text{Log } x_{A1} + \text{Log } x_{A2} + \text{Log } m_A \quad \text{s.t.}$$

$$x_{A1} = 2 - \lambda/p_1,$$
$$x_{A2} = \lambda/p_2,$$

yielding immediately $\tilde{\lambda}_A = p_1$. We find $\tilde{\lambda}_B = p_2$ similarly, so that the actual volume of trade will be $\lambda^* = \min(p_1, p_2)$ and the final holdings

$$x_A = \left(2 - \frac{\min(p_1, p_2)}{p_1}, \frac{\min(p_1, p_2)}{p_2}\right), \qquad m_A = 1,$$

$$x_B = \left(\frac{\min(p_1, p_2)}{p_1}, 2 - \frac{\min(p_1, p_2)}{p_2}\right), \qquad m_B = 1,$$

which can easily be shown to satisfy the condition of p-efficiency. We should, however, make an important remark before leaving this example: in the case considered here, a *direct* barter exchange between two agents was enough to restore efficiency. This is clearly due to the highly aggregated character of the economy. As soon as the economy studied is a

---

[4] For a more general treatment of barter exchange at non-Walrasian prices and the related efficiency properties, see Appendix N.

little more complex and involves more agents, a chain of exchanges, thus involving some indirect barter, would be necessary to reestablish efficiency (for an example of this, see Appendix M).

6. The Nature of Inefficiency

As we have seen in the preceding paragraphs, there is more in the inefficiency properties of Keynesian equilibria than the inefficiency associated with nonflexible prices. There is also an informational and signaling problem, since transactors will often fail to realize trades that are both possible and profitable to everybody. We shall now investigate some aspects of this informational failure.

Money and Barter

The first possible cause of inefficiency we shall scrutinize is the monetary nature of exchange. We saw from the example given in Section 5 that reestablishing some form of barter by opening trading posts for all pairs of goods would restore efficiency. Pursuing the same line of inquiry, in Appendix N we study a fictitious indirect barter economy where a trading post exists for all pairs of goods. It is shown that fixprice equilibria in this economy are efficient with respect to our criterion.

A comparison of the efficiency properties of monetary and (fictitious) barter economies at non-Walrasian prices might tempt us to ascribe the inefficiencies studied in the previous sections to the monetary nature of exchange. More specifically, since effective demands are expressed against money, information on the desired real counterparts is not transmitted, and hence some fruitful exchanges between real goods may be missed. As Leijonhufvud (1968, p. 90) says, giving the example of a Keynesian unemployment situation:

> The workers looking for jobs ask for money, not for commodities. Their notional demand for commodities is not communicated to producers; not being able to perceive this potential demand for their products, producers will not be willing to absorb the excess supply of labor. . . .[5]

From this and from the efficiency properties derived for barter economies one might be tempted to claim that money is the cause of inefficiency and that the problem would be solved by reestablishment of barter exchange. Unfortunately, this is not the case, and the above results must be interpreted with the greatest caution. Indeed, real economies, unlike

[5] Reprinted from A. Leijonhufvud, *On Keynesian Economics and the Economics of Keynes,* Oxford University Press, London and New York, 1968, by permission of the publisher.

the economy studied in Section 5, are characterized by lack of mutual coincidence of wants. Consequently the trades leading to an improvement would be extremely indirect and thus for informational reasons would be almost impossible to organize by decentralized units (as we discuss briefly in Appendix A). Therefore the superiority of the indirect barter equilibrium over the monetary equilibrium is irrelevant because the lack of mutual coincidence of wants would prevent the barter equilibrium from being informationally attainable. As Leijonhufvud (1968, p. 90) notes:

> The fact that there exists a potential barter bargain of goods for labor services that would be mutually agreeable to producers as a group and labor as a group is irrelevant to the motion of the system. The individual steel-producer cannot pay a newly hired worker by handing over to him his physical product (nor will the worker try to feed his family on a ton-and-a-half of cold rolled sheet a week). The lack of any "mutual coincidence of wants" between pairs of individual employers and employees is what dictates the use of a means of payment in the first place.[5]

Thus, to summarize, monetary exchange cannot be taken as the cause of inefficiencies. Rather, the ultimate cause must be sought in the informational problems created by the lack of mutual coincidence of wants. These same problems are one of the causes of the emergence of monetary exchange (cf. Appendix A).

Inefficiency and Expectations

Another cause of inefficiency that comes naturally to mind after reading the previous sections is that current prices are "wrong" (that is, different from market-clearing prices). We want to show here, however, that the notion of "wrong" prices is extremely ambiguous in this context because of the role of expectations.

Indeed, as we showed in previous chapters, the values of all current variables, including the level of market-clearing prices, depend very much on expectations. Thus the fact that current prices differ from *temporary* Walrasian equilibrium prices that would clear the current markets does not mean that they are intrinsically "wrong". Instead, current market disequilibria may be due to incorrect quantitative expectations, owing to the fact that agents cannot transmit to each other information regarding the quantities they would like to exchange on future markets. This point was particularly well made and stressed by Keynes (1936, pp. 210–11):

> An act of individual saving means—so to speak—a decision not to have dinner to-day. But it does *not* necessitate a decision to have a dinner or to buy a pair of boots a week hence or a year hence or to consume any specified thing at any specified date. Thus it depresses the business of preparing to-day's dinner without stimulating the business of making ready for some future act of consumption. It is not a substitution of future consumption-demand for present consumption-demand,—it is a net diminution of such demand. Moreover, the expectation of future consumption is so largely based on current experience of present consumption that a reduction in the latter is likely to depress

the former, with the result that the act of saving will not merely depress the price of consumption-goods and leave the marginal efficiency of existing capital unaffected, but may actually tend to depress the latter also. In this event it may reduce present investment-demand as well as present consumption-demand.

If saving consisted not merely in abstaining from present consumption but in placing simultaneously a specific order for future consumption, the effect might indeed be different. For in that case the expectation of some future yield from investment would be improved, and the resources released from preparing for present consumption could be turned over to preparing for the future consumption. . . .

The trouble arises, therefore, because the act of saving implies, not a substitution for present consumption of some specific additional consumption which requires for its preparation just as much immediate economic activity as would have been required by present consumption equal in value to the sum saved, but a desire for "wealth" as such, that is, for a potentiality of consuming an unspecified article at an unspecified time.[6]

We shall now study a simple model inspired by Keynes's remarks, where the absence of information on future trades leads the economy into a Keynesian unemployment situation even though prices are at their *intertemporal* Walrasian equilibrium values.

7. The Role of Expectations: An Example

In our model inspired by the quotation from Keynes,[7] there will be two agents, a household and a firm, with a horizon of two periods. We shall assume that price and wage correspond to those of the intertemporal Walrasian equilibrium. In spite of this we shall see that the current-period equilibrium may be one with unemployment if the household and firm do not have perfect foresight about each other's quantity decisions in the future period.

The Model

Our model has a horizon of two periods, current and future. Variables in the second period have a superscript e. In each period there are two spot markets, one for goods and one for labor, but no futures markets. The agents consist of a household and a firm.

The firm has a production function F, assumed to be the same in the two periods:

$$q = F(l), \qquad q^e = F(l^e).$$

It can store the produced good without cost from the first to the second

[6] Reproduced from J. M. Keynes, *The General Theory of Employment, Interest and Money*, Harcourt, Brace, Jovanovich, New York, 1936, by permission of Harcourt, Brace, Jovanovich, Inc.; the Royal Economic Society; and Macmillan, London and Basingstoke.

[7] A dynamic model illustrating the same point can be found in Appendix O.

period. It maximizes the undiscounted sum of profits and distributes all profits to the household in each period.

The household has an initial endowment of labor l_0 in both periods and an initial quantity of money $\bar{m}$ at the outset of the first period. Further, the household has a utility function defined over its consumptions c and c^e in the first and second periods and its money holdings m^e at the end of the second period:

$$U(c, c^e, m^e) = (\alpha - \delta) \text{ Log } c + (\alpha + \delta) \text{ Log } c^e + \beta \text{ Log } m^e,$$

where α, β, and δ are real positive parameters such that $\delta \leq \alpha$. Since the household's utility does not depend on its leisure, the supply of labor is l_0 in both periods, and full employment production is equal to $F(l_0)$.

Intertemporal Walrasian Equilibrium

The model has been parametrized so that the intertemporal Walrasian equilibrium price and wage are the same in the two periods and are independent of δ. They can easily be computed as

$$p_0 = \alpha \bar{m} / \beta F(l_0), \qquad w_0 = p_0 F'(l_0).$$

In what follows, we shall assume that the price and wage are fixed and equal to these values.

Equilibrium with Perfect Foresight

If we assume that the firm correctly forecasts the demand that will be addressed to it and that the household perfectly anticipates its income, then the current equilibrium is one of full employment: the firm produces $q_0 = F(l_0)$. Current demand is $(\alpha - \delta)q_0/\alpha$ and the firm thus stores $\delta q_0/\alpha$, expecting (correctly) that demand in the future period will be $(\alpha + \delta)q_0/\alpha$.

However, we must remark that in this context the perfect foresight assumption is totally unrealistic, since it implies that the firm, observing a demand $(\alpha - \delta)q_0/\alpha$, which is lower than full employment output q_0, forecasts a demand $(\alpha + \delta)q_0/\alpha$, higher than full employment output. We shall now investigate what will be the current equilibrium under a more realistic expectations pattern.

Static Expectations

We assume that the firm and household have static expectations; that is, the firm expects the same demand and the household expects the same income as in the current period. Since the firm expects an unchanged demand, it will produce exactly for current demand: $q = y$. Since the household expects an unchanged income, its effective demand for goods will be

$$\tilde{c} = \frac{\alpha - \delta}{2\alpha + \beta} \left(\frac{\bar{m}}{p} + 2y \right).$$

The equilibrium level of sales is given by $\tilde{c} = y$, yielding

$$y^* = \frac{\alpha - \delta}{\beta + 2\delta} \frac{\bar{m}}{p},$$

or, since $p = p_0$, using the value found above,

$$q^* = y^* = \frac{\alpha - \delta}{\alpha} \frac{\beta}{\beta + 2\delta} F(l_0).$$

As soon as $\delta > 0$, this corresponds to a multiplier equilibrium with a level of employment lower than l_0.

An Interpretation

To interpret the above results, it is useful to compare the case $\delta > 0$ with the "reference" situation where $\delta = 0$. When $\delta = 0$, the consumer wants to consume the same amount in the two periods. The two equilibria corresponding to static expectations and perfect foresight are then the same and correspond to full employment.

As compared to this reference case, when $\delta > 0$, the household decides to transfer some consumption from the first to the second period. If there is perfect foresight, the producer knows this and will compensate for the reduced consumption today by expanding its inventories to cover increased consumption tomorrow, that is, by investing.[8]

As we already pointed out, however, it is not realistic to assume this perfect foresight. Indeed, as Keynes stressed, only the signal of reduced consumption today is transmitted to the market, not the signal of increased consumption tomorrow. As a result of this lack of communication, the economy ends up in a multiplier state with unemployment, which is inefficient.

8. Conclusions

In this chapter we studied the efficiency properties of K-equilibria. We shall now reexamine them briefly and draw policy implications.

A main result is that at a K-equilibrium, for prices differing from the

[8] Note that the same effect would be obtained if there were, in the current period, markets for future consumption and labor, that is, futures markets.

Walrasian ones, there may be the possibility of trades that are beneficial to all involved but that remain unachieved. Eliminating the trivial case of inefficient markets, we showed that these trades would involve subsets of goods all in excess demand or all in excess supply. In particular, we saw that inefficiencies were likely to be associated with the presence of multiplier effects. Assuming that prices may remain at non-Walrasian values for some time (because of either institutional rigidities or imperfect competition), we may search for possible means of eliminating or reducing these inefficiencies.

Since the potential unachieved trades are indirect barter exchanges, one might first jump to the conclusion that establishing generalized barter trading posts would solve the problem. We saw, however, that the absence of mutual coincidence of wants and the multilateral nature of the beneficial barter trades would make these trades prohibitively expensive to find, for informational reasons, in a decentralized economy.

We also saw that inefficiency in the current period could result from lack of coordination between the future plans of the agents. Unfortunately, to eliminate this lack of coordination it would be necessary to organize a full set of futures markets. Clearly the cost of such a measure would be prohibitive in most cases and thus could not realistically be implemented. In addition, it is not likely that agents would want to commit themselves to such future purchases since, as Keynes stressed, they would prefer to hold their savings in a more liquid form.

One may thus want next to reexamine the case of government intervention. Traditional wisdom (in this case, the classical tradition) holds that government intervention can only be at the expense of some agents in the economy. (For example, it has been argued that government expenses "crowd out" or displace private investment.) However, our efficiency results point clearly in another direction when multiplier effects are in operation. Indeed, in such cases there is a possibility that all agents will be better off, provided that a method is found that will increase the level of their transactions. Government action through public spending, tax cuts, or other "Keynesian" measures can be one such way. And if, owing to some sluggishness in the price system, the return to Walrasian equilibrium is slow, the benefits from government intervention may be very substantial.

From our results, however, we would expect government intervention to be beneficial only for some configurations of excess demands. This will be confirmed in the next chapter, where we study the problem of unemployment at the aggregate level.

PART III

MACROECONOMICS

11

A Model of Unemployment

1. Classical versus Keynesian Theories of Unemployment[1]

Two dissenting theories of unemployment are traditionally found in textbooks and policy-oriented works. The "classical" theory blames unemployment on excessively high real wages, the "Keynesian" on insufficient effective demand. The associated economic policies advised are no less different: "classicals" prescribe a reduction in real wages, attained by the free market mechanism or by adequate incomes and price policies, whereas "Keynesians" prescribe increased public spending, tax reductions, or incentives for encouragement of investment and consumption.

These two theories are easy to illustrate graphically. Let the productive capacity of the economy be represented by a production function $F(l)$. To simplify the analysis let us assume an inelastic supply of labor l_0, and thus a given full employment income $y_0 = F(l_0)$.

In classical theory it is assumed that firms hire an amount of labor chosen so as to maximize profits, taking the real wage w/p as given. This yields the "classical" demand function for labor l_c,

$$l_c(w/p) = F'^{-1}(w/p),$$

to which corresponds a supply of goods y_c,

$$y_c(w/p) = F(F'^{-1}(w/p)).$$

[1] The model in this chapter is inspired by the well-known work of Barro and Grossman (1971, 1976). Other adaptations were made in Benassy (1974, 1977a) and in Malinvaud (1977), to which the "classical–Keynesian" distinction is due. See also the early works of Solow and Stiglitz (1968) and Younès (1970).

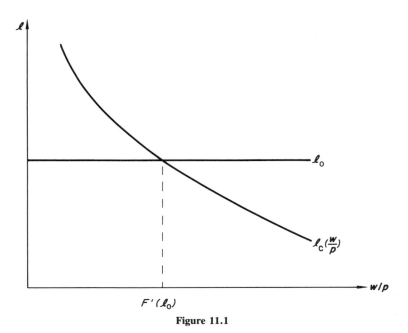

Figure 11.1

A comparison of the supply and demand for labor (Fig. 11.1) shows that there is unemployment if and only if the real wage is above its equilibrium value $F'(l_0)$.

In Keynesian theory the effective demand on the goods market is emphasized instead as the main determinant of income and production, and thus of employment. Keynesians plot aggregate effective demand versus the level of real income y (Fig. 11.2). Aggregate effective demand is defined as the sum of consumption, investment, and government demand, all of which are taken to be functions of income and "other" given variables (including, notably, expectations). Equilibrium income y_K is determined by the intersection with the 45° line. Employment settles at the level necessary to produce the corresponding quantity, that is, $F^{-1}(y_K)$. Clearly, in this model, unemployment is due to y_K's being smaller than y_0 and thus to insufficient aggregate effective demand. This can be remedied by government spending, tax cuts, or other Keynesian measures aimed at sustaining demand.

We see immediately from this description and from the graphs that each theory completely ignores an important element. Classical theory forgets that, away from Walrasian equilibrium, firms may not succeed in selling all the output they want—which will of course change their demand function of labor. Conversely, Keynesian theory ignores the fact that the

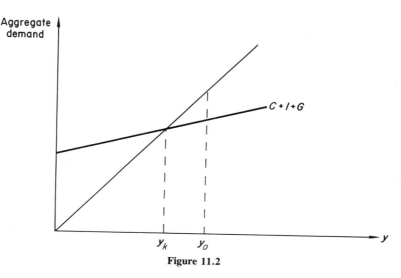

Figure 11.2

Walrasian supply of output by the firms, $y_c(w/p)$, may be smaller than effective demand, in which case sales of goods will be supply determined. This ruins the Keynesian diagnosis, since we may have unemployment with "too high" effective demand, that is, with y_K higher than y_0 (Fig. 11.3).

These simple remarks clearly show that we should try not to determine which theory is *the* correct one, but rather to construct a model that shows in which circumstances each of the two above cases and their associated policy recommendations are relevant.

2. The Model

A Fixprice Model

It is clear that a model aimed at comparing classical and Keynesian theories of unemployment should display some rigidity in both prices and wages: effective demand problems are generally associated in Keynesian models with price–wage stickiness, and the "too high real wages" of the classical models obviously requires some rigidity in real wages. We shall here push these rigidities to the extreme and use for our study a model of fixprice equilibrium.[2] In order to remain close to traditional macromodels, the economy will be treated at the simplest and most aggregated level.

---

[2] The general structure of fixprice equilibria has been described in Chapter 7. A macroeconomic model displaying less price rigidity will be studied in Chapter 13.

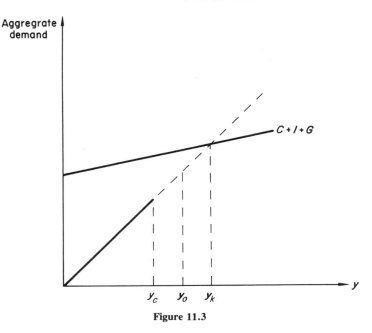

Figure 11.3

Markets and Agents

We shall consider here a simple monetary economy with three representative economic agents — a household, a firm, and the government — and three commodities — a consumption good (output), labor, and money. Accordingly there are two current markets, one on which the good is exchanged against money at the price p, another on which labor is exchanged against money at the wage w. The household demands output and supplies labor, the firm demands labor and supplies output, and the government demands output. Each market is assumed frictionless, so that transactions realized are equal to the minimum of supply and demand. We shall study the determinants of the current equilibrium levels of employment l^* and sales of good y^* for different values of p and w. First, however, we shall describe in more detail the agents and their behavior.

The Firm

The representative firm has a short-run production function that relates its production q to the quantity of labor employed l,

$$q = F(l),$$

with the traditional properties

$$F(0) = 0, \qquad F'(l) > 0, \qquad F''(l) < 0.$$

The firm does not use or build up inventories in the period considered, so that, in equilibrium, production q will be equal to output sales y. The firm attempts to maximize profits $\pi = py - wl$ under the constraint $y \leq q$. These profits are entirely distributed to the household during the period considered. Household real income is thus equal to y. (The case of partial profit distribution is considered in Appendix P.)

The Household

The representative household consumes a quantity c of the aggregate consumption good, sells l units of labor, and saves a quantity of money m. It has an initial quantity of money $\bar{m}$ and an endowment of labor l_0. Sales of labor cannot be greater than this endowment: $l \leq l_0$. Let τ be the tax rate on household income. The household's budget constraint is

$$pc + m = \bar{m} + (1 - \tau)\, py.$$

We assume that the household has no utility for leisure, so that its supply of labor is constant and equal to l_0. Its effective demand for goods $\tilde{c}$ is described by a consumption function that depends on real income (here equal to y), the price level p, initial money holdings $\bar{m}$, and tax rate τ:

$$\tilde{c} = C(y, p, \bar{m}, \tau).$$

This consumption function may be thought of as derived from an intertemporal program of utility maximization, subject to a sequence of budget constraints such as the one above,[3] where expected future real incomes, prices, and tax rates are functions of the current values. We assume[4]

$$0 \leq C_y \leq \delta < 1, \qquad C_p < 0, \qquad C_{\bar{m}} > 0, \qquad C_\tau < 0.$$

In what follows we shall sometimes use, as an explicit example, a consumption function linear in real disposable income $(1 - \tau)y$ and real money balances $\bar{m}/p$:

$$\tilde{c} = \alpha(1 - \tau)\, y + \beta\, \bar{m}/p,$$

with

$$0 < \alpha < 1, \qquad 0 < \beta < 1.$$

---

[3] The general method for dealing with such programs was studied in Chapter 8.

[4] Here and in what follows, subscripts to a function refer to partial derivatives, for example, $C_y = \partial C/\partial y$.

Government

The government taxes income at the rate τ and expresses an effective demand for output equal to $\tilde{g}$. Actual purchases will be denoted by g^*. Any budget deficit will be financed through monetary creation.

3. Equilibrium and Disequilibrium

The temporary Walrasian equilibrium price and wage are determined by the conditions of equilibrium on the goods and labor markets. Let p_0 and w_0 denote these equilibrium values. Equilibrium on the labor market implies

$$F'^{-1}(w_0/p_0) = l_0,$$

or

$$w_0/p_0 = F'(l_0).$$

That is, the Walrasian equilibrium real wage is equal to marginal productivity of labor at full employment. Equilibrium on the goods market requires that full employment output be equal to the sum of consumption for full employment income and government spending. This is written

$$C(y_0, p_0, \bar{m}, \tau) + \tilde{g} = y_0.$$

We assume that the consumption function and the values of the parameters are such that this equation has a solution (though this is not necessary in what follows). For example, in the case of the linear consumption function introduced above we obtain[5]

$$p_0 = \frac{\beta\bar{m}}{y_0[1 - \alpha(1 - \tau)] - \tilde{g}}.$$

The Walrasian equilibrium values of price and wage are not our main concern here, however. Rather, we are interested in determining for which values of the exogenously given parameters p, w, $\tilde{g}$, τ, and $\bar{m}$ Keynesian and classical unemployment will occur. Before doing that, we shall have to express the two theories in the framework of our model.

Conflicting Diagnoses

We now have a simple model in which it is possible to compare the classical and Keynesian diagnoses. Classicals would simply say that there is

---

[5] We note that in this case a temporary Walrasian equilibrium exists only if $\tilde{g}$ is smaller than $[1 - \alpha(1 - \tau)]y_0$. If, alternatively, the government fixes its spending in nominal terms, that is, $\tilde{g} = G/p$, the equilibrium price always exists.

unemployment because the real wage is above its equilibrium value, that is, because

$$w/p > F'(l_0).$$

Keynesians would compute the "Keynesian equilibrium" level of income y_K by the following equation in y:

$$C(y, p, \bar{m}, \tau) + \tilde{g} = y.$$

Because we assumed $0 < C_y \le \delta < 1$, this equation always has a unique solution, which we denote functionally as

$$y_K(p, \bar{m}, \tilde{g}, \tau).$$

For example, for the linear consumption function introduced above we find for y_K a traditional Keynesian multiplier formula

$$y_K = \frac{1}{1 - \alpha(1 - \tau)} \left(\frac{\beta \bar{m}}{p} + \tilde{g} \right).$$

Keynesians would simply say that there is unemployment because $y_K < y_0$ or, equivalently, because $F^{-1}(y_K) < l_0$. To determine which parameter changes would increase y_K, we compute the following partial derivatives:

$$\frac{\partial y_K}{\partial \tilde{g}} = \frac{1}{1 - C_y} > 1,$$

$$\frac{\partial y_K}{\partial \tau} = \frac{C_\tau}{1 - C_y} < 0,$$

$$\frac{\partial y_K}{\partial p} = \frac{C_p}{1 - C_y} < 0,$$

$$\frac{\partial y_K}{\partial \bar{m}} = \frac{C_{\bar{m}}}{1 - C_y} > 0.$$

Thus y_K will be increased by an increase in $\tilde{g}$ or $\bar{m}$, or by a decrease in τ or p.

The Labor Demand Function

Clearly, the form of the labor demand function, whether it appears implicitly or explicitly in the models, is a major difference between the two theories: classicals take a labor demand equal to $F'^{-1}(w/p)$, whereas Keynesians implicitly use a labor demand $F^{-1}(y_K)$. Actually, these two forms can be obtained as effective demand for labor, provided that the firm takes into account a quantity constraint on the goods market. Indeed, let $\bar{y}$ denote the maximum possible sales of the firm; $\bar{y}$ is actually equal to the total demand for goods $\tilde{c} + \tilde{g}$. Effective demand for labor is then the solution in l of the following program:

$$\text{Maximize} \quad py - wl \quad \text{s.t.}$$

$$y \leq q = F(l),$$
$$y \leq \bar{y} = \tilde{c} + \tilde{g},$$

which yields

$$\bar{l}^{\text{d}} = \min[F'^{-1}(w/p), F^{-1}(\bar{y})].$$

We see that the effective demand for labor is of the Keynesian type if the constraint on the goods market is binding and of the classical type if it is not.

4. The Different Regimes

As one might expect after the preceding section, the determination of employment and income will vary considerably, depending on the sign of excess demand on each market. With two markets, one would expect *a priori* four main cases, since each market may be in excess demand or in excess supply. However, anticipating a little what follows, we shall see that in this simple model there are only three types of fixprice equilibria, depending on the values of the parameters p, w, $\bar{m}$, $\tilde{g}$, and τ:

• *Keynesian unemployment,* with excess supply of labor and goods[6],
• *Classical unemployment,* with excess supply of labor and excess demand of goods,
• *Repressed inflation,* with excess demand of labor and goods.

We should note that the simple association of excess demand for goods with classical unemployment, and of excess supply of goods with Keynesian unemployment, is valid only in this simplified model. The introduction of stocks in the next chapter will invalidate this association. Notice further that owing to the absence of stocks, the fourth possibility (excess supply of goods, excess demand for labor) degenerates to a limit case, between the regions of Keynesian unemployment and repressed inflation, as we shall see later.

We shall now determine the level of employment l^* and sales y^* in each of these three cases and then determine for which values of the parameters they are relevant.

---

[6] One should actually say ''demand-determined transactions'' instead of ''excess supply,'' and ''supply-determined transactions'' instead of ''excess demand.''

Keynesian Unemployment

This case corresponds to the traditional Keynesian situation of excess supply on the two markets. Since transactions are demand determined, sales of goods are equal to the aggregate demand for goods, that is,

$$y = \tilde{c} + \tilde{g} = C(y, p, \bar{m}, \tau) + \tilde{g}.$$

We already denoted by y_K the solution to this equation. Equilibrium sales of goods and income are

$$y^* = y_K(p, \bar{m}, \tilde{g}, \tau).$$

This is a traditional multiplier formula, with

$$\frac{\partial y_K}{\partial \tilde{g}} = \frac{1}{1 - C_y} > 1, \qquad \frac{\partial y_K}{\partial \tau} = \frac{C_\tau}{1 - C_y} < 0.$$

Consumption c^* is equal to $y_K - \tilde{g}$. Note that consumption is an increasing function of government spending $\tilde{g}$, as

$$\frac{\partial c^*}{\partial \tilde{g}} = \frac{\partial y_K}{\partial \tilde{g}} - 1 = \frac{C_y}{1 - C_y}.$$

Employment l^* is equal to $F^{-1}(y_K)$. Unemployment will thus be reduced by an increase in $\tilde{g}$ or a decrease in the tax rate τ, standard Keynesian results. A decrease in the price p will also reduce unemployment, and so will an increase in $\bar{m}$. A change in the wage level w changes the factor distribution of income but here has no effect on activity or consumption since the household receives all income, and thus w does not appear in the consumption function. This last conclusion must be modified, however, when we take a different pattern of income distribution (Appendix P).

Classical Unemployment

As indicated above, this is the case of excess supply on the labor market and excess demand on the goods market. The household is constrained on both markets, but the firm is unconstrained on the two markets and is thus able to realize its Walrasian employment and sales plan. The corresponding values for l^* and y^* are therefore

$$l^* = l_c(w/p) = F'^{-1}(w/p),$$
$$y^* = y_c(w/p) = F(F'^{-1}(w/p)).$$

This region is called classical for a simple reason: the demand for labor has the classical form and determines the level of employment. Only a decrease in the real wage can diminish the level of unemployment, in accordance with the classical prescription. The "Keynesian" measures, increasing $\tilde{g}$ or reducing τ, would only increase the excess demand on the goods market.

If we assume that government is served before the household on the goods market, government purchases and private consumption will be given by

$$g^* = \min(\tilde{g}, y_c),$$
$$c^* = y_c - \min(\tilde{g}, y_c).$$

We see that in this case an increase in $\tilde{g}$ will reduce private consumption by the same amount but will have no effect on aggregate income.

Repressed Inflation

Here we are in a situation of excess demand on the two markets. Since the household is on the short side of the labor market, the level of employment is equal to the inelastic labor supply l_0. Accordingly production and sales are equal to full employment production $F(l_0)$:

$$l^* = l_0,$$
$$y^* = y_0 = F(l_0).$$

Assuming again that government has priority on the goods market, private consumption is equal to

$$c^* = y_0 - \min(\tilde{g}, y_0)$$

and thus varies inversely with government demand. Variations in the real wage, government spending, or the tax rate do not affect the level of employment. However, an increase in $\tilde{g}$ or a decrease in τ will further augment the excess demand for goods.

5. The Complete Picture: Determination of the Regime

In the previous section we determined the employment level l^* and sales y^* in each of the relevant combinations of excess demands and supplies. We now want to determine which values of the parameters p, w, $\bar{m}$, $\tilde{g}$, and τ correspond to each of the three cases.[7]

In a fixprice equilibrium, the transactions of each agent are the "best" with respect to his criterion, taking account of all the constraints he faces.

[7] The method we use here was suggested by Michel (1980).

(This property was shown in Chapter 7.) In particular, the transactions of the firm maximize its profits, subject to all constraints. This implies that l^*, y^*, and q^* are the solution of the following program, where p and w are given:

$$\text{Maximize} \quad py - wl \quad \text{s.t.}$$

$$y \le q = F(l),$$
$$l \le l_0,$$
$$y \le \tilde{y} = \tilde{c} + \tilde{g}.$$

As $\tilde{c} = C(y, p, \bar{m}, \tau)$, the condition $y \le \tilde{c} + \tilde{g}$ is equivalent to $y \le y_K(p, \bar{m}, \tilde{g}, \tau)$. Therefore the above program can be rewritten as

$$\text{Maximize} \quad py - wl \quad \text{s.t.}$$

$$y \le q = F(l),$$
$$l \le l_0,$$
$$y \le y_K,$$

whose solution is

$$l^* = \min[F^{-1}(y_K), F'^{-1}(w/p), l_0],$$
$$q^* = y^* = F(l^*).$$

From this we also see that the rigid relation between employment and sales, due to the absence of stocks, prevents the firm from being constrained on both markets and thus suppresses the potential "fourth case" where the firm would be on the "long side" of the two markets.

Rewriting the solution for y^* as a function of the "exogenous" variables of the model, we obtain

$$y^* = \min[y_K(p, \bar{m}, \tilde{g}, \tau), F(F'^{-1}(w/p)), y_0].$$

Using this formula, we could now classify the three regions according to the values of the parameters p, w, $\bar{m}$, $\tilde{g}$, and τ. But actually l^* and y^* are functions of only two fundamental parameters: the real wage w/p and the "Keynesian" level of sales $y_K(p, \bar{m}, \tilde{g}, \tau)$. Therefore we can represent the resulting classification in a two-dimensional diagram (Fig. 11.4), which has the advantage of being invariant with respect to changes in the five original parameters. The values of w/p and y_K corresponding to a Walrasian equilibrium are, respectively, $F'(l_0)$ and y_0. The Keynesian region has been pictured as K, the classical as C, and the repressed inflation as R.

Alternatively these regions can be depicted in price–wage space,

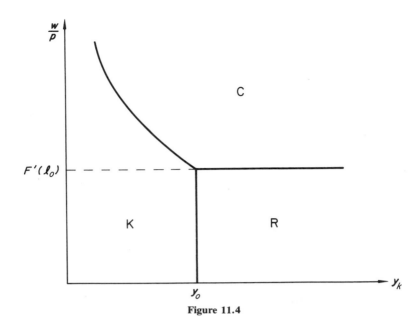

Figure 11.4

keeping $\bar{m}$, $\tilde{g}$, and τ constant (Fig. 11.5), with p_0 and w_0 the Walrasian equilibrium price and wage. We should stress that in contrast to the above invariant diagram, the representation in (p, w) space will shift if $\bar{m}$, $\tilde{g}$, or τ changes.

A few points are of particular interest. Point W is, of course, the Walrasian equilibrium, and points on the boundary between the Keynesian and classical regions correspond to the "textbook Keynesian" model where prices "clear" the goods market. The corresponding equilibria will be studied in Chapter 13.

We should remark that the distinction between classical and Keynesian unemployment is a local property. For example, in the subregion in Fig. 11.4 characterized by $y_K < y_0$ and $w/p > F'(l_0)$, it would be necessary to increase y_K and decrease w/p to totally suppress unemployment; that is, *both* classical and Keynesian measures would be necessary.

6. Efficiency

We have shown in Chapter 10 that in some fixprice equilibria, and particularly multiplier equilibria, a peculiar kind of inefficiency develops in which potential trades that would make everybody better off are not car-

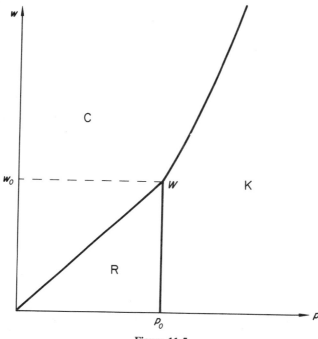

Figure 11.5

ried out. This we shall now study in our simple example. Of course, in order to remain in the fixprice logic, we must look for trades that improve everybody's situation at the given prices.

Clearly such trades do not exist in the classical and repressed-inflation regions: in the classical region the firm realizes its unconstrained profit-maximizing employment l_c and in the repressed-inflation region the household sells its maximum amount of work l_0. Therefore in both cases at least one of the two agents would not want to trade more.

If we are in the interior of the Keynesian region, however, there is clearly some room for more trade. Imagine, in fact, that some central authority were to impose a level of employment equal to $\min(l_0, l_c)$ and force the household to buy all production not taken by the government: the profits of the firm would increase and so would the household's consumption and thus its utility. But unfortunately this better situation cannot be attained in a decentralized way in our monetary economy, since employment will settle at the level $F^{-1}(y_K) < \min(l_0, l_c)$. It is interesting to note, however, that these transactions could be attained in a hypothetical barter economy where "aggregate labor" would be exchanged directly against "aggregate goods" between the household and the firm. In such an economy, the household would supply l_0 units of labor, and the firm would demand the usual "neoclassical" quantity $F'^{-1}(w/p) = l_c$. The transaction would settle at the minimum of these two; that is, if we call l_B^* the level of employment in the "barterized" economy,

$$l_B^* = \min(l_0, l_c).$$

However, as we noted in Chapter 10, the fact that such a barter trade would exist if there were a single firm and a single household exchanging a single good and a single type of labor is totally irrelevant for real economies. Indeed, with a multiplicity of goods, firms, and households, the absence of mutual coincidence of wants between individual firms and individual households makes such beneficial trades unrealizable in a decentralized way at the microeconomic level.

7. Conclusions

The fixprice model of this chapter (a simple special case of the general model developed in Chapter 7) has allowed us to show that both classical and Keynesian unemployment can arise in the same model; which form of unemployment actually occurs depends on the values of some of the model's parameters. The two types of unemployment can be distinguished on the basis of both the determinants of the level of employment and the adequate type of corrective policy measures.

In the classical case, only a reduction in real wages can bring about an improvement in the employment situation. This may be attained by a policy of laissez-faire: unemployment exerts a downward pressure on wages, the excess demand for goods exerts an upward pressure on prices, and both effects thus contribute to lowering the real wage. If price and wage adjustments are too sluggish, or if wages are geared to prices so as to prevent a sufficiently rapid reduction of the real wage, then an active incomes policy may be desirable. Traditional "Keynesian" measures would clearly have unwanted effects: lowering the tax rate τ would only increase the excess demand for goods; augmenting public demand $\tilde{g}$ could in addition reduce private consumption.

In the Keynesian case, on the other hand, an increase in government spending $\tilde{g}$ or a decrease in the tax rate τ will reduce unemployment *and* increase private consumption. A decrease in price p will lower unemployment (through a positive effect on consumption demand), but a variation in the nominal wage w will have no effect. This last result must be modified, however, when, as in Appendix P, we introduce income distributional effects by assuming, for example, that profits are only partly distributed to the household during the period considered.

We must point out, however, that the clear-cut dichotomy between classical and Keynesian unemployment in this model resulted from simplifying assumptions. In a more disaggregated model we could find some sectors in a "Keynesian" situation and others in a "classical" one. Furthermore, as we shall see in Chapters 12 and 13, even at the extreme level of aggregation that we chose, the simple Keynesian–classical dichotomy is upset by the introduction of either expectations or price flexibility.

12

Unemployment and Expectations

1. Introduction

To the simple model considered in the previous chapter we shall now add the possibility of holding inventories for the firm. As a result, we shall be able to see in a simple and direct manner how expectations influence the current equilibrium.[1] A number of results will be obtained from this exercise. First, we shall see that the occurrence of full employment or of Keynesian or classical unemployment depends not only on current or expected prices but also on quantity expectations. Second, our model will exhibit the "fourth" region of excess demand for labor and excess supply of goods. Third, we shall see that the traditional association of a type of unemployment (classical or Keynesian) with specific patterns of excess demands and supplies is no longer valid—an issue somewhat overlooked in the literature. For example, classical unemployment may occur with either an excess demand for or an excess supply of goods.

2. The Model

We shall now explicitly extend the horizon of the model to an additional period so that there will be two periods, current and future. Variables per-

[1] The role of expectations in similar models of unemployment was studied by Hildenbrand and Hildenbrand (1978) and by Muellbauer and Portes (1978).

taining to the current period will have the same notation as in the previous chapter. Variables pertaining to the future period will have a superscript e (denoting "expected").

For simplicity of exposition, the household and government will be taken to behave in the same way as in the model of Chapter 11. The government taxes income at the rate τ and expresses an effective demand for goods $\tilde{g}$. The household has a supply of labor l_0 and a consumption function

$$\tilde{c} = C(y, p, \bar{m}, \tau).$$

As we shall concentrate on the firm's expectations, we do not make explicit the household's expectations embedded in this consumption function. We turn now to a description of the firm.

The Firm

The firm is assumed to have the same production function in both periods:

$$q = F(l), \qquad q^e = F(l^e).$$

We shall assume that goods not sold in the first period can be stored at no cost until the second period and that the firm has no initial inventories at the outset of the first period. Thus, if I is the level of inventories transferred to the second period and y and y^e are sales in the current and future periods, the physical constraints are

$$y + I = q, \qquad I \geq 0,$$
$$y^e \leq I + q^e,$$

which can also be written

$$y \leq q,$$
$$y + y^e \leq q + q^e.$$

The firm is assumed to maximize the sum of current and expected profits,[2] that is, to maximize

$$\pi + \pi^e = py - wl + p^e y^e - w^e l^e.$$

We note that if $p^e = p$ (which we shall assume below), the firm may not care if it sells now or later. We shall assume, however, that in this situation the firm always prefers to sell now (which would be the case if there were even an infinitesimal rate of discount or depreciation).

---

[2] The assumptions of zero rates of discount and depreciation of inventories are made only to yield simple calculations.

Expectations

The firm forms some expectations about future prices and quantity constraints. To keep the exposition simple, we shall concentrate on only one expectational variable. We shall thus take as a parameter the constraint $\bar{y}^e$ on the future goods market, that is, the future level of demand expected by the firm. We shall further assume that no constraint on the labor market is expected and that the price and wage in the future period are expected to be the same as in the current period:

$$p^e = p, \qquad w^e = w.$$

3. The Effective Demand for Labor

The form of the effective demand for labor by the firm will be quite important in determining whether the situation is one of Keynesian or of classical unemployment. The effective demand for labor is obtained by maximizing the objective function of the firm, subject to quantity constraints on all markets other than the current labor market, that is, $\bar{y}$ on the current goods market, $\bar{y}^e$ on the future goods market. It is given by the solution in l of the following program:

Maximize $\quad py - wl + py^e - wl^e \qquad$ s.t.

$$q = F(l), \qquad q^e = F(l^e),$$
$$y \le q,$$
$$y + y^e \le q + q^e,$$
$$y \le \bar{y},$$
$$y^e \le \bar{y}^e,$$

which yields

$$\tilde{l}^d = \min\{F'^{-1}(w/p), F^{-1}(\max[\bar{y}, (\bar{y} + \bar{y}^e)/2])\}.$$

We recognize immediately a "classical" and a "Keynesian" demand. The effective demand for labor has the classical form if only one, or neither, of the two constraints $\bar{y}$ and $\bar{y}^e$ is binding. It has the Keynesian form if both constraints are binding. In the latter case, two possibilities may occur: if $\bar{y} \ge \bar{y}^e$, the firm will produce to meet current demand exactly; if $\bar{y} \le \bar{y}^e$, the firm will produce in the first period half of the total demand for the two periods, $\bar{y} + \bar{y}^e$ in order to minimize total production costs.

We notice that the "Keynesian" demand for labor now depends not only on current effective demand $\bar{y} = \tilde{c} + \tilde{g}$ but also on the expected demand in the future period $\bar{y}^e$. We also see that even if the constraint $\bar{y}$ on current sales is binding, the producer may want to produce beyond $\bar{y}$, if $\bar{y}^e$ is greater than $\bar{y}$, piling up inventories for later sales. As a result the demand for labor may have the classical form even if the firm faces current sales difficulties.

4. The Different Regions

We shall now determine the level of employment and income according to the pattern of excess demand or supply on the current labor and goods markets. Whenever unemployment is present, we shall pay particular attention to its nature, classical or Keynesian. A detailed discussion of the effects of changes in exogenous parameters will be omitted here, as it would be very similar to that of the previous chapter.

Excess Supply on the Two Markets

In this case, the sales of goods are equal to the aggregate demand for goods,

$$y = \tilde{c} + \tilde{g} = C(y, p, \bar{m}, \tau) + \tilde{g},$$

which yields the equilibrium level of sales and income y^*,

$$y^* = y_K(p, \bar{m}, \tilde{g}, \tau).$$

The level of y^* is thus given by a multiplier formula, the same formula as in Chapter 11. Sales determination in this case is thus Keynesian. Employment l^* is equal to the effective demand for labor, which yields, since $\bar{y}$ is equal to y_K,

$$l^* = \min\{F'^{-1}(w/p), F^{-1}(\max[y_K, (y_K + \bar{y}^e)/2])\}.$$

We see that this expression differs in several respects from the expression obtained in Chapter 11 in the model without stocks, that is, $F^{-1}(y_K)$. First, in the case of optimistic sales expectations $\bar{y}^e$, employment may be pushed to its "classical" value $F'^{-1}(w/p)$. Unemployment will thus be classical in this case, and Keynesian measures augmenting y_K will have no effect on employment, even though we are in the region of general excess supply. Second, even when unemployment is "Keynesian," the level of employment may be higher than what is necessary to produce for current demand. In such a case the employment multiplier will be smaller than the usual Keynesian multiplier, as inventories absorb half of current demand variations.

To summarize, the region with excess supply on both markets is separated into two subregions in both of which sales are given by a Keynesian multiplier formula. However, in one of the subregions, which we shall denote by K in Figs. 12.1 and 12.2 below, unemployment will be Keynesian and in the other, denoted by CK, it will be classical.

Excess Supply of Goods, Excess Demand for Labor

Since there is an excess supply of goods, sales of goods are again demand determined and are given by a multiplier formula

$$y^* = y_K(p, \bar{m}, \tilde{g}, \tau).$$

Since there is an excess demand for labor, employment is determined by the inelastic supply:

$$l^* = l_0.$$

We note that this is a "new" region that appeared only as a limiting case in the model without stocks in Chapter 11. What happens is that, in spite of deficient current demand, optimistic expectations lead the firm to hire all the labor force and to store inventories for future sales. For this region to exist, the effective demand for labor must be greater than l_0, even though current demand for goods y_K is smaller than y_0, which means that there must be optimistic expectations, specifically, $\bar{y}^e > y_0$. We shall denote this region by FK, since it is characterized by full employment, with sales of goods determined in a Keynesian manner.

Excess Demand for Goods, Excess Supply for Labor

Given excess demand for goods in the current period, the demand for labor has the classical form. Employment is demand determined and is thus equal to this classical demand:

$$l^* = F'^{-1}(w/p).$$

The sales of goods are supply determined and thus are equal to production:

$$y^* = F(F'^{-1}(w/p)).$$

This region is thus characterized by classical unemployment. We shall denote it by C.

Excess Demand on the Two Markets

In this region, all transactions are supply determined: employment is equal to the inelastic supply l_0 and sales are given by full employment production:

$$l^* = l_0,$$
$$y^* = y_0$$

We shall again call this the repressed-inflation region, and denote it by R in the figures below.

5. The Complete Picture

It now remains for us to determine for which values of the parameters p, w, $\bar{m}$, g, τ, and $\bar{y}^e$ we obtain each of the above possibilities. We know that current employment l^*, sales y^*, and production q^* are the solutions of the optimization program of the firm, taking into account all current and expected quantity constraints; that is, they are solutions of the following program[3]:

Maximize $py - wl + py^e - wl^e$ s.t.

$q = F(l),$ $q^e = F(l^e),$
$y \leq q,$
$y + y^e \leq q + q^e,$
$y \leq \bar{y} = \tilde{c} + \tilde{g},$
$y^e \leq \bar{y}^e,$
$l \leq l_0.$

As in chapter 11, the constraint $y \leq \bar{y} = \tilde{c} + \tilde{g}$ can be replaced with the equivalent constraint $y \leq y_K(p, \bar{m}, \tilde{g}, \tau)$. The program then yields the following solutions:

$y^* = \min[F(l_0), F(F'^{-1}(w/p)), y_K],$
$l^* = \min\{l_0, F'^{-1}(w/p), F^{-1}(\max[y_K, (y_K + \bar{y}^e)/2])\},$
$q^* = F(l^*).$

As before, with these formulas we can draw the different regions, using w/p and y_K as our basic variables. This is done in Fig. 12.1 for different values of the parameter $\bar{y}^e$.

Alternatively, we may draw the different regions in (p, w) space, this

---

[3] Remember that, by assumption, the firm expects to be unconstrained on the future labor market.

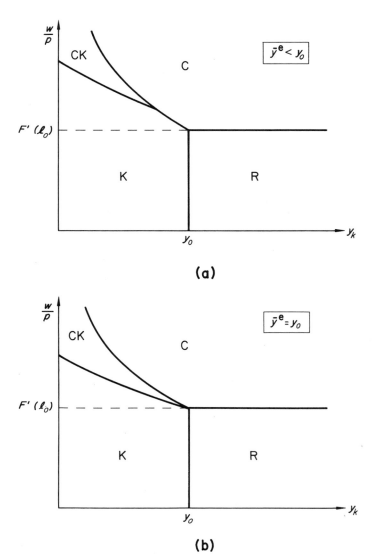

Figure 12.1

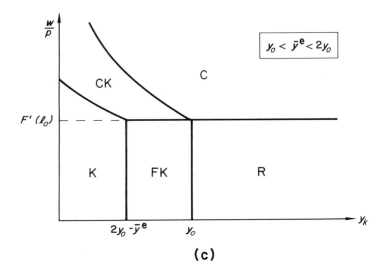

(c)

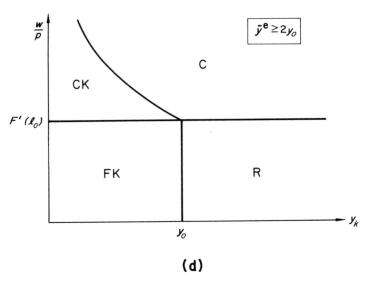

(d)

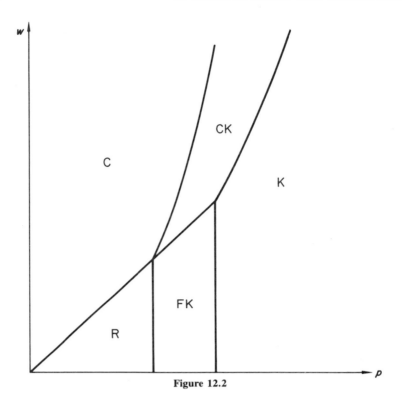

Figure 12.2

time taking $\bar{m}$, $\tilde{g}$, τ, and $\bar{y}^e$ as given. One example is presented in Fig. 12.2, which depicts the case where $y_0 < \bar{y}^e < 2y_0$.

6. Conclusions

The model of this chapter demonstrated, in a simple macroeconomic setting, the influence of expectations on the nature of current equilibria. For the same values of all current parameters, including the price and wage, we saw that, depending on quantity expectations, we could obtain (i) a state of Keynesian unemployment *or* full employment, or (ii) a state of classical *or* Keynesian unemployment. To keep the model very simple, we concentrated on only one expectational variable, $\bar{y}^e$, the level of demand expected by the firm. One would predict that with several expectational variables (quantities and prices) even more striking examples of the influence of expectations would be obtained.

Another result of the exercise is that one cannot draw direct policy conclusions by considering only the signs of excess demands on all markets. We saw, for example, that both Keynesian *and* classical unemployment can occur in the region of general excess supply.

After this simple extension of the model of Chapter 11 to include the consideration of expectations, we shall now make another modification and introduce some price flexibility.

13

A Model of Unemployment with Flexible Price

1. Introduction

In the models of the two previous chapters, price and wage were assumed fixed, as in some Keynesian IS–LM models. This extreme assumption led us to consider equilibria with rationing on the goods market—a phenomenon seldom observed when administrative constraints are not imposed on prices. It will therefore be interesting to consider models where the wage is still assumed fixed but the price is flexible, a line of approach adopted in a number of Keynesian models. The models we shall consider here are very similar to the model of Chapter 11, but whereas the wage is still given, the price now adjusts in one of two ways. In the first model we shall consider, the price clears the market for goods in a "competitive" manner; in the second model, the firm sets the price on the basis of perceived demand curves, as described in Chapters 5 and 9.

For both these arrangements, we shall see that there are two types of equilibria (when they exist): one displays full employment, the other unemployment. We shall also see that, as a result of introducing price flexibility, the classical–Keynesian distinction breaks down because in the case of unemployment both classical and Keynesian measures will reduce the unemployment rate.

Finally we shall study the problem of existence of equilibria. In particular, we shall demonstrate the possibility of having an equilibrium with fixed wage and flexible price for any wage level even though a Walrasian equilibrium does not exist.

The Structure of the Model

Our model has the same ingredients as that of Chapter 11. There are two markets (labor and goods) and three agents (a household, a firm, and the government). The household has a fixed supply of labor l_0 and a consumption function $C(y, p, \bar{m}, \tau)$. The government demands a quantity of goods $\tilde{g}$ and taxes income at the rate τ. The firm has a production function $q = F(l)$. The wage rate w is given and fixed during the period considered. The exogenous parameters are thus w, $\bar{m}$, $\tilde{g}$, and τ.

The price p of the good and the sales y on the goods market are determined simultaneously, either by the equality of supply and demand in the competitive case or by the price-making behavior of the firm when it sets the price. The resulting equilibria we shall simply call fixwage equilibria. We shall first discuss the competitive case.

2. The Competitive Case

In the competitive case, the price p and the level of transactions y on the goods market are determined by the condition that y is equal to the demand and supply on the goods market. We shall therefore examine the demand and supply sides of the goods market.

The Demand Side

The effective demand for goods is equal to the sum of the demand for consumption by the household and government demand, that is, $\tilde{c} + \tilde{g}$. Thus, for the level of transactions y to be equal to demand, the condition is

$$y = \tilde{c} + \tilde{g} = C(y, p, \bar{m}, \tau) + \tilde{g},$$

or

$$y = y_K(p, \bar{m}, \tilde{g}, \tau).$$

We recognize here the "Keynesian" level of transactions seen in Chapter 11. Note, however, that the price is now an endogenous variable.

The Supply Side

The effective supply of the firm is given by profit maximization subject to the constraint l_0 on the labor market. The level of supply is therefore the solution in y of the following program (where p and w are given):

$$\text{Maximize} \quad py - wl \quad \text{s.t.}$$

$$y \leq q = F(l),$$
$$l \leq l_0,$$

yielding

$$y = \min[F(F'^{-1}(w/p)), F(l_0)].$$

In what follows, we write this in the compact form

$$y = \min[S(p, w), y_0],$$

with

$$S(p, w) = F(F'^{-1}(w/p)), \quad S_p > 0, \quad S_w < 0.$$

Fixwage Equilibria

We have just obtained the necessary conditions for y to be equal to effective demand and supply on the goods market. Combining these, we obtain the equilibrium conditions

$$y = y_K(p, \bar{m}, \tilde{g}, \tau),$$
$$y = \min[S(p, w), y_0].$$

In what follows, it will be convenient for graphical analysis to work with "demand" and "supply" curves in (p, y) space. We shall thus define

$$\hat{D}(p) = y_K(p, \bar{m}, \tilde{g}, \tau),$$
$$\hat{S}(p) = \min[S(p, w), y_0].$$

Of course, these are not true demand and supply curves but rather the loci of values of p and y consistent, respectively, with the behavior of the demand and supply sides of the goods market.

3. The Two Types of Equilibria

Assuming for the moment that an equilibrium exists, we see from the equations represented graphically in Fig. 13.1 that we have two different types of equilibria, depending on whether or not the "demand" curve cuts the "supply" curve in its horizontal part. We call the two types, for short, *unemployment* and *full employment* equilibria.

We shall now study the effects of changes in the exogenous parameters

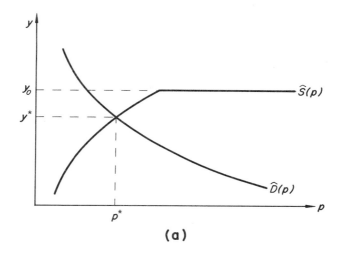

(a)

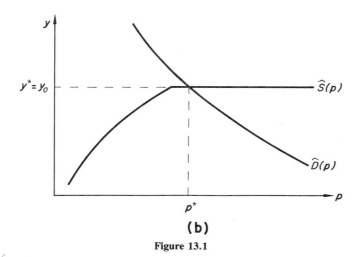

(b)

Figure 13.1

for each type of equilibrium. To do that, we shall rewrite the two equilibrium conditions in the following form, which will make the determination of these effects easier:

$$y = C(y, p, \bar{m}, \tau) + \tilde{g},$$
$$y = \min[S(p, w), y_0].$$

Unemployment Equilibria

This is the case traditionally studied in Keynesian models. The equilibrium values y^* and p^* are given by the system of equations

$$y = C(y, p, \bar{m}, \tau) + \tilde{g},$$
$$y = S(p, w).$$

An equilibrium corresponding to this case is pictured in Fig. 13.1a. In this case, both Keynesian and classical measures will increase the level of activity: equilibrium sales will be augmented by an increase in $\tilde{g}$ or a decrease in τ or w,[1]

$$\frac{\partial y^*}{\partial \tilde{g}} = \frac{S_p}{S_p(1 - C_y) - C_p} > 0,$$

$$\frac{\partial y^*}{\partial \tau} = \frac{S_p C_\tau}{S_p(1 - C_y) - C_p} < 0,$$

$$\frac{\partial y^*}{\partial w} = \frac{-C_p S_w}{S_p(1 - C_y) - C_p} < 0.$$

Notice that the multiplier for government purchases is smaller than the "fixprice" multiplier $1/(1 - C_y)$ obtained in Chapter 11 because of the associated price increase. We may also note that "Keynesian" and "classical" measures have opposite effects on the price level: an increase in $\tilde{g}$ or a decrease in τ increases the equilibrium price, but a wage reduction decreases it,

$$\frac{\partial p^*}{\partial \tilde{g}} = \frac{1}{S_p(1 - C_y) - C_p} > 0,$$

$$\frac{\partial p^*}{\partial \tau} = \frac{C_\tau}{S_p(1 - C_y) - C_p} < 0,$$

$$\frac{\partial p^*}{\partial w} = \frac{-S_w(1 - C_y)}{S_p(1 - C_y) - C_p} > 0.$$

Full Employment Equilibria

In this case (Fig. 13.1b), the level of production and sales is blocked by the inelastic supply of labor: $y^* = y_0 = F(l_0)$. The equilibrium price p^* is the solution in p of

$$y_0 = C(y_0, p, \bar{m}, \tau) + \tilde{g}.$$

---

[1] Some of these results are slightly modified if the consumption function depends on w. See Appendix P.

A change in the wage rate has no influence on the price or on employment,[2] unless the change is so drastic as to move the equilibrium into the unemployment region. Keynesian measures increase the equilibrium price:

$$\frac{\partial p^*}{\partial \tilde{g}} = -\frac{1}{C_p} > 0, \qquad \frac{\partial p^*}{\partial \tau} = -\frac{C_\tau}{C_p} < 0.$$

Comparison with K-Equilibria

To relate the results obtained here to those of Chapter 11, it may be useful to compare the fixwage equilibria with those with fixed wage *and* price obtained for the same model. To make this comparison, we consider the figure in (p, w) space introduced in Chapter 11, still assuming that a temporary Walrasian equilibrium exists (Fig. 13.2). It is easy to see that

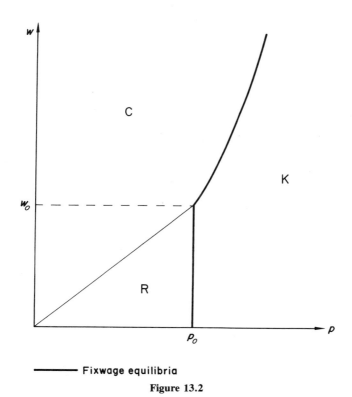

——— Fixwage equilibria

Figure 13.2

[2] However, see in Appendix P how this conclusion has to be modified if consumption demand depends on w.

the set of fixwage equilibria consists of (i) the frontier between the Keynesian and classical regions (unemployment equilibria) and (ii) the frontier
between the Keynesian and repressed inflation regions (full employment
equilibria).

4. Fixwage Equilibrium with a Price-Setting Firm

We have assumed up to now that the price on the goods market was determined by the equality of supply and demand. We shall now study the
more realistic case where the price is fixed by the firm. In Chapter 5 we
saw that in such a case the firm should estimate its demand curve in order
to evaluate the effect of its price decisions on the quantity demanded.
Thus we shall assume here that the firm has a family of potential perceived demand curves. To simplify our calculations, we shall assume here
that these perceived demand curves are defined up to a multiplicative
parameter θ; that is, the expected demand for price p is

$$\theta g(p), \quad \text{with} \quad g'(p) < 0.$$

We shall also assume that the elasticity of these perceived demand curves
is greater than 1 in absolute value. (Otherwise the program below giving
the optimal price of the firm might not have a finite solution.)

$$\epsilon(p) = -pg'(p)/g(p) > 1.$$

The Supply Side

For a given value of the parameter θ, the firm faces the quantity constraint $\theta g(p)$ on the goods market and the fixed constraint l_0 on the labor
market. The following program gives the profit-maximizing price, sales,
and production:

$$\text{Maximize} \quad py - wl \quad \text{s.t.}$$

$$y \le q = F(l),$$
$$y \le \theta g(p),$$
$$l \le l_0.$$

The profit-maximizing price and sales are both functions of θ. In order
to get a representation of the supply side analogous to that studied above
in the competitive case, we want to obtain a direct relation between p and
y, which we can do by eliminating the parameter θ. The relation between y

and p derived from the solutions of the above program can be written as

$$y = \min\left[F\left(F'^{-1}\left(\frac{\epsilon(p)}{\epsilon(p) - 1} \cdot \frac{w}{p}\right)\right), F(l_0)\right].$$

Indeed, when solving the above program two cases can occur:

• If the constraint $l \leq l_0$ is effective, then $y = F(l_0) = y_0$.
• If the constraint $l \leq l_0$ is ineffective, the solution is characterized by the usual equality between marginal revenue and marginal cost, that is,

$$p\left[1 - \frac{1}{\epsilon(p)}\right] = \frac{w}{F'(l)} = \frac{w}{F'(F^{-1}(y))}.$$

Combining the two cases, we obtain the above formula. We may note that this relation may be written in the form

$$y = \min[S(p, w), y_0],$$

with[3]

$$S(p, w) = F\left(F'^{-1}\left(\frac{\epsilon(p)}{\epsilon(p) - 1} \cdot \frac{w}{p}\right)\right), \qquad S_p > 0, \quad S_w < 0.$$

The representation obtained is thus very similar to that of the competitive case, though with a different function $S(p, w)$. We should note that this relation between y and p cannot be considered a true supply curve; it is, rather, a relation between price and sales combinations that are acceptable to the firm. We shall continue to denote this relation in the figures as

$$y = \hat{S}(p) = \min[S(p, w), y_0].$$

In Chapter 14 we shall consider the particular case of isoelastic perceived demand curves:

$$\theta g(p) = \theta p^{-\epsilon}, \qquad \epsilon > 1.$$

In this case the "supply curve" has the simple form

$$y = \min\left[F\left(F'^{-1}\left(\frac{\epsilon}{\epsilon - 1} \cdot \frac{w}{p}\right)\right), y_0\right].$$

We may remark that for ϵ going to infinity, we obtain the competitive case as the "limit" case.

The Demand Side

We know from Chapters 5 and 9 that in an equilibrium where the firm sets the price of goods, the firm will satisfy the demand for goods ad-

---

[3] The property $S_p > 0$ is actually verified only if marginal revenue is an increasing function of the price, which we shall assume here.

dressed to it. Hence the level of sales will be equal to the total demand, that is,

$$y = C(y, p, \bar{m}, \tau) + \tilde{g},$$

or

$$y = y_K(p, \bar{m}, \tilde{g}, \tau).$$

This relation is exactly the same as in the competitive case, and we shall denote it in the figures as

$$y = \hat{D}(p) = y_K(p, \bar{m}, \tilde{g}, \tau).$$

Fixwage Equilibria

A fixwage equilibrium is defined as a solution of the following set of equations (where w is given):

$$y = C(y, p, \bar{m}, \tau) + \tilde{g},$$
$$y = \min[S(p, w), y_0].$$

As above, there are two types of equilibria—with unemployment and with full employment—and the comparative statics properties that can be derived are similar to those in the competitive case (see Section 3). We thus do not state them here. Since the function $S(p, w)$ in the above equation is different from that obtained in the competitive case, the equilibria will generally be different for the same set of exogenous parameters. This may be seen, for example, by plotting the corresponding equilibria in the (p, w) plane (Fig. 13.3) and comparing the resulting figure with that obtained in the competitive case (Fig. 13.2).

5. The Existence of Equilibria

Up to now we have assumed that an equilibrium exists. However, Chapter 9 showed us that when some prices are flexible, existence is not guaranteed under the standard assumptions. Therefore we shall now investigate the problem of existence of fixwage equilibria, and compare the existence conditions obtained with those of the temporary Walrasian equilibrium. Owing to the simplified character of the model, most of the discussion can be conducted graphically. It will be convenient to start by analyzing the existence conditions for the temporary Walrasian equilibrium.

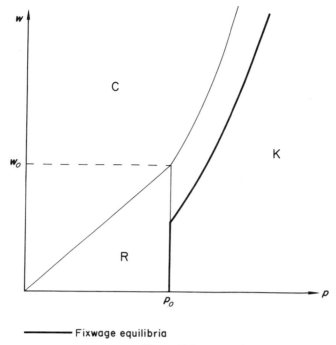

———— Fixwage equilibria

Figure 13.3

Existence
of a Temporary Walrasian Equilibrium

We saw in Chapter 11, Section 3, that the temporary Walrasian equilibrium price and wage p_0 and w_0 are defined by the two equations

$$w_0/p_0 = F'(l_0),$$
$$y_0 = C(y_0, p_0, \bar{m}, \tau) + \tilde{g}.$$

The second equation can be rewritten as

$$y_0 = y_K(p_0, \bar{m}, \tilde{g}, \tau).$$

A necessary and sufficient condition for existence is thus that the "demand curve" $\hat{D}(p) = y_K(p, \bar{m}, \tilde{g}, \tau)$ intersect the horizontal line $y = y_0$, as shown in Fig. 13.4. There are obviously two cases in which equilibrium does not exist: if the curve $\hat{D}(p)$ is (i) entirely above or (ii) entirely below

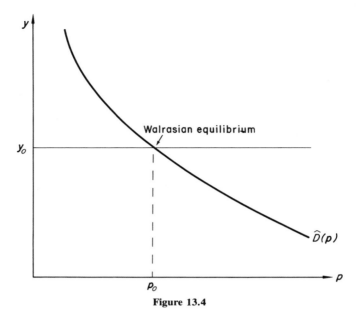

Figure 13.4

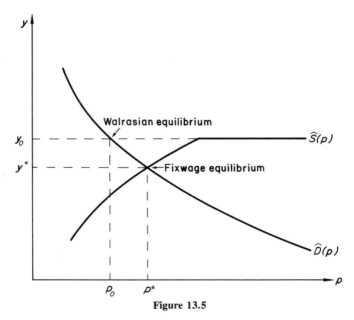

Figure 13.5

the line $y = y_0$. These two cases, the plausibility of which we shall not discuss here, are pictured in Fig. 13.6 and 13.7.

Existence of Fixwage Equilibria

A fixwage equilibrium exists if the "supply" curve $\hat{S}(p)$ intersects the "demand" schedule $\hat{D}(p)$. There are three possibilities:

1. If a temporary Walrasian equilibrium exists, then a fixwage equilibrium exists whatever the level of the wage. It may be either of the full employment or of the unemployment type. This last case is pictured in Fig. 13.5.

2. If a temporary Walrasian equilibrium does not exist because the demand curve is *above* the line $y = y_0$, then no fixwage equilibrium exists either, whatever the level of the wage (Fig. 13.6).

3. If a temporary Walrasian equilibrium does not exist because the "demand" curve is *below* the line $y = y_0$, then a fixwage equilibrium still exists, and it is of the unemployment type (Fig. 13.7). We notice that this situation is similar to the "liquidity trap" case in Keynesian models—a situation in which a Keynesian equilibrium exists even though the Walrasian equilibrium does not.

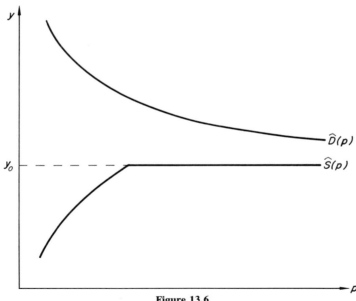

Figure 13.6

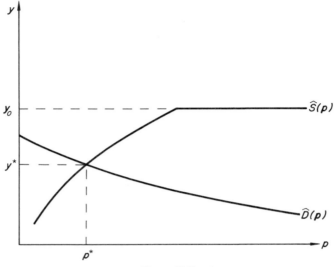

Figure 13.7

6. Conclusions

In this chapter we saw that the introduction of price flexibility into the model of unemployment caused the distinction between classical and Keynesian unemployment to vanish. As a result, the fixwage equilibria studied in this chapter were of only two types: with full employment or with unemployment. In the latter case, both classical measures (a reduction in nominal wages) and Keynesian measures (an increase in government spending or a tax reduction) can be used to reduce unemployment. The classical and Keynesian measures have opposite effects on the price level, however. These results were obtained in two types of models: one where the price is determined by the equality of supply and demand on the goods market, another where the price is determined directly by the firm.

We also studied the problem of existence of fixwage equilibria and saw that there are cases where they exist for all wages even though a temporary Walrasian equilibrium does not exist. Conversely, we saw that fixwage equilibria do not always exist. In the case of nonexistence one should return to the study of equilibria with fixed wage *and* price, which always exist.

We shall now use the model of this chapter to study alternative theories of inflation.

14

A Model of Inflation

1. Cost Push versus Demand Pull

The cost push–demand pull debates about the causes and cures of inflation have been no less heated and no more conclusive than those about unemployment—perhaps because of the lack of a common theoretical ground between the two sides.[1] We intend here to build a simple model where cost and demand inflations occur as responses to different shocks. The two types of inflation will correspond to different regimes of the *same* model.

The Basic Structure

We shall study an aggregate model very similar to that of the previous chapter, with three commodities—money, labor, and a consumption good (output)—and three aggregate agents—a firm, a household, and the government. But we shall now consider the evolution of such a model in time.

Time will be represented by a discrete sequence of periods indexed by *t*. During each period a complete cycle of production and exchange takes place. Prices and quantities exchanged are determined by a temporary equilibrium of the type studied in Chapter 13. The wage level is assumed to be indexed with respect to prices, though with a certain lag. As we shall

[1] For a well-known survey of the two lines of thought see Bronfenbrenner and Holzman (1963).

see, such a simple structure is enough to generate dynamic evolutions corresponding to demand and cost inflations. Before showing this, we shall describe the complete model in more detail.

2. The Model: Markets and Agents

In each period there are two markets, one for labor at the wage w and one for output at the price p. We shall now describe how these markets function, as well as the behavior of the different agents.

Labor Market and Wage Formation

Wages are assumed to be collectively bargained with the purpose of obtaining a "target real wage," denoted by $\omega(t)$ for period t. However, the object of the negotiation is the money wage $w(t)$, which we shall assume is given by the formula

$$w(t) = \omega(t)\, p(t - 1).$$

We use $p(t - 1)$ instead of $p(t)$ to reflect in the simplest way the idea that there is some lag in wage adjustments.[2] At this level of the wage, the household supplies the inelastic quantity of labor l_0.

The Firm and the "Supply" Curve

The firm produces the consumption good with labor. Production q and employment l are related by a production function with decreasing returns:

$$q = F(l), \qquad F'(l) > 0, \qquad F''(l) < 0.$$

We assume that the firm sets the price of the good, taking into account a family of isoelastic perceived demand curves:

$$\theta g(p) = \theta p^{-\epsilon}, \qquad \epsilon > 1.$$

We saw in Chapter 13, Section 4, that in this case the price p and sales y of the firm are related by

$$y = \min\left[F\left(F'^{-1}\left(\frac{\epsilon}{\epsilon - 1} \cdot \frac{w}{p} \right) \right),\ F(l_0) \right] = \hat{S}(p).$$

We shall continue to call this relation, pictured in Fig. 14.1, the supply

---

[2] A more complex lag system for a similar model is studied in the appendix of Benassy (1978).

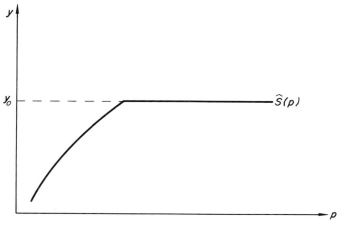

Figure 14.1

curve, though it is actually only a relation between acceptable levels of sales and price. We may remark that the nonhorizontal part of this "supply" curve may be rewritten as a "price equation":

$$p = \frac{\epsilon}{\epsilon - 1} \frac{w}{F'(F^{-1}(y))} = \frac{\epsilon}{\epsilon - 1} \frac{w}{F'(l)}.$$

This says that the price is equal to marginal cost multiplied by a markup, which is itself a function of the elasticity of the perceived demand curve.

Government

The government taxes income at the rate τ and undertakes public spending, financed by taxes or by issuing money. Government's effective demand for output is denoted by $\tilde{g}$, its actual purchases by g^*. Note that these two quantities will be equal in the equilibria considered hereafter, as the firm will satisfy the total demand for goods. The government may set $\tilde{g}$ exogenously or to achieve stabilization goals. For computational simplicity it will sometimes be more convenient to take government demand as a given ratio γ of real income, in which case $g^* = \tilde{g} = \gamma y$. The monetary deficit of the government is equal to

$$pg^* - \tau py = p\gamma y - \tau py.$$

The Household

The household has a fixed supply of labor l_0. As in the previous chapter, its demand behavior is described by a consumption function of the general form

$$\tilde{c} = C(y, p, \bar{m}, \tau).$$

In order to obtain simple calculations, in the rest of this chapter we shall use a particular specification of this consumption function that is linear in real disposable income $(1 - \tau)y$ and real money balances $\bar{m}/p$:

$$\tilde{c} = \alpha(1 - \tau) y + \beta \bar{m}/p.$$

3. Temporary Equilibria and Dynamics

With the preceding elements, the structure in any specific period is the same as that studied in the previous chapter. The wage is given at the outset of the period, from which the "supply" curve $\hat{S}(p)$ is determined as

$$\hat{S}(p) = \min\left[F\left(F'^{-1}\left(\frac{\epsilon}{\epsilon - 1} \cdot \frac{w}{p} \right) \right), F(l_0) \right].$$

The consumption function and government demand determine the "demand" curve $\hat{D}(p)$ as follows.

Let us first consider the case where government demand is fixed in real terms $\tilde{g}$. The condition that sales equal total demand can be written

$$\tilde{c} + \tilde{g} = y.$$

Using the explicit formula for $\tilde{c}$ given above, we obtain

$$\alpha(1 - \tau) y + \beta \bar{m}/p + \tilde{g} = y,$$

which yields the usual multiplier formula

$$y = \frac{1}{1 - \alpha(1 - \tau)} \left(\frac{\beta \bar{m}}{p} + \tilde{g} \right) = \hat{D}(p).$$

However, in the rest of this chapter we shall work chiefly with the case where government demand is fixed as a fraction γ of national income, that is, $\tilde{g} = \gamma y$.[3] In that case the above equation must be modified as

$$\tilde{c} + \gamma y = y.$$

Using again the explicit function for $\tilde{c}$, we obtain

$$\alpha(1 - \tau) y + \beta \bar{m}/p + \gamma y = y,$$

[3] Calculations using $\tilde{g}$ instead of γ are found in Appendix Q.

which yields

$$y = \frac{\beta}{1 - \gamma - \alpha(1 - \tau)} \frac{\bar{m}}{p} = \hat{D}(p).$$

We may remark that the "demand" curve is defined only if

$$\gamma < 1 - \alpha(1 - \tau),$$

an assumption maintained in all that follows.

Having constructed the "demand" and "supply" curves $\hat{D}(p)$ and $\hat{S}(p)$, we know from the previous chapter, and we can see graphically (Fig. 14.2), that two cases can occur, depending on whether the temporary equilibrium level of employment is below or equal to full employment. Which case occurs depends on the decisions of the government (γ and τ) and on the values of w and the initial money holdings $\bar{m}$. We shall now say a few words about the evolution of these parameters.

The Dynamics

As we indicated at the outset, the evolution of the economy over time will be represented by a succession of temporary equilibria of the type just described. The link between successive periods is made through the wage equation (stated above),

$$w(t) = \omega(t) \, p(t - 1),$$

and the following equation characterizing the evolution of the household's initial money holdings:

$$\bar{m}(t + 1) = \bar{m}(t) + \gamma(t) \, p(t) \, y(t) - \tau(t) \, p(t) \, y(t);$$

that is, money holdings are simply augmented by the amount of the government's deficit. The evolution of the "exogenous" parameters $\omega(t)$, $\gamma(t)$, and $\tau(t)$ will determine the path of the system over time. In what follows, we shall model different shocks as changes in these exogenous variables and associate them with the traditional demand and cost inflations.

4. Demand Inflation

The cause of inflation here is an increase in government demand above the level that can be financed by taxes. Assuming a constant rate of taxation τ, the maximum stationary fraction of national income that can be financed through taxes is $\gamma_0 = \tau$. Assume now that the government tries

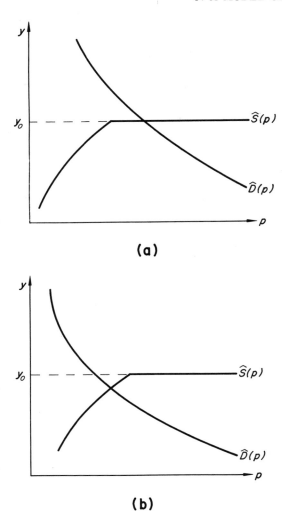

(a)

(b)

Figure 14.2

to increase permanently the share of its spending from γ_0 to $\gamma > \gamma_0$ without raising τ. As we shall see, this will create successive rounds of inflation, generating the "forced savings" necessary to match the increased government expenditure. We shall now formalize this process using our model.

Temporary Equilibria and Dynamics

At least a few periods after the government has increased its spending, we shall be in the situation where the demand curve cuts the supply curve in its horizontal portion[4] (Fig. 14.2a). Employment and production are thus blocked at their maxima, l_0 and $y_0 = F(l_0)$, respectively. We find the price level by equating to y_0 the level of income given by the demand curve seen above, that is,

$$\frac{\beta}{1 - \gamma(t) - \alpha(1 - \tau)} \frac{\bar{m}(t)}{p(t)} = y_0,$$

which yields

$$p(t) = \frac{\beta \bar{m}(t)}{[1 - \gamma(t) - \alpha(1 - \tau)]y_0}.$$

Accordingly, and taking a constant target real wage through time ω, the dynamic equations governing the nominal values in the system are

$$w(t) = \omega p(t - 1),$$

$$p(t) = \frac{\beta \bar{m}(t)}{[1 - \gamma(t) - \alpha(1 - \tau)]y_0},$$

$$\bar{m}(t + 1) = \bar{m}(t) + \gamma(t) p(t) y_0 - \tau p(t) y_0.$$

Combining the last two equations and lagging appropriately, we obtain

$$\frac{p(t)}{p(t - 1)} = \frac{\beta[\gamma(t - 1) - \tau] + 1 - \gamma(t - 1) - \alpha(1 - \tau)}{1 - \gamma(t) - \alpha(1 - \tau)}.$$

The rate of inflation in a steady state i can be computed by taking $\gamma(t) = \gamma(t - 1) = \gamma$:

$$i = \frac{\beta(\gamma - \tau)}{1 - \gamma - \alpha(1 - \tau)},$$

[4] Of course, the "target real wage" must not be too high; otherwise we might fall into the case of cost inflation studied in the next section.

which takes a finite value, provided, as we assumed above, that $\gamma < 1 - \alpha(1 - \tau)$.

Financing of Public Spending

We indicated earlier that the increased government spending is somehow "financed" by real forced savings. We shall now see more precisely how this occurs. Let us rewrite the equation describing the evolution of initial money holdings:

$$\bar{m}(t + 1) = \bar{m}(t) + \gamma p(t) \, y_0 - \tau p(t) \, y_0.$$

In a steady state $\bar{m}(t + 1) = (1 + i) \, \bar{m}(t)$, so that

$$\gamma p(t) \, y_0 = i\bar{m}(t) + \tau p(t) \, y_0.$$

Dividing by $p(t)$ and calling μ the steady-state level of real balances, we obtain

$$(\gamma - \tau) \, y_0 = i\mu;$$

that is, the additional government spending in real terms $(\gamma - \tau)y_0$ is financed by the "inflation tax" on real balances $i\mu$. We should stress that this result is due to the particular specification retained here. An alternative specification is treated in Benassy (1978), where the displacement of income from wages to profits also plays a role in generating the forced savings.

5. Cost Inflation

The cause of inflation is now an increase in the target real wage ω. The initial result of this increase is a shifting of the nonhorizontal part of the supply curve to the right. This increases the price level, which will induce wage increases because of indexation, and then price increases, and so on. However, as we shall see later on, it turns out that this "wage–price spiral" will not develop indefinitely unless the demand curve itself shifts upwards. Such upward shifts can be produced in our model by the increase in government spending that results from an antiunemployment policy. In what follows we shall study the dynamics of the model with or without such an endogenous spending policy.

Unemployment versus Inflation

At least a few periods after the increase in ω, we shall be in a situation where the demand curve cuts the supply curve in the nonhorizontal part

(Fig. 14.2b). Thus $y(t)$ and $p(t)$ are related by

$$y(t) = F\left(F'^{-1}\left(\frac{\epsilon}{\epsilon - 1} \cdot \frac{w(t)}{p(t)}\right)\right).$$

Since $y(t) = F(l(t))$ and $w(t) = \omega(t) p(t - 1)$, we can rewrite the above relation as

$$\frac{p(t)}{p(t - 1)} = \frac{\epsilon}{\epsilon - 1} \frac{\omega(t)}{F'(l(t))}.$$

It we let $u(t)$ denote the unemployment level at time t and use $l(t) = l_0 - u(t)$, this equation can be written as

$$1 + i(t) = \frac{\epsilon}{\epsilon - 1} \frac{\omega(t)}{F'(l_0 - u(t))},$$

which gives the relation between inflation and unemployment in each period. Define

$$\chi(t) = \frac{\epsilon}{\epsilon - 1} \frac{\omega(t)}{F'(l_0)},$$

where $\chi(t)$ is an index of the degree of inconsistency between the target real wage of the workers $\omega(t)$ and the pricing behavior of firms, summarized in the parameter ϵ. If $\chi(t) > 1$, these are inconsistent with simultaneous full employment and price stability. We thus obtain a family of inflation–unemployment tradeoff curves, indexed by χ and pictured in Fig. 14.3:

$$1 + i = \chi F'(l_0)/F'(l_0 - u).$$

Note that $\chi(t) > 1$ if $\omega(t) > F'(l_0)(\epsilon - 1)/\epsilon$. Thus we may have inconsistency, that is, $\chi(t) > 1$, even if the target real wage is smaller than the Walrasian equilibrium real wage $F'(l_0)$.

The movements along and final position on each curve are determined by the government policy, summarized in the parameters γ and τ. In Section 6, we shall study the steady states that the system will reach. Before doing so, we shall report on a few dynamic simulations, investigating the role of government spending in the process.

Government Policy and the Process of Income Inflation

With the help of our model, we shall address the following question: is inconsistency between the strategies of workers and firms (that is, $\chi > 1$) a sufficient condition for a perpetual inflationary wage–price spiral, or is some kind of monetary accommodation, here via public spending, neces-

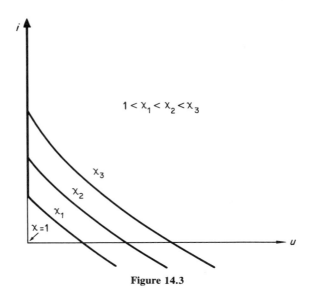

Figure 14.3

sary for inflation to persist? Rather than answering this question in general we shall present the results of some simple simulations that show the dynamic effects of an increase in χ, with or without an accommodating government policy. Two types of policies will be investigated: a financially "neutral" policy, corresponding to $\gamma(t) = \tau$, and an endogenous stabilization policy that can be modeled as

$$\gamma(t) - \gamma(t - 1) = \eta[u(t - 1) - \bar{u}],$$

where $\bar{u}$ is a "target" unemployment rate and η a reaction coefficient.

Assume first that $\chi(t)$ increases from 1 to $\chi > 1$, with the government remaining "neutral," that is, maintaining $\gamma(t) = \tau$. In our simulation we obtain the evolution of $u(t)$ and $i(t)$ pictured in Fig. 14.4. After $\chi(t)$ has taken the value χ, all points lie along the "inflation–unemployment" curve associated with χ. However, after an initial burst of inflation and a sudden increase in unemployment (point A), the rate of inflation returns to zero but the rate of unemployment continues to increase, converging to a new positive equilibrium level (point B). In this model, without an accommodating policy, cost inflation does not persist. In the long run, inconsistent claims lead instead to unemployment.

Next we assume that the government adopts a "Keynesian" policy for fighting unemployment, of the form

$$\gamma(t) - \gamma(t - 1) = \eta[u(t - 1) - \bar{u}].$$

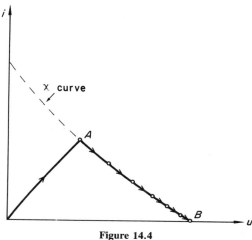

Figure 14.4

Assuming we now start from point B, our simulation gives the evolution pictured in Fig. 14.5 (provided that η is sufficiently small not to make the system oscillatory or unstable). Points still lie along the χ curve. Unemployment falls, asymptotically approaching the level $\bar{u}$, and γ and i stabilize at stationary levels $i > 0$ and $\gamma > \tau$ (point C). At least in this case, an accommodating government policy appears to be a necessary condition for persistent cost inflation.

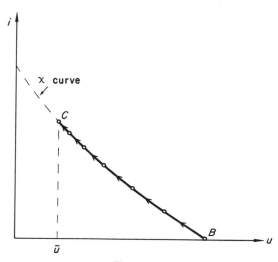

Figure 14.5

6. Steady States

Stationary values of ω, γ, and τ will normally (that is, unless no equilibria exist) generate steady states with constant values of i and u. We shall now compute these.

Inflation

Let us rewrite the equations describing the "demand" schedule on the goods market and the evolution of the money stock, for given values of ω, γ, and τ:

$$y(t) = \frac{\beta \bar{m}(t)}{[1 - \gamma - \alpha(1 - \tau)]p(t)},$$

$$\bar{m}(t + 1) = \bar{m}(t) + \gamma p(t) y(t) - \tau p(t) y(t).$$

Combining and lagging appropriately, we obtain

$$\frac{p(t)y(t)}{p(t - 1)y(t - 1)} = 1 + \frac{\beta(\gamma - \tau)}{1 - \gamma - \alpha(1 - \tau)}.$$

In a steady state $y(t) = y(t - 1)$, so the stationary rate of inflation is

$$i = \frac{\beta(\gamma - \tau)}{1 - \gamma - \alpha(1 - \tau)}.$$

Unemployment

The variation in prices from one period to the next is characterized by the following inequality, derived from the "supply" curve:

$$\frac{p(t)}{p(t - 1)} \geq \chi(t) \frac{F'(l_0)}{F'(l_0 - u(t))},$$

where equality holds if unemployment is positive. In the steady state, $\chi(t) = \chi$, $u(t) = u$, and from the expression of i derived above

$$\frac{p(t)}{p(t - 1)} = 1 + i = 1 + \frac{\beta(\gamma - \tau)}{1 - \gamma - \alpha(1 - \tau)}.$$

We thus have

$$1 + \frac{\beta(\gamma - \tau)}{1 - \gamma - \alpha(1 - \tau)} \geq \chi \frac{F'(l_0)}{F'(l_0 - u)}.$$

Again equality holds if u is positive. Two cases can occur:

$$\chi - 1 \leq \frac{\beta(\gamma - \tau)}{1 - \gamma - \alpha(1 - \tau)} \tag{a}$$

In this case, there is full employment.

$$\chi - 1 \geq \frac{\beta(\gamma - \tau)}{1 - \gamma - \alpha(1 - \tau)}. \tag{b}$$

In this case, unemployment in the steady state is given by the formula

$$1 + \frac{\beta(\gamma - \tau)}{1 - \gamma - \alpha(1 - \tau)} = \chi \frac{F'(l_0)}{F'(l_0 - u)},$$

from which we see that the steady-state level of unemployment is an increasing function of χ and a decreasing function of γ.

Classification of Steady States

Using the preceding formulas, we can now show the types of steady states according to the level of inflation and unemployment. This is done in Fig. 14.6 on a (γ, χ) graph, keeping the value of τ constant. The equation of the dividing line between the zone of unemployment and the zone

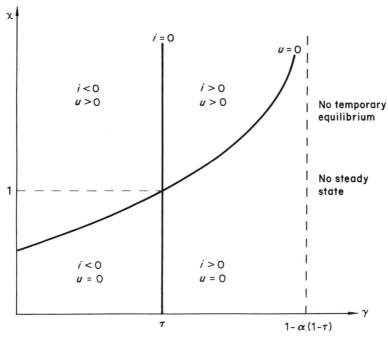

Figure 14.6

of full employment (denoted as $u = 0$ on the graph) is

$$\chi - 1 = \frac{\beta(\gamma - \tau)}{1 - \gamma - \alpha(1 - \tau)}.$$

7. Conclusions

This chapter showed us that we could formalize cost and demand inflation in a unified way, since both occurred as the response of the same system to different "shocks." In order to do that, we studied the dynamic evolution in time of the model of temporary equilibrium analyzed in the previous chapter. Different strategic parameters were singled out: the target real wage of workers ω, the tax rate τ, and the level of public spending g (often measured by its ratio γ to the level of income). We saw that an autonomous increase in public spending (g or γ) with constant tax rate τ would yield sustained demand inflation (the same result would have been obtained with an autonomous reduction in τ, g or γ remaining constant). Conversely, an autonomous increase in the target real wage ω would induce cost inflation, which could be sustained indefinitely, however, only if the government had an accommodating policy of monetary creation. We noticed that cost inflation could occur even if the target real wage ω remained below the Walrasian real wage. This could happen if the firms had some degree of monopoly power on the goods markets.

We kept the model extremely simple by assuming that the wage determination process was characterized by a simple lag structure and that the "strategic" parameters were exogenous (we relaxed this assumption, however, when we studied an endogenous antiunemployment government policy), and then deriving the associated path of the other "endogenous" variables, notably the levels of unemployment u and inflation i.

In reality, however, both the wage bargaining process and the government's spending and monetary creation policies are the outcome of complex sociopolitical processes in which lag structures may vary and in which the "exogenous" variables are actually subject to both economic and political feedback from the levels of unemployment and inflation. The study of such processes, at aggregated and disaggregated levels, should be a fruitful subject of research.

APPENDIXES

Appendix A

Barter Exchange

In this appendix we shall study very briefly the representation and working properties of a barter economy.[1] In particular, we shall consider a "trading post" barter economy as invoked by Walras (1874), where a trading post, or market, exists for each pair of goods. If r goods are exchanged in the economy, there will be $r(r - 1)/2$ such trading posts. To make the discussion simpler, we shall assume that the rates of exchange prevailing at all trading posts correspond to those of a Walrasian general equilibrium. (Trading at prices different from Walrasian equilibrium prices will be considered in Appendix N.)

Markets, Agents, and Exchanges

We shall thus consider n agents, indexed by $i = 1, \ldots, n$, exchanging a set of r goods, indexed by $h = 1, \ldots, r$. Agent i has a vector of initial endowments $\omega_i \in R^r_+$, with components $\omega_{ih} \geq 0$. We shall denote by $x_i \in R^r_+$ the vector of agent i's final holdings after all trades have been completed. Since the price system corresponds to that of a Walrasian equilibrium, the rates of exchange at the $r(r - 1)/2$ trading posts can be expressed in terms of *numeraire prices*. We shall denote by p_h the numeraire price of good h. The rate of exchange at trading post (h, k) will be of $1/p_h$ units of good h against $1/p_k$ units of good k.

We may remark that in such an economy the notion of a "demand for a good" expressed on a market does not exist. Instead there will be a specific demand for a good against each of the other goods. Let us make this formal and define λ_{ihk} as the volume of the transactions of agent i on market (h, k), the "unit" transaction consisting of the purchase of $1/p_h$ units of good h against $1/p_k$ units of good k. After trade on market (h, k), agent i's holdings of good h have increased by λ_{ihk}/p_h and his holdings of good k have decreased by λ_{ihk}/p_k. Agent i's final holding of good h, x_{ih}, is

---

[1] Many themes in this appendix have already been studied, notably by Veendorp (1970), Ostroy (1973), and Ostroy and Starr (1974).

given by aggregating these elementary trades over the $r - 1$ markets where good h is traded:

$$x_{ih} = \omega_{ih} + \sum_{k \neq h} \frac{\lambda_{ihk}}{p_h}.$$

Since the λ_{ihk} are trades on a market, they must balance for all agents; that is, we must have for all pairs (h, k)

$$\sum_{i=1}^{n} \lambda_{ihk} = 0.$$

Using this property and the identity $\lambda_{ihk} + \lambda_{ikh} = 0$, we can compute that

$$\sum_{h=1}^{r} p_h x_{ih} = \sum_{h=1}^{r} p_h \omega_{ih} \qquad \forall \; i,$$

$$\sum_{i=1}^{n} x_{ih} = \sum_{i=1}^{n} \omega_{ih} \qquad \forall \; h.$$

That is, the allocation vectors x_i obtained through these barter exchanges automatically satisfy the "budget constraints" and "physical balance" conditions of traditional Walrasian analysis.

The Problem

The problem we shall address here is: how will the agents' desires for exchange be converted into trades at the $r(r - 1)/2$ trading posts, and will the agents actually be able to achieve their desired exchanges?

The desires for exchange of all agents at the Walrasian equilibrium price system will be described by the matrix of their Walrasian excess demands. The matrix has n lines and r columns. The entry e_{ih} in line i and column h is the Walrasian excess demand of good h by agent i. Since the numbers e_{ih} in the matrix correspond to a Walrasian equilibrium, they must satisfy

$$\sum_{h=1}^{r} p_h e_{ih} = 0 \qquad \text{for all} \quad i,$$

$$\sum_{i=1}^{n} e_{ih} = 0 \qquad \text{for all} \quad h.$$

Now, the agents will be able to achieve their desired exchanges if they can find through decentralized trading on all markets a set of consistent λ_{ihk} (there are $r(r - 1)/2$ such quantities for each agent i) such that $x_{ih} - \omega_{ih} = e_{ih}$ for all i and h; that is, one must find values for all λ_{ihk} satisfying the following set of equations:

$$\sum_{k \neq h} \frac{\lambda_{ihk}}{p_h} = e_{ih} \qquad \forall\ i,\ \forall\ h, \qquad\qquad (\alpha)$$

$$\sum_{i=1}^{n} \lambda_{ihk} = 0 \qquad \forall\ (h, k). \qquad\qquad (\beta)$$

We shall now study, with respect to this problem, two types of barter arrangements, direct and indirect.

Direct Barter

In direct barter, an agent will supply a good in an individual exchange only if he is a net supplier of this good, and he will acquire a good in an individual exchange only if he is a net demander of it; that is, he will engage only in trades λ_{ihk} such that

$$\begin{aligned} \lambda_{ihk} > 0 &\Rightarrow e_{ih} > 0 \quad \text{and} \quad e_{ik} < 0, \\ \lambda_{ihk} < 0 &\Rightarrow e_{ih} < 0 \quad \text{and} \quad e_{ik} > 0. \end{aligned} \qquad (\gamma)$$

Thus no good is used as a medium of exchange (that is, demanded for the purpose of being resold), and goods go directly from an ultimate supplier to an ultimate demander.

Although very simple, trading in a direct barter system may lead in some cases to little trade or no trade at all. Mathematically, the system of equations (α) and (β) very often has no solution under the constraints (γ). Let us, for example, consider the following matrix of Walrasian excess demands for three agents (A, B, C) and three goods (1, 2, 3), where numeraire prices are all equal to 1:

$$\begin{array}{c} \\ A \\ B \\ C \end{array} \begin{array}{ccc} 1 & 2 & 3 \end{array} \\ \begin{bmatrix} -1 & +1 & 0 \\ 0' & -1 & +1 \\ +1 & 0 & -1 \end{bmatrix}.$$

Clearly no direct barter trade can occur. The economy is blocked in a no-trade situation, even though prices are the Walrasian equilibrium ones. Generally, direct barter will not allow exchanges that require some degree of multilateral trading, such as the exchanges in the above example. Rather, it will only allow the achievement of exchanges that fulfill the condition of "mutual coincidence of wants." Although this condition may be met frequently in primitive economies, it would lead to almost no exchange in modern economies, where the circuits of exchange are much more complex than simple bilateral trades. One is naturally led to allow the existence of more indirect trades and thus to study indirect barter.

Indirect Barter

The distinguishing feature of indirect barter is that, *a priori,* any good can be used as a medium of exchange. Of course, in reality some goods cannot be used as media of exchange because of rapid perishability, but quite a number of goods will qualify as media of exchange on the basis of "physical" qualities and will be demanded for the sole purpose of being reexchanged.

However, this situation of indirect barter with multiple media of exchange is likely to present agents with huge informational problems. These have been studied by Ostroy (1973) and Ostroy and Starr (1974). Indeed, for an individual agent who wants to achieve a given final net exchange, it is not at all clear which sequence of individual transactions he should engage in or which media of exchange he should use. In mathematical terms, this indeterminateness is reflected in the fact that the set of equations

$$\sum_{k \neq h} \frac{\lambda_{ihk}}{p_h} = e_{ih} \qquad \forall\, h, \tag{α}$$

$$\sum_{i=1}^{n} \lambda_{ihk} = 0 \qquad \forall\, (h, k) \tag{β}$$

generally has an infinity of solutions in λ_{ihk} when there is no sign constraint on the λ_{ihk} and when the e_{ih} satisfy the budget and material balance constraints

$$\sum_{h=1}^{r} p_h\, e_{ih} = 0 \qquad \forall\, i,$$

$$\sum_{i=1}^{n} e_{ih} = 0 \qquad \forall\, h.$$

As a result, in an indirect barter economy where exchanges are not coordinated by a central authority and where there are more than a few goods, it is quite likely that in the process of exchange some agents will demand some goods as media of exchange that they will not be able to resell. The following example, adapted from Veendorp (1970), will illustrate this point. Let us consider an economy with four agents (A, B, C, D) and four goods (1, 2, 3, 4). The general equilibrium price vector is (1, 1, 1, 1). Walrasian excess demands are pictured in the following matrix:

	1	*2*	*3*	*4*
A	−1	1	0	0
B	0	−1	1	0
C	0	0	−1	1
D	1	0	0	−1

We have here a typical case of lack of mutual coincidence of wants, where some indirect exchanges are necessary if any trade at all is to be completed. In the first "round" of trading, nothing will happen if agents want to achieve direct exchanges. In the second "round" they will be trying to engage in indirect exchanges of "length 1" (that is, with only one intermediate commodity between what they supply and what they demand). For example, A, who wants some good 2, will have noticed that on market (2, 3) there was a supply of good 2 against good 3 (actually coming from trader B). He will thus go to market (1, 3) to buy good 3 against good 1, with the purpose of reselling it afterwards on market (2, 3) against good 2. In a similar fashion, we will find that

A	will demand	3	against	1,
C	will demand	1	against	3,
B	will demand	4	against	2,
D	will demand	2	against	4.

There will thus be exchanges on markets (1, 3) and (2, 4) that lead to a new excess demand matrix

	1	*2*	*3*	*4*
A	0	1	−1	0
B	0	0	1	−1
C	−1	0	0	1
D	1	−1	0	0

We are again in a situation where no direct exchange can take place. The problem arises because agents, making their choices in an uncoordinated manner, have all chosen a different medium of exchange (A chose 3, B chose 4, C chose 1, D chose 2), and thus ended up not being able to resell it against what they really wanted.

Of course, this problem does not arise in a monetary economy, where the medium of exchange is institutionally given and where there thus cannot be a wrong choice.

Appendix B

Effective Demand on a Single Market: Uncertainty, Transaction Costs

In this appendix we shall study the problem of determining effective demand on a single market where the expected quantity signals are forecasted probabilistically and where transaction costs may be present.

Perceived Rationing Scheme

As noted in Chapter 3, in a dynamic context the perceived rationing scheme on a market may be stochastic and may thus be represented by a probability distribution on the transaction, conditional on the effective demand or supply expressed. For example, for a demander the perceived rationing scheme will be denoted by $\Phi_i(\cdot \mid \tilde{d}_i)$, where

$$\Phi_i(\delta \mid \tilde{d}_i) = \text{Prob}\{d_i^* \leq \delta \mid \tilde{d}_i\}.$$

Similarly, for a supplier it will be denoted by $\Phi_i(\cdot \mid \tilde{s}_i)$, where

$$\Phi_i(\eta \mid \tilde{s}_i) = \text{Prob}\{s_i^* \leq \eta \mid \tilde{s}_i\}.$$

In this probabilistic framework the property of voluntary exchange is expressed by the property that the transaction belongs to the interval between zero and the demand (or supply) with probability 1, that is,

$$\text{Prob}\{0 \leq d_i^* \leq \tilde{d}_i\} = 1 \quad \text{or} \quad \Phi_i(\tilde{d}_i \mid \tilde{d}_i) = 1,$$
$$\text{Prob}\{0 \leq s_i^* \leq \tilde{s}_i\} = 1 \quad \text{or} \quad \Phi_i(\tilde{s}_i \mid \tilde{s}_i) = 1.$$

Effective Demand

Assuming as in Chapter 3 that agent i ranks his trades according to a utility index $V_i(d_i)$, effective demand will be given by the property that it maximizes the expected utility of the resulting transaction; that is, it will be the solution in $\tilde{d}_i$ of the following program:

$$\text{Maximize} \quad \int_0^\infty V_i(d_i) \, d\Phi_i(d_i \mid \tilde{d}_i).$$

The Nonmanipulable Case

In the stochastic nonmanipulable case, the perceived rationing scheme can be written

$$d_i^* = \min(\tilde{d}_i, \bar{d}_i^e),$$

where $\bar{d}_i^e$, the expected constraint, has a cumulative probability distribution $\psi_i(\cdot)$, with

$$\psi_i(\delta) = \text{Prob}\{\bar{d}_i^e \le \delta\}.$$

Maximizing the expected utility of the transaction is then equivalent to maximizing

$$\int_0^\infty V_i(\min(\tilde{d}_i, \bar{d}_i^e)) \, d\psi(\bar{d}_i^e) = \int_0^{\tilde{d}_i} V_i(\bar{d}_i^e) \, d\psi(\bar{d}_i^e) + \int_{\tilde{d}_i}^\infty V_i(\tilde{d}_i) \, d\psi(\bar{d}_i^e).$$

Computing the derivative with respect to $\tilde{d}_i$ of this function, we find

$$[1 - \psi_i(\tilde{d}_i)]V'(\tilde{d}_i).$$

As in Chapter 3, let us call $\hat{d}_i$ the target transaction of agent i, which corresponds to the unconstrained maximum of $V_i(d_i)$. We see immediately that if $\psi_i(\hat{d}_i) < 1$, that is, if there is *some* chance of being unconstrained, then $\hat{d}_i$ is the only solution of the above maximization problem.

Transaction Costs and the Revelation of Desired Transactions

The previous section showed us that an agent would usually announce his target transaction $\hat{d}_i$ in the nonmanipulable case. We shall now see, by studying a simple example, that if transaction costs are associated with the fact of expressing demands, the expectation of rationing may induce individuals not to express their target transactions on a market.

Consider a demander i on a market. If he expresses a demand $\tilde{d}_i$, he will realize a transaction $d_i = \min(\tilde{d}_i, \bar{d}_i^e)$, where $\bar{d}_i^e$ has a probability distribution $\psi_i(\cdot)$. The cost of expressing a demand is

$$\kappa_i(\tilde{d}_i) = \begin{cases} 0 & \text{if} \quad \tilde{d}_i = 0, \\ \kappa & \text{if} \quad \tilde{d}_i > 0, \end{cases}$$

where κ is a positive number. The objective function is to maximize the expected utility of the trade diminished by the cost of expressing the demand, that is,

$$\text{Maximize} \quad \int_0^\infty V_i(\min(\tilde{d}_i, \bar{d}_i^e))\, d\psi_i(\bar{d}_i^e) - \kappa_i(\tilde{d}_i).$$

It is clear from the previous section that if any positive demand is expressed, it should be $\hat{d}_i$, since it maximizes the expected utility of the transaction for all ψ_i. However, it may be possible that for pessimistic expectations the cost of expressing the demand is higher than the expected utility of the resulting transaction. This will happen if, specifically,

$$\int_0^\infty V_i(\min(\hat{d}_i, \bar{d}_i^e))\, d\psi_i(\bar{d}_i^e) - V_i(0) < \kappa.$$

In such a case, effective demand will be equal to zero, not to $\hat{d}_i$. The rule giving effective demand is thus

$$\tilde{d}_i = \begin{cases} \hat{d}_i & \text{if} \quad \int_0^\infty V_i(\min(\hat{d}_i, \bar{d}_i^e))\, d\psi_i(\bar{d}_i^e) - V_i(0) \geq \kappa, \\[2ex] 0 & \text{if} \quad \int_0^\infty V_i(\min(\hat{d}_i, \bar{d}_i^e))\, d\psi_i(\bar{d}_i^e) - V_i(0) < \kappa. \end{cases}$$

We should note that this phenomenon of nonrevelation of the desired transaction will also occur with a deterministic constraint. If $\bar{d}_i^e$ is the expected constraint, the above switching rule will be

$$\tilde{d}_i = \begin{cases} \hat{d}_i & \text{if} \quad V_i(\min(\hat{d}_i, \bar{d}_i^e)) - V_i(0) \geq \kappa, \\ 0 & \text{if} \quad V_i(\min(\hat{d}_i, \bar{d}_i^e)) - V_i(0) < \kappa. \end{cases}$$

Appendix C

Price and Quantity Decisions of a
Firm under Stochastic Demand

We shall derive here the optimal employment, production, and price decisions of a firm faced with uncertain demand. We shall first solve the problem with a given price, then consider the price-making behavior of the firm.

The Model with Given Price[1]

The problem considered here was described in Chapter 4, Section 3. Let us recall it briefly. The firm considered has a constant returns-to-scale production function $q_t = l_t/\lambda$. It must choose the best strategy in terms of production levels q_t, $t \geq 0$, for maximizing the expected value of discounted profits from period zero until infinity:

$$\text{Maximize} \quad E\left[\sum_{t=0}^{\infty} \delta^t(ps_t - w\lambda q_t)\right].$$

Sales and inventories are given by the following equations:

$$s_t = \min(q_t + I_t, \xi_t),$$
$$I_{t+1} = \gamma(I_t + q_t - s_t).$$

Expected demands ξ_t are assumed to be independently distributed random variables, with a common cumulative probability distribution $\psi(\xi_t)$. As usual in such multiperiod stochastic models, we shall find the solution by using the methods of dynamic programming (Bellman 1957) and constructing recursively a valuation function for inventories. The valuation function at time t, $V_t(I_t)$, is the expected value of discounted profits from time t onward when an optimal production policy is followed, condi-

---

[1] See Arrow *et al.* (1958) and Bellman (1957) for a more general treatment of the inventory problem.

tional on the level of inventories at the outset of period t, that is,

$$V_t(I_t) = \max_{\{q_\tau | \tau \geq t\}} E\left[\sum_{\tau=t}^{\infty} \delta^{\tau-t}(ps_\tau - w\lambda q_\tau)\right].$$

Since the problem is stationary, this valuation function is the same in all periods, and we shall denote it by $V(I)$. It is determined recursively by the following equation, which also yields the optimal production q (we omit the time index, since the problem is stationary):

$$V(I) = \max_{q \geq 0}\left\{\int_0^{q+I} [p\xi + \delta V(\gamma(q + I - \xi))\, d\psi(\xi)]\right.$$
$$\left. + \int_{q+I}^{\infty} [p(q + I) + \delta V(0)]\, d\psi(\xi) - \lambda wq\right\}. \tag{1}$$

Assuming an interior solution for q, we obtain by differentiating the above expression with respect to q the following equation:

$$\int_0^{q+I} \gamma\, \delta V'(\gamma(q + I - \xi))\, d\psi(\xi) + \int_{q+I}^{\infty} p\, d\psi(\xi) - \lambda w = 0. \tag{2}$$

Equation (2) is actually an equation in $q + I$, admitting as a solution $q + I = \hat{I}$. However, since q is constrained to be positive, the decision rule will be

$$q = \begin{cases} \hat{I} - I & \text{if } I \leq \hat{I}, \\ 0 & \text{if } I \geq \hat{I}. \end{cases}$$

This implies that $V(I)$ is linear in the range $0 \leq I \leq \hat{I}$; indeed, Eq. (1) yields for this range

$$V(I) = \int_0^{\hat{I}} [p\xi + \delta V(\gamma(\hat{I} - \xi))]\, d\psi(\xi)$$
$$+ \int_{\hat{I}}^{\infty} [p\hat{I} + \delta V(0)]\, d\psi(\xi) - \lambda w(\hat{I} - I),$$

and thus $V'(I) = \lambda w$ for $0 \leq I \leq \hat{I}$. Let us continue to assume that $I \leq \hat{I}$. Then $q + I = \hat{I}$ and $V'(\gamma(q + I - \xi)) = \lambda w$ for $0 \leq \xi \leq q + I$. Using these equalities, Eq. (2) becomes

$$\int_0^{\hat{I}} \gamma\, \delta\lambda w\, d\psi(\xi) + \int_{\hat{I}}^{\infty} p\, d\psi(\xi) - \lambda w = 0,$$
$$\gamma\, \delta\lambda w\psi(\hat{I}) + p[1 - \psi(\hat{I})] - \lambda w = 0,$$
$$\psi(\hat{I}) = \frac{p - \lambda w}{p - \gamma\, \delta\lambda w},$$

the expression used in Chapter 4.

The Model with Endogenous Price

Instead of taking the price as given, we shall assume that it is determined by the firm, which now faces an uncertain demand depending on the price it chooses. Expected demands are assumed to be given by stochastic perceived demand curves with multiplicative uncertainty; that is, the expected demand in period t, ξ_t, is given by

$$\xi_t = \theta_t\, g(p_t),$$

where $g(p)$ is the "mean demand curve" and the variables θ_t are independently distributed random variables with mean 1 and a common cumulative probability distribution $\varphi(\theta_t)$. The firm must now choose the best strategy in terms of production levels q_t. As in the previous problem, the solution is found by constructing a valuation function for inventories, which we shall again denote by V. This function, and the optimal price and production, are determined by the following recursive equation (the time index is omitted, since the problem is stationary):

$$V(I) = \max_{\substack{q \geq 0 \\ p \geq 0}} \left\{ \int_0^{(q+I)/g(p)} [p\theta g(p) + \delta V(\gamma(q + I - \theta g(p)))]\, d\varphi(\theta) \right.$$
$$\left. + \int_{(q+I)/g(p)}^{\infty} [p(q + I) + \delta V(0)]\, d\varphi(\theta) - \lambda w q \right\}. \tag{3}$$

Assuming an interior solution (that is, that, in particular, I is small enough for production to be positive), we obtain the optimal values for q and p by equating to zero the partial derivatives with respect to q and p of the right-hand side of Eq. (3). This yields the following equations:

$$\int_0^{(q+I)/g(p)} \gamma\, \delta V'(\gamma(q + I - \theta g(p)))\, d\varphi(\theta)$$
$$+ \int_{(q+I)/g(p)}^{\infty} p\, d\varphi(\theta) - \lambda w = 0, \tag{4}$$

$$\int_0^{(q+I)/g(p)} [g(p) + pg'(p) - \gamma\, \delta g'(p)V'(\gamma(q + I - \theta g(p)))]\theta\, d\varphi(\theta)$$
$$+ \int_{(q+I)/g(p)}^{\infty} (q + I)\, d\varphi(\theta) = 0. \tag{5}$$

We notice that Eqs. (4) and (5) are actually equations in $q + I$ and p. Thus, provided that I is smaller than a value $\hat{I}$, the optimal price is independent of I and the solution in q has the form

$$q = \hat{I} - I.$$

Inserting these optimal values into Eq. (3), we find that $V'(I) = \lambda w$ for

$I \leq \hat{I}$. Using this equality in Eqs. (4) and (5), we obtain the following two equations, which yield the optimal p and $\hat{I}$:

$$\varphi\left(\frac{\hat{I}}{g(p)}\right) = \frac{p - \lambda w}{p - \gamma \, \delta \lambda w}, \tag{6}$$

$$\int_0^{\hat{I}/g(p)} [g(p) + pg'(p) - \gamma \, \delta \lambda w g'(p)]\theta \, d\varphi(\theta) + \int_{\hat{I}/g(p)}^{\infty} \hat{I} \, d\varphi(\theta) = 0. \tag{7}$$

Equations (6) and (7) generally do not admit a simple explicit solution. We may remark that in the limit case where $\theta = 1$ with certainty, that is, when the firm has deterministic expected demand curves $g(p)$ in each period, we find

$$\hat{I} = g(p),$$

$$p\left[1 + \frac{g(p)}{pg'(p)}\right] = \lambda w;$$

that is, the price is such that marginal revenue equals marginal cost and $\hat{I}$ equals expected demand at that price—a very natural result.

Appendix D

Effective Demand in a Sequence of Markets

Using the notation of Part II, we shall study here the determination of effective demand in a sequence of markets. After indicating the general setting, we shall consider first the case of deterministic expected quantity constraints and then the stochastic case.

The Setting

We consider an agent i visiting a sequence of markets labeled $h = 1, \ldots r$. To simplify the exposition, we assume prices given on these markets, or expected with certainty. Let p_h be the price of good h, p the price vector. Agent i initially holds a quantity of money $\bar{m}_i$ and has an endowment ω_{ih} of good h. Call z_{ih} the net trade of agent i carried out on market h, z_i the vector of these trades. Let x_{ih} be agent i's final holding of good h, m_i his final holding of money after trading on the r markets. These are related to the net trades z_i by the following relations:

$$x_{ih} = \omega_{ih} + z_{ih}, \qquad h = 1, \ldots, r,$$
$$m_i = \bar{m}_i - p z_i.$$

The vector $z_i = (z_{i1}, \ldots, z_{ir})$ must belong to a compact convex set K_i, which represents the positivity constraints for x_{ih} and m_i as well as any additional constraints resulting from the sequentiality of trading. Agent i is assumed to try to maximize a utility function $U_i(x_i, m_i)$. To simplify the exposition, we shall use a utility function V_i that depends directly on the net trades z_i and is determined from U_i by the following equation:

$$V_i(z_i) = U_i(\omega_i + z_i, \bar{m}_i - p z_i).$$

We assume that $V_i(z_i)$ is strictly concave in its arguments. In this setting, the Walrasian demands correspond to the solution in z_i of the following program:

$$\text{Maximize} \quad V_i(z_i) \quad \text{s.t.}$$

$$z_i \in K_i.$$

Deterministic Constraints

Let us assume that agent i is currently visiting market h, having completed transactions z_{ik}^* on markets prior to h ($k < h$) and expecting constraints $\underline{z}_{ik}$, $\bar{z}_{ik}$ on markets following h ($k > h$). As indicated in Chapter 4, effective demand on market h is the trade that maximizes the criterion of the agent, taking into account exchanges already realized on past markets and expected constraints on future markets. Thus $\tilde{z}_{ih}$ will be the solution in z_{ih} of the program

$$\text{Maximize} \quad V_i(z_i) \quad \text{s.t.}$$

$$z_i \in K_i,$$
$$z_{ik} = z_{ik}^*, \qquad k < h,$$
$$\underline{z}_{ik} \leq z_{ik} \leq \bar{z}_{ik}, \qquad k > h.$$

An argument similar to that developed in Chapter 3, Section 4, shows that this effective demand leads to the optimal expected transaction, whatever the value of $\underline{z}_{ih}$ and $\bar{z}_{ih}$.

Stochastic Constraints

We now consider the problem of effective demand determination in a sequential framework when expectations about future quantity constraints are stochastic.[1] We describe, in particular, the case where the trader has an ex ante cumulative probability distribution for the quantity constraints on each market, that is, for market h,

$$\psi_{ih}(\bar{z}_{ih}, \underline{z}_{ih}).$$

These are assumed to be independent across markets. Agent i tries to maximize the expected utility of his stream of transactions given these probability distributions, that is,

$$\text{Maximize} \quad E[V_i(z_{i1}, \ldots, z_{ir})].$$

As is traditional in this dynamic-programming type problem (Bellman 1957), the solution is obtained by constructing successive evaluation functions by backward induction. Consider a sequence of transactions $z_{i1}, \ldots, z_{ih}$ and call $V_{ih}(z_{i1}, \ldots, z_{ih})$ the expected utility resulting from this initial stream of transactions, provided optimal actions are taken in the future. Clearly the function V_{ir} for the full sequence is the original

---

[1] An argument like the one in this section was developed in the two-market case by Futia (1975).

utility function

$$V_{ir}(z_{i1}, \ldots, z_{ir}) \equiv V_i(z_{i1}, \ldots, z_{ir}).$$

The functions V_{ih} for $h < r$ are determined recursively through the following relation:

$$V_{ih-1}(z_{i1}, \ldots, z_{ih-1})$$

$$= \max_{z_{ih} \in K_{ih}} \int V_{ih}(z_{i1}, \ldots, z_{ih-1}, \min[\bar{z}_{ih}, \max(\underline{z}_{ih}, \tilde{z}_{ih})]) \, d\psi_{ih}(\bar{z}_{ih}, \underline{z}_{ih}).$$

The set $K_{ih} = K_{ih}(z_{i1}, \ldots, z_{ih-1})$ over which the maximization is carried out is the set of feasible trades z_{ih}, given the previous transactions $z_{i1}, \ldots, z_{ih-1}$.[2] This maximization simultaneously yields the effective demand $\tilde{z}_{ih}$. Our previous exercises with a single market under uncertainty (see especially Appendix B) give us the intuitive idea that the effective demand $\tilde{z}_{ih}$ is also determined more simply by the maximum in z_{ih} of $V_{ih}(z_{i1}, \ldots, z_{ih-1}, z_{ih})$, subject to $z_{ih} \in K_{ih}$. This is easily verified using the fact that V_{ih} is concave in its arguments. The proof is left to the reader.

We may remark that the effective demand on market h depends on transactions on markets $k < h$ and constraints expected on markets $k > h$, but not on the constraints on market h itself (that is, upon ψ_{ih}). Of course, this result would no longer hold if the expectations were interdependent (as V_{ih} would then depend on $\bar{z}_{ih}$ and $\underline{z}_{ih}$ via expectations of future constraints) or if there were transaction costs, as we saw in Appendix B.

---

[2] More precisely, K_{ih} is the set of z_{ih} such that $(z_{i1}, \ldots, z_{ih-1}, z_{ih})$ belongs to the projection of K_i onto the space of the first h trades.

Appendix E

Rationality of the Effective Demand Function

We want to show here that the effective demand vector function $\tilde{\zeta}_i(p, \bar{z}_i, \underline{z}_i)$ defined in Chapter 7 leads to the optimal transaction vector ζ_i^* when the utility function is strictly concave in x_i (Proposition 7.1). Before stating the property and the proof more precisely, let us recall the definitions of ζ_i^* and $\tilde{\zeta}_i$. $\zeta_i^*(p, z_i, \underline{z}_i)$ is the vector solution in z_i of the following program:

$$\text{Maximize} \quad U_i(x_i, m_i) \quad \text{s.t.}$$

$$
\begin{aligned}
x_i &= \omega_i + z_i \geq 0, \\
m_i &= \bar{m}_i - pz_i \geq 0, \\
\underline{z}_{ik} &\leq z_{ik} \leq \bar{z}_{ik} \quad \forall k = 1, \ldots, r.
\end{aligned}
\tag{A}
$$

The effective demand for good h, $\tilde{\zeta}_{ih}(p, \bar{z}_i, \underline{z}_i)$, is the solution in z_{ih} of the following program:

$$\text{Maximize} \quad U_i(x_i, m_i) \quad \text{s.t.}$$

$$
\begin{aligned}
x_i &= \omega_i + z_i \geq 0, \\
m_i &= \bar{m}_i - pz_i \geq 0, \\
\underline{z}_{ik} &\leq z_{ik} \leq \bar{z}_{ik}, \quad k \neq h.
\end{aligned}
\tag{C}
$$

Note that because of the strict concavity of U_i in x_i, the solutions of programs (A) and (C) are unique. We shall now prove the following proposition, equivalent to Proposition 7.1:

Proposition E.1 *If U_i is concave in (x_i, m_i) with strict concavity in x_i, then for all values of p, z_i, $\underline{z}_i$*

$$\zeta_i^*(p, \bar{z}_i, \underline{z}_i) = \min\{\bar{z}_i, \max[\underline{z}_i, \tilde{\zeta}_i(p, \bar{z}_i, \underline{z}_i)]\}.$$

Proof Define z_i^* as

$$z_i^* = \min\{\bar{z}_i, \max[\underline{z}_i, \tilde{\zeta}_i(p, \bar{z}_i, \underline{z}_i)]\}.$$

We want to show the equality of z_i^* and ζ_i^* component by component; that is, we shall show that $z_{ih}^* = \zeta_{ih}^*$ for all h. Three possibilities can occur:

$$\underline{z}_{ih} \leq \tilde{\zeta}_{ih} \leq \bar{z}_{ih}. \tag{a}$$

In this case the constraints on market h are not binding and the solutions of the two programs (A) and (C) are the same, which implies $\tilde{\zeta}_{ih} = \zeta_{ih}^*$.

On the other hand, $\underline{z}_{ih} \leq \tilde{\zeta}_{ih} \leq \bar{z}_{ih}$ implies by the definition of z_{ih}^* that $z_{ih}^* = \tilde{\zeta}_{ih}$.

Hence $z_{ih}^* = \zeta_{ih}^*$.

$$\tilde{\zeta}_{ih} > \bar{z}_{ih}. \tag{b}$$

In this case $\bar{z}_{ih}$ is a binding constraint, and by the concavity of U_i we have $\zeta_{ih}^* = \bar{z}_{ih}$.

$\tilde{\zeta}_{ih} > \bar{z}_{ih}$ implies by the definition of z_{ih}^* that $z_{ih}^* = \bar{z}_{ih}$.
Hence $z_{ih}^* = \zeta_{ih}^*$.

$$\tilde{\zeta}_{ih} < \underline{z}_{ih}. \tag{c}$$

In this case $\underline{z}_{ih}$ is a binding constraint, and by the concavity of U_i we have $\zeta_{ih}^* = \underline{z}_{ih}$.

$\tilde{\zeta}_{ih} < \underline{z}_{ih}$ implies by the definition of z_{ih}^* that $z_{ih}^* = \underline{z}_{ih}$.
Hence $z_{ih}^* = \zeta_{ih}^*$.   Q.E.D.

Appendix F

Fixprice Equilibrium with Involuntary Exchange

In Chapter 7 we developed the concept of fixprice equilibrium under the assumption of voluntary exchange. Though convenient for the exposition, this assumption is not necessary for the development of the concept, and we shall thus treat here the case of rationing schemes that are continuous and nonmanipulable but that need not satisfy the voluntary exchange assumption. Continuity and nonmanipulability imply that the rationing schemes have the following simple form:

$$F_{ih}(\tilde{z}_{ih}, \tilde{Z}_{ih}) = \min\{\bar{G}_{ih}(\tilde{Z}_{ih}), \max[\underline{G}_{ih}(\tilde{Z}_{ih}), \tilde{z}_{ih}]\},$$

with $\underline{G}_{ih} \leq \bar{G}_{ih}$. We see that this is formally quite similar to the rationing schemes used in Chapters 6–10. However, since voluntary exchange is not assumed, we need not have $\underline{G}_{ih}(\tilde{Z}_{ih}) \leq 0$ or $\bar{G}_{ih}(\tilde{Z}_{ih}) \geq 0$, and the relation between the demand of an agent $\tilde{z}_{ih}$ and his transaction z_{ih}^* may thus look as in Fig. F.1, where we have restricted the picture to positive net demands. Notice that in the particular limit case where $\underline{G}_{ih} = \bar{G}_{ih}$, the transaction of agent i on market h is totally determined by his trading partners.

Quantity Signals, Effective Demands

Again we define the perceived constraints as

$$\bar{z}_{ih} = \bar{G}_{ih}(\tilde{Z}_{ih}),$$
$$\underline{z}_{ih} = \underline{G}_{ih}(\tilde{Z}_{ih}).$$

Given a set of price and quantity signals $(p, \bar{z}_i, \underline{z}_i)$, we define the best attainable transaction $\zeta_i^*(p, \bar{z}_i, \underline{z}_i)$ and the effective demand function $\tilde{\zeta}_i(p,$

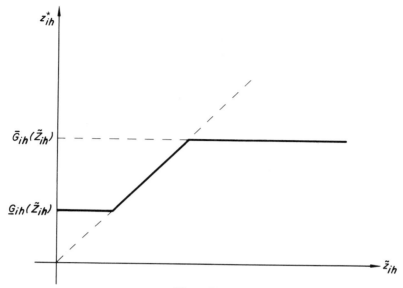

Figure F.1

$\bar{z}_i$, $\underline{z}_i$) as in Chapter 7. $\zeta_i^*(p, \bar{z}_i, \underline{z}_i)$ is the vector solution in z_i of the program

$$\text{Maximize} \quad U_i(x_i, m_i) \quad \text{s.t.}$$

$$\begin{aligned}
x_i &= \omega_i + z_i \geq 0, \\
m_i &= \bar{m}_i - pz_i \geq 0, \\
\underline{z}_{ik} &\leq z_{ih} \leq \bar{z}_{ik} \quad \forall\, k.
\end{aligned} \tag{A}$$

The effective demand for good h, $\tilde{\zeta}_{ih}(p, \bar{z}_i, \underline{z}_i)$, is the solution in z_{ih} of the program

$$\text{Maximize} \quad U_i(x_i, m_i) \quad \text{s.t.}$$

$$\begin{aligned}
x_i &= \omega_i + z_i \geq 0, \\
m_i &= \bar{m}_i - pz_i \geq 0, \\
\underline{z}_{ik} &\leq z_{ik} \leq \bar{z}_{ik}, \quad k \neq h.
\end{aligned} \tag{C}$$

The same proof as in Appendix E can be used to show that the vector of effective demands obtained in this way, $\tilde{\zeta}_i(p, \bar{z}_i, \underline{z}_i)$, leads to the best transaction, $\zeta_i^*(p, \bar{z}_i, \underline{z}_i)$. As in Chapter 7, we say that a constraint $\underline{z}_{ih}$ or $\bar{z}_{ih}$ is binding if it is binding in program (A) above. The effective demand

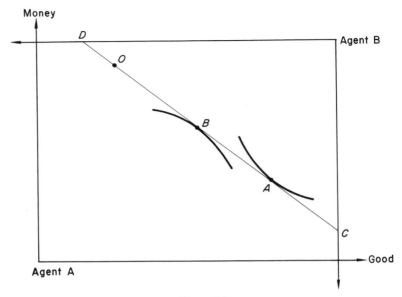

Figure F.2

function reveals when an agent is constrained in the sense that

$$\bar{z}_{ih} \quad \text{is binding} \Rightarrow \tilde{\zeta}_{ih} > \zeta_{ih}^* = \bar{z}_{ih},$$
$$\underline{z}_{ih} \quad \text{is binding} \Rightarrow \tilde{\zeta}_{ih} < \zeta_{ih}^* = \underline{z}_{ih}.$$

However, a main difference is that we may have $|\tilde{\zeta}_{ih}| < |\zeta_{ih}^*|$; that is, the effective demand on a market h may be smaller in absolute value than the optimal transaction, in which case involuntary exchange will be present.

Fixprice Equilibrium

A fixprice equilibrium consists of a set of effective demands $\tilde{z}_i$, transactions z_i^*, and quantity constraints $\bar{z}_i$ and $\underline{z}_i$ such that

$$\tilde{z}_i = \tilde{\zeta}_i(p, \bar{z}_i, \underline{z}_i) \qquad \forall \ i, \tag{1}$$

$$z_i^* = F_i(\tilde{z}_i, \tilde{Z}_i) \qquad \forall \ i, \tag{2}$$

$$\bar{z}_i = \bar{G}_i(\tilde{Z}_i) \qquad \forall \ i, \tag{3}$$

$$\underline{z}_i = \underline{G}_i(\tilde{Z}_i) \qquad \forall \ i.$$

The proof of existence of such an equilibrium is the same as that given in Chapter 7, and is thus omitted here.

An Example

We again consider the Edgeworth box example (Fig. F.2), representing a single market where two agents A and B exchange a good against money. However, we now consider the particular rationing scheme where the transaction is always equal to the effective demand of trader A. In the case depicted in Fig. F.2, the equilibrium transaction is, for both agents, equal to OA, which is A's effective demand. Agent B expresses an effective supply OB but perceives a *lower* binding constraint on his supply equal to OA. He is thus forced to trade more than he wants.

Appendix G

Fixprice Equilibrium with an Effective Demand Correspondence

In Chapter 7, we worked with an effective demand function $\tilde{\zeta}_i$. We shall now restate the theory using a generalized definition of effective demand $\tilde{\Delta}_i$, which will in general be a correspondence. Note that such a correspondence should be used in any case if the utility function $U_i(x_i, m_i)$ is not strictly concave in x_i.

Effective Demand Generalized

There are two properties of the effective demand function $\tilde{\zeta}_i(p, \bar{z}_i, \underline{z}_i)$ that we particularly emphasized, and that we shall also require of the effective demand correspondence $\tilde{\Delta}_i(p, \bar{z}_i, \underline{z}_i)$: (i) it must lead to the best possible transactions, and (ii) it must reveal an agent's being constrained. Since the set of effective demands yielding the best transactions is the set $\Delta_i(p, \bar{z}_i, \underline{z}_i)$ seen in Chapter 7, we are naturally led to the following definition of the generalized effective demand $\tilde{\Delta}_i(p, \bar{z}_i, \underline{z}_i)$:

Definition *The set $\tilde{\Delta}_i(p, \bar{z}_i, \underline{z}_i)$ consists of all the vectors $\tilde{z}_i$ such that:*

(a) $\tilde{z} \in \Delta_i(p, \bar{z}_i, \underline{z}_i)$
(b) $\tilde{z}_{ih} > \bar{z}_{ih}$ *if and only if $\bar{z}_{ih}$ is binding.*
(c) $\tilde{z}_{ih} < \underline{z}_{ih}$ *if and only if $\underline{z}_{ih}$ is binding.*

It is easy to check that if the U_i are strictly concave in x_i, this set of effective demands has the following structure:

• If $\bar{z}_{ih}$ is binding, $\tilde{\Delta}_{ih}$ consists of all $z_{ih} > \bar{z}_{ih} = \zeta_{ih}^*(p, \bar{z}_i, \underline{z}_i)$.
• If $\underline{z}_{ih}$ is binding, $\tilde{\Delta}_{ih}$ consists of all $z_{ih} < \underline{z}_{ih} = \zeta_{ih}^*(p, \bar{z}_i, \underline{z}_i)$.
• If no constraint is binding, $\tilde{\Delta}_{ih}$ is single valued and equal to $\zeta_{ih}^*(p, \bar{z}_i, \underline{z}_i)$.

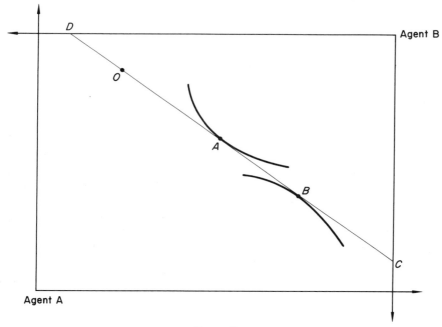

Figure G.1

Fixprice Equilibrium

Using the above definition of effective demand, we can now give a modified definition of fixprice equilibrium.

Definition *A fixprice equilibrium associated with a price system p and rationing schemes represented by functions F_i is a set of vectors of effective demands $\tilde{z}_i$, transactions z_i^*, and quantity constraints $\bar{z}_i$ and $\underline{z}_i$ such that*

$$\tilde{z}_i \in \tilde{\Delta}_i(p, \bar{z}_i, \underline{z}_i), \tag{1}$$
$$z_i^* = F_i(\tilde{z}_i, \tilde{Z}_i), \tag{2}$$
$$\bar{z}_i = \bar{G}_i(\tilde{Z}_i), \tag{3}$$
$$\underline{z}_i = \underline{G}_i(\tilde{Z}_i).$$

These are exactly the same conditions as in the definition of Chapter 7, except for (1), where the enlarged definition of effective demand has replaced the simpler function $\tilde{\zeta}_i$. It is easy to check that fixprice equilibria with this enlarged definition of effective demand have the same properties that were shown to hold in Chapter 7: they are Nash equilibria with respect to the effective demands, and transactions are the best taking all quantity constraints into account. Moreover, if the rationing scheme is frictionless on a market h, there will not be constrained demanders and constrained suppliers simultaneously on that market. We shall now consider an example that illustrates how the sets of equilibria obtained under the two definitions are related to each other.

An Example

Let us again consider the Edgeworth box example (Fig. G.1). Under the new definition there are now many fixprice equilibria. However, all of them yield the *same level of transactions OA*. A always perceives a nonbinding constraint and expresses a demand OA. B perceives a binding constraint OA but expresses a supply that can be anywhere between OA and OC (but strictly greater than OA). As compared with the result of Chapter 7 (see especially Fig. 7.1 in Section 4), we see that the transactions and effective demands of unconstrained agents are the same. The effective demands of constrained agents, however, may be of arbitrary magnitude, as long as they remain greater than the transaction.

Appendix H

Single-Market Efficiency Properties of Fixprice Equilibria

In Chapter 7, we characterized in a very simple manner the efficiency properties of K-equilibria pertaining to a single market when the rationing scheme is frictionless. In that case we were able to use the Drèze criterion and show that it is not possible to have constrained demanders and constrained suppliers simultaneously on a frictionless market. We saw in Chapter 2, however, that the assumption of frictionless markets could not be retained in general. Therefore we shall now provide a characterization of nonfrictionless rationing schemes. Unfortunately, the Drèze criterion applies only to frictionless schemes, and we must use different criteria to characterize the fixprice allocations.

We shall investigate two characterizations of nonfrictionless schemes. The first will use an intuitive extension of the Drèze criterion; the second will use a more game-theoretic approach and will show that no collective action on a single market can improve the state of the traders.

A First Characterization

Before giving our first characterization, we must define the notion of connectedness on a market.

Definition *Two agents i and j are connected through the rationing scheme on market h if for all possible values of $\bar{z}_{1h}, \ldots, \bar{z}_{nh}$ we have*

$$(\bar{z}_{ih} - z_{ih}^*)(\bar{z}_{jh} - z_{jh}^*) \geq 0.$$

Otherwise they are not connected.

This definition is quite intuitive if we think of a rationing scheme as resulting from the decentralized meeting of a number of agents. In such a system some pairs of agents meet, some do not. Only the pairs that meet will be connected through the corresponding rationing scheme. As an example of application, take the case of a market that is the aggregation of a number of frictionless submarkets. Then agents on the same submarket are connected and agents on different submarkets are not connected.

We are now ready to state the efficiency property.

Proposition H.1 *In a K-equilibrium, it is impossible to find on a market h a buyer and a seller who are constrained at the same time if they are connected on that market.*

Proof Assume that one can find a constrained buyer i and a constrained seller j. Then, since effective demands "reveal" that they are constrained, we have $\tilde{z}_{ih} - z_{ih}^* > 0$ and $\tilde{z}_{jh} - z_{jh}^* < 0$. Consequently $(\tilde{z}_{ih} - z_{ih}^*)(\tilde{z}_{jh} - z_{jh}^*) < 0$ and, by the definition of connectedness, i and j cannot be connected. Q.E.D.

A Second Characterization

We shall here characterize K-equilibria by the levels of utility attained through the agents' actions (i.e., their effective demands). More specifically, we shall show that it is impossible for any subset of agents to find *cooperatively* on a single market a new set of effective demands that increase their utility.

Since we shall be dealing with the efficiency properties of actions on a single market, we shall use an indirect utility function bearing on the trades on this market, $V_{ih}(z_{ih})$, constructed as follows. $V_{ih}(z_{ih})$ is the maximum value of the objective function of the following program, where z_{ih} is given:

$$V_{ih}(z_{ih}) = \max\ U_i(x_i, m_i) \qquad \text{s.t.}$$

$$x_i = \omega_i + z_i \geq 0,$$
$$m_i = \bar{m}_i - pz_i \geq 0,$$
$$\underline{z}_{ik} \leq z_{ik} \leq \bar{z}_{ik}, \qquad k \neq h.$$

That is, $V_{ih}(z_{ih})$ is the maximum level of utility that agent i expects to obtain if he carries out the trade z_{ih} on market h and realizes the best trades possible on all other markets, subject to his quantity constraints. $V_{ih}(z_{ih})$ is strictly concave in z_{ih} if $U_i(x_i, m_i)$ is strictly concave in x_i, which we assume.

The rationing scheme on market h is described through a set of n functions

$$F_{ih}(\tilde{z}_{1h}, \ldots, \tilde{z}_{nh}) = F_{ih}(\tilde{z}_{ih}, \tilde{Z}_{ih}), \qquad i = 1, \ldots, n.$$

We assume here that the rationing scheme is nonmanipulable and that each function F_{ih} is nondecreasing in $\tilde{z}_{ih}$ and nonincreasing in $\tilde{z}_{jh}$, $j \neq i$. We can now state the following result.

Proposition H.2 *At a K-equilibrium characterized by effective demands $\tilde{z}_{ih}$ and transactions z_{ih}^* it is impossible to find a new set of effective demands on market h, $\tilde{z}_{ih}'$, for all $i = 1, \ldots, n$ that yields new transactions $z_{ih}' = F_{ih}(\tilde{z}_{1h}', \ldots, \tilde{z}_{nh}')$ such that $V_{ih}(z_{ih}') \geq V_{ih}(z_{ih}^*)$ for all i, with strict inequality if $\tilde{z}_{ih}' \neq \tilde{z}_{ih}$.*

Proof The proof will proceed in five steps.

(a) Let us first consider the unconstrained agents. Since by construction the function V_{ih} attains its maximum for $z_{ih} = \tilde{z}_{ih}$, no change in effective demand would improve the situation for them, and the same is true for all unconstrained agents $\tilde{z}_{ih}' = \tilde{z}_{ih}$.

(b) Let us now consider the set of constrained agents. In order for their new effective demands $\tilde{z}_{ih}'$ to at least maintain the same level of utility, we should have

$$\tilde{z}_{ih}' \geq \tilde{z}_{ih} = z_{ih}^* \qquad \text{for constrained demanders,}$$
$$\tilde{z}_{ih}' \leq \tilde{z}_{ih} = z_{ih}^* \qquad \text{for constrained suppliers.}$$

One can move from the "old" to the "new" situation by choosing an arbitrary order for the constrained agents and by successively changing the effective demands from $\tilde{z}_{ih}$ to $\tilde{z}_{ih}'$. We shall now see whether this changes any transaction.

(c) Let us take the first constrained agent on the list (index i) and assume that he is a demander. (The proof proceeds identically for a supplier.) Let us thus shift his effective demand from $\tilde{z}_{ih} > z_{ih}^*$ to $\tilde{z}_{ih}' \geq z_{ih}^*$ and examine the characteristics of the new situation. Recall that

$$F_{ih}(\tilde{z}_{ih}, \tilde{Z}_{ih}) = \min[\tilde{z}_{ih}, \bar{G}_{ih}(\tilde{Z}_{ih})].$$

Since effective demands other than $\tilde{z}_{ih}$ do not move, $\bar{G}_{ih}(\tilde{Z}_{ih})$ remains constant, and thus the transaction of agent i remains constant.

Since we assumed above that the F_{jh}, $j \neq i$, are nonincreasing functions of $\tilde{z}_{ih}$, the variations in all other agents' transactions should have the same sign as $\tilde{z}_{ih} - \tilde{z}_{ih}'$. But since these variations sum to zero, the transactions of the other agents do not change.

Finally, since neither the effective demands of the other constrained agents nor their transactions have changed, these agents remain constrained under the new situation.

(d) We can repeat the same operation for all constrained agents, in the

order chosen. At each step, using similar reasoning, we find that no transaction has changed and that the remaining constrained agents on the list
are still constrained.

(e) Thus, summing up the whole process, passage from the $\bar{z}_{ih}$ to a new
set of $\bar{z}'_{ih}$ such that no agent's utility is decreased leads to the same transactions, hence the proposition.   Q.E.D.

Appendix I

Perceived Rationing Schemes, Effective Demand, and Fixprice Equilibria

In Part II we concentrated on the study of nonmanipulable rationing schemes since, as we showed in Chapter 3, manipulability would usually lead to no equilibrium. Accordingly the quantity signals considered had the form of upper and lower bounds on trades. In this appendix we shall develop a little further the concept of a perceived rationing scheme sketched in Chapter 3. We shall use this concept to extend the notion of effective demand in a multimarket setting to the case where some rationing schemes may be manipulable and then present a definition of a fixprice equilibrium in this case. The problems encountered will be sketched briefly.

The Perceived Rationing Scheme

Traditional demand and supply theory is based on the assumption that, at least ex ante, transactions will be equal to demands; that is, in the notation of Part II,

$$z_{ih}^* = \tilde{z}_{ih} \qquad \text{for all} \quad i \text{ and } h.$$

We saw, however, that a rational agent must abandon this assumption if the markets do not clear at all times. But he should still perceive *some* relation between his net demands and transactions in order to link his actions (the effective demands) and their consequences (the transactions). We called this relation the perceived rationing scheme, by an obvious analogy with the "true" relation, that is, the rationing scheme F_{ih}. The perceived scheme of agent i on market h will most naturally be conditional upon the quantity signals received by the agent on the market. These we shall denote by q_{ih}. The perceived rationing scheme will thus be written (we assume here a deterministic relation)

$$z_{ih} = \phi_{ih}(\tilde{z}_{ih}, q_{ih}).$$

201

We shall generally assume that the perceived scheme is continuous in its arguments and nondecreasing in $\bar{z}_{ih}$. It may also (but need not) have the property of voluntary exchange, written as

$$\phi_{ih}(\bar{z}_{ih}, q_{ih}) \cdot \bar{z}_{ih} \geq 0 \quad \text{and} \quad |\phi_{ih}(\bar{z}_{ih}, q_{ih})| \leq |\bar{z}_{ih}|.$$

Manipulability

We have insisted several times on the importance of the distinction between manipulable and nonmanipulable rationing schemes. This distinction will be made for perceived rationing schemes in the same way as for "true" rationing schemes F_{ih}. Let us define

$$\bar{\zeta}_{ih}(q_{ih}) = \max\{\bar{z}_{ih} \mid \phi_{ih}(\bar{z}_{ih}, q_{ih}) = \bar{z}_{ih}\},$$
$$\underline{\zeta}_{ih}(q_{ih}) = \min\{\bar{z}_{ih} \mid \phi_{ih}(\bar{z}_{ih}, q_{ih}) = \bar{z}_{ih}\}.$$

The perceived rationing scheme is nonmanipulable if and only if

$$\phi_{ih}(\bar{z}_{ih}, q_{ih}) = \min\{\bar{\zeta}_{ih}(q_{ih}), \max[\underline{\zeta}_{ih}(q_{ih}), \bar{z}_{ih}]\}.$$

Otherwise the scheme is manipulable. The two types of schemes are pictured in Fig. I.1, where voluntary exchange is implicitly assumed.

Consistency with Observations

The purpose of constructing perceived schemes is to make the agent's perception of his trading possibilities consistent with his observations. The observations in a given period include at least the demand expressed $\bar{z}_{ih}$ and the transaction realized z_{ih}^*. We say that a perceived rationing scheme is consistent with these observations if

$$\phi_{ih}(\bar{z}_{ih} \mid q_{ih}) = z_{ih}^*.$$

As we saw in Chapter 3, Section 5, and as Fig. I.2 suggests, this condition does not uniquely determine the perceived rationing scheme in the case of manipulation.

Effective Demand

For given quantity signals q_{ih} on all markets $h = 1, \ldots, r$, and thus given perceived rationing schemes, an optimal vector of effective demands must maximize the utility of the resulting transactions. Consider

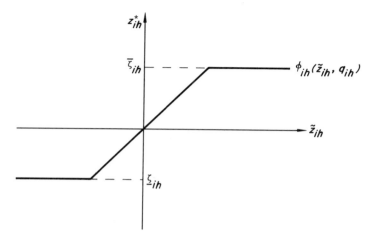

Nonmanipulable

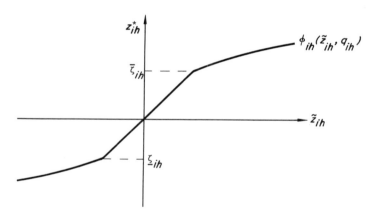

Manipulable

Figure I.1

the program

$$\text{Maximize} \quad U_i(x_i, m_i) \quad \text{s.t.}$$

$$\begin{aligned}
x_i &= \omega_i + z_i \geq 0, \\
m_i &= \bar{m}_i - pz_i \geq 0, \\
z_{ih} &= \phi_{ih}(\tilde{z}_{ih}, q_{ih}), \quad h = 1, \dots, r.
\end{aligned} \tag{A}$$

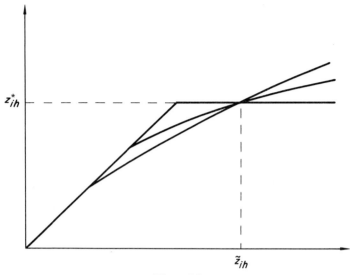

Figure I.2

The best attainable transaction vector is the solution in z_i of this program. We denote it functionally by $\zeta_i^*(p, q_i)$, where q_i is the vector of quantity signals on all markets. The set of effective demands leading to these optimal transactions are the solutions $\tilde{z}_i$ of this program, and they are denoted by $\Delta_i(p, q_i)$.

As before, we shall require that the effective demand reveal when an agent is constrained on a market. So we shall say that agent i is constrained on market h if releasing all quantity constraints on that market would make him better off. Mathematically agent i is constrained on market h if the maximum utility given by program (A) above is inferior to that given by program (B) below, where quantity constraints on market h have been deleted:

$$\text{Maximize} \quad U_i(x_i, m_i) \quad \text{s.t.}$$

$$
\begin{aligned}
x_i &= \omega_i + z_i \geq 0, \\
m_i &= \bar{m}_i - pz_i \geq 0, \\
z_{ik} &= \phi_{ik}(\tilde{z}_{ik}, q_{ik}), \qquad k \neq h \\
z_{ih} &= \tilde{z}_{ih}.
\end{aligned}
\tag{B}
$$

We can now define an effective demand correspondence $\tilde{\Delta}_i(p, q_i)$ as follows:

Definition *The set $\tilde{\Delta}_i(p, q_i)$ consists of all the vectors $\tilde{z}_i$ such that:*

(a) $\tilde{z}_{ih} \in \Delta_i(p, q_i)$.
(b) $\tilde{z}_{ih} \neq \zeta^*_{ih}(p, q_i)$ *if and only if i is constrained on market h.*

Fixprice Equilibrium

A fixprice equilibrium for a price system p consists of a set of effective demands $\tilde{z}_i$, transactions z^*_i, and quantity signals q_i such that

$$\tilde{z}_i \in \tilde{\Delta}_i(p, q_i) \qquad \text{for all } i, \tag{1}$$

$$z^*_i = F_i(\tilde{z}_i, \tilde{Z}_i) \qquad \text{for all } i, \tag{2}$$

$$\phi_i(\tilde{z}_i, q_i) = z^*_i \qquad \text{for all } i. \tag{3}$$

We may make a few remarks about this type of fixprice equilibrium. First, if all schemes are nonmanipulable, we obtain an equilibrium concept similar to that described in Appendix G. Second, if some markets have manipulable rationing schemes, and if there is more than one agent on the long side of one of these markets, an equilibrium does not exist, because of the overbidding phenomenon described in Chapter 3, Section 4. In such a case, in order to restore the existence of equilibrium, we have to impose some bounds on the level of effective demands in markets where the rationing scheme is manipulable and add the corresponding constraints in program (A) above. With these additional constraints, effective demands will remain bounded in spite of manipulability, and an equilibrium will exist.

Appendix J

Perceived Constraints

Throughout Part II we made the assumption that the quantity signals received by an agent on a market with a nonmanipulable rationing scheme were the "objective" bounds on his trades. Specifically, the perceived constraints of agent i on market h, $\bar{z}_{ih}$ and $\underline{z}_{ih}$, were taken as equal, respectively, to $\bar{G}_{ih}(\tilde{Z}_{ih})$ and $\underline{G}_{ih}(\tilde{Z}_{ih})$, as defined in Chapter 6, Section 6. We shall now briefly extend the theory to cases where the perceived constraints may differ from these. Anticipating what follows, we may remark that this will occur only when the agent is not rationed on the market considered.

Indeed, we note first that (as will be shown below) we always have $\bar{z}_{ih} = \bar{G}_{ih}(\tilde{Z}_{ih})$ when agent i is rationed on his demand and $\underline{z}_{ih} = \underline{G}_{ih}(\tilde{Z}_{ih})$ when agent i is rationed on his supply. The perception of the constraint is thus fully objective. In the case where the agent is not rationed, however, the perceived constraints are not as determinate, and they may differ from the values given by the functions $\bar{G}_{ih}$ and $\underline{G}_{ih}$. Let us indicate two types of reasons.

1. If the rationing scheme is centralized, the quantity signals transmitted may be different from $\bar{G}_{ih}(\tilde{Z}_{ih})$ and $\underline{G}_{ih}(\tilde{Z}_{ih})$. We shall consider an example of this below by studying the uniform rationing scheme.

2. If the rationing scheme is decentralized, transactions are generally the result of sequential meetings between pairs of agents. An unrationed agent typically stops trading as soon as he has fulfilled his demand or supply. Therefore he most likely will not know the exact extent of the extra demands or supplies that might have been available to him, and his perception of his constraints will be subjective and thus possibly biased.

In all these cases, perceived constraints should be functions of all quantity signals generated on the market. As these signals are themselves functions of all effective demands expressed on the market, we shall now describe perceived constraints by two new functions,

$$\bar{z}_{ih} = \bar{G}'_{ih}(\tilde{z}_{1h}, \ldots, \tilde{z}_{nh}) = \bar{G}'_{ih}(\tilde{z}_{ih}, \tilde{Z}_{ih}),$$
$$\underline{z}_{ih} = \underline{G}'_{ih}(\tilde{z}_{1h}, \ldots, \tilde{z}_{nh}) = \underline{G}'_{ih}(\tilde{z}_{ih}, \tilde{Z}_{ih}).$$

Note that this formulation is more general mathematically than that used in the main body of this book, where perceived constraints are taken as equal to the "objective" constraints $\bar{G}_{ih}(\tilde{Z}_{ih})$ and $\underline{G}_{ih}(\tilde{Z}_{ih})$.

Properties of Perceived Constraints

We shall now explore a number of properties that we may demand the functions $\bar{G}'_{ih}$ and $\underline{G}'_{ih}$ to fulfill.

(a) First, the perceived constraints must be consistent with the observations, which consist of the effective demand $\tilde{z}_{ih}$ and the transaction $z^*_{ih} = F_{ih}(\tilde{z}_{ih}, \tilde{Z}_{ih})$. Consistency thus implies that the perceived constraints $\bar{z}_{ih}$ and $\underline{z}_{ih}$ must satisfy the condition

$$z^*_{ih} = \min[\bar{z}_{ih}, \max(\tilde{z}_{ih}, \underline{z}_{ih})],$$

which can also be expressed, using the functional expressions of z^*_{ih}, $\bar{z}_{ih}$, and $\underline{z}_{ih}$ seen above, as

$$F_{ih}(\tilde{z}_{ih}, \tilde{Z}_{ih}) = \min\{\bar{G}'_{ih}(\tilde{z}_{ih}, \tilde{Z}_{ih}), \max[\tilde{z}_{ih}, \underline{G}'_{ih}(\tilde{z}_{ih}, \tilde{Z}_{ih})]\}.$$

This condition, which is a particular case of the more general condition on perceived rationing schemes given in Appendix I, can be split into the following three simpler conditions:

$$\underline{z}_{ih} \le z^*_{ih} \le \bar{z}_{ih},$$
$$\bar{z}_{ih} = z^*_{ih} \quad \text{if} \quad z^*_{ih} < \tilde{z}_{ih},$$
$$\underline{z}_{ih} = z^*_{ih} \quad \text{if} \quad z^*_{ih} > \tilde{z}_{ih},$$

which can be expressed functionally as

$$\underline{G}'_{ih}(\tilde{z}_{ih}, \tilde{Z}_{ih}) \le F_{ih}(\tilde{z}_{ih}, \tilde{Z}_{ih}) \le \bar{G}'_{ih}(\tilde{z}_{ih}, \tilde{Z}_{ih}),$$
$$\bar{G}'_{ih}(\tilde{z}_{ih}, \tilde{Z}_{ih}) = F_{ih}(\tilde{z}_{ih}, \tilde{Z}_{ih}) \quad \text{if} \quad F_{ih}(\tilde{z}_{ih}, \tilde{Z}_{ih}) < \tilde{z}_{ih},$$
$$\underline{G}'_{ih}(\tilde{z}_{ih}, \tilde{Z}_{ih}) = F_{ih}(\tilde{z}_{ih}, \tilde{Z}_{ih}) \quad \text{if} \quad F_{ih}(\tilde{z}_{ih}, \tilde{Z}_{ih}) > \tilde{z}_{ih}.$$

The last two conditions express the idea that a rationed agent perceives a quantity constraint that is equal to his transaction and is thus fully objective—a property emphasized above.

(b) Second, we would like these perceived constraints to indicate some "slack" in trading opportunities whenever the "objective" constraints indicate such a slack; that is, mathematically,

$$\bar{G}'_{ih}(\tilde{z}_{ih}, \tilde{Z}_{ih}) > \tilde{z}_{ih} \Leftrightarrow \bar{G}_{ih}(\tilde{Z}_{ih}) > \tilde{z}_{ih},$$
$$\underline{G}'_{ih}(\tilde{z}_{ih}, \tilde{Z}_{ih}) < \tilde{z}_{ih} \Leftrightarrow \underline{G}_{ih}(\tilde{Z}_{ih}) < \tilde{z}_{ih}.$$

(c) Finally, we would like the functions $\bar{G}'_{ih}$ and $\underline{G}'_{ih}$ to be continuous in all their arguments. We may note that the continuity property for the functions $\bar{G}_{ih}$ and $\underline{G}_{ih}$ was derived from the continuity of the rationing function F_{ih}. Here continuity must be assumed.

Under the three sets of assumptions just presented, all of the theory in Chapters 7–10 and Appendices E–I can be rewritten simply by replacing the functions $\bar{G}_{ih}(\tilde{Z}_{ih})$ and $\underline{G}_{ih}(\tilde{Z}_{ih})$ with $\bar{G}'_{ih}(\tilde{z}_{ih}, \tilde{Z}_{ih})$ and $\underline{G}'_{ih}(\tilde{z}_{ih}, \tilde{Z}_{ih})$. No result will be changed in any substantial manner, and thus we will not repeat anything here.

An Example: The Uniform Rationing Scheme

We shall now study briefly the uniform rationing scheme (without stocks) and show that the quantity signals transmitted are often different from those given by the functions $\bar{G}_{ih}$ and $\underline{G}_{ih}$. The uniform rationing scheme is described by the following rules, corresponding to three possible cases depending on the sign of excess aggregate demand on the market:

1. Market h is in equilibrium. Then

$$z^*_{ih} = \tilde{z}_{ih} \quad \forall \, i.$$

2. Market h is in excess demand. In this case demanders are given a uniform bound $\bar{\zeta}_h \geq 0$, which does not affect the suppliers. Transactions are given by

$$z^*_{ih} = \min(\tilde{z}_{ih}, \bar{\zeta}_h) \quad \forall \, i,$$

and $\bar{\zeta}_h$ is determined so as to balance transactions. It is the unique solution of

$$\sum_{i=1}^{n} \min(\tilde{z}_{ih}, \bar{\zeta}_h) = 0.$$

3. Market h is in excess supply. Here suppliers are given a uniform bound $\underline{\zeta}_h \leq 0$ that does not affect the demanders. Transactions are given by

$$z^*_{ih} = \max(\tilde{z}_{ih}, \underline{\zeta}_h) \quad \forall \, i,$$

and $\underline{\zeta}_h$ is the unique solution of

$$\sum_{i=1}^{n} \max(\tilde{z}_{ih}, \underline{\zeta}_h) = 0.$$

The uniform signals $\bar{\zeta}_h$ or $\underline{\zeta}_h$ correspond to the values given by the functions $\bar{G}_{ih}$ and $\underline{G}_{ih}$, only for rationed traders. This may be checked by computing the values of $\bar{G}_{ih}(\tilde{Z}_{ih})$ and $\underline{G}_{ih}(\tilde{Z}_{ih})$ as the unique solutions of the following equations:

$$\bar{G}_{ih}(\tilde{Z}_{ih}) + \sum_{j \neq i} \min[\bar{G}_{ih}(\tilde{Z}_{ih}), \tilde{z}_{jh}] = 0,$$

$$\underline{G}_{ih}(\tilde{Z}_{ih}) + \sum_{j \neq i} \max[\underline{G}_{ih}(\tilde{Z}_{ih}), \tilde{z}_{jh}] = 0.$$

Appendix K

The Indirect Utility of Price Makers

In Chapter 8 we derived the indirect utility function of a price taker $U_i(x_i, m_i, \sigma_i)$ from his direct utility function and the pattern of his expectations. We shall now do the same for a price maker i. We shall again assume that his horizon extends over two periods, current and future, and that he has a direct utility function over his intertemporal consumption stream $W_i(x_i, x_i^e)$.

Expectations

The form of expectations about future trading opportunities will vary depending on whether or not agent i controls the price of the good considered. Let us call H_i^e the set of goods whose price is set by agent i in the future period.

For goods $h \notin H_i^e$ not controlled by agent i, the agent forecasts the price p_h^e and the quantity constraints $\bar{z}_{ih}^e$ and $\underline{z}_{ih}^e$. These expected values depend on the set of current signals σ_i (and on past signals, which we omit, since they are a given datum). This we express functionally by denoting them as

$$p_h^e(\sigma_i), \qquad \bar{z}_{ih}^e(\sigma_i), \qquad \underline{z}_{ih}^e(\sigma_i).$$

For goods $h \in H_i^e$ controlled by agent i, the agent himself will have to quote the prices, and we denote the corresponding vector by p_i^e. He forecasts his trading opportunities in the form of perceived demand and supply curves that are dependent on the price p_i^e he will announce and also on a set of parameters summarized in the vector θ_i^e. We thus denote these perceived curves as

$$\bar{Z}_{ih}^e(p_i^e, \theta_i^e) \qquad \text{and} \qquad \underline{Z}_{ih}^e(p_i^e, \theta_i^e).$$

The parameters θ_i^e are derived by an estimation procedure that uses the stream of price–quantity signals for the past and current periods. Since

210

the past is given, we make explicit only the dependence on current signals, and thus write

$$\theta_i^e = \theta_i^e(\sigma_i).$$

The Indirect Utility

We are now ready to determine the indirect utility function. Let us assume that agent i has consumed x_i in the first period and transfers a quantity of money m_i. For given first-period price and quantity signals σ_i, future expectations are determined as we just saw, and the optimal second-period consumption plan is the solution in x_i^e of the following program:

Maximize $W_i(x_i, x_i^e)$ s.t.

$$x_i^e = \omega_i^e + z_i^e \geq 0,$$
$$p^e z_i^e \leq m_i,$$
$$p_h^e = p_h^e(\sigma_i), \qquad\qquad\qquad h \notin H_i^e,$$
$$\underline{z}_{ih}^e(\sigma_i) \leq z_{ih}^e \leq \bar{z}_{ih}^e(\sigma_i), \qquad\qquad h \notin H_i^e,$$
$$\underline{Z}_{ih}^e(p_i^e, \theta_i^e(\sigma_i)) \leq z_{ih}^e \leq \bar{z}_{ih}^e(p_i^e, \theta_i^e(\sigma_i)), \quad h \in H_i^e.$$

The optimal second-period consumption depends on x_i, m_i, and σ_i, and we denote it functionally as

$$\mathcal{X}_i^e(x_i, m_i, \sigma_i).$$

The indirect utility function U_i is then immediately constructed from W_i as

$$U_i(x_i, m_i, \sigma_i) = W_i(x_i, \mathcal{X}_i^e(x_i, m_i, \sigma_i)).$$

Appendix L

K-Equilibria with Price Makers: A Tâtonnement Process

In Chapter 9, Section 4, we studied the concept of a *K*-equilibrium with price makers. Price making was described in Section 3, and we noted that, as a result of the instantaneous interaction implicitly contained in the equilibrium notion, some variables appeared at the same time both as the result of a decision process and as information variables in the same process. This was the case notably for the subvectors p_i of prices controlled by the agents. Indeed, p_i is both the outcome of the function $\mathcal{P}_i^*(\sigma_i)$ and part of the information vector subsumed in σ_i. We shall now sketch briefly a mixed tâtonnement process in prices and quantities in which this problem is avoided and which has the *K*-equilibrium with price makers as a fixed point.[1]

In order to do that, we shall adopt the following time structure. We shall consider a sequence of periods, indexed by t. (These periods are actually fictitious and correspond only to successive steps of the tâtonnement process.) At the outset of each period, all price makers announce their prices on the basis of information collected in the previous period. After all prices have been announced, quantity adjustments, which we assume infinitely fast, take place, and a fixprice equilibrium is established. This will generate new information, on which price decisions of the next period will be based, and so on. A *K*-equilibrium with price makers is a fixed point of this process. We shall now describe the process in more detail, showing its evolution from one period to the next.

Let us first consider period $t - 1$. Price makers announce their prices $p_i(t - 1)$. The given prices are at their fixed values throughout all periods, and the vector $p(t - 1)$ is thus fully known. We assume that a fixprice equilibrium corresponding to $p(t - 1)$ is then established. (From the analyses of Chapters 7 and 8 we know that such an equilibrium always exists.) To this equilibrium correspond for agent i vectors of effective demands

---

[1] Note that this is only one possible process among many having these properties. This one has been chosen for its simplicity.

$\tilde{z}_i(t - 1)$, transactions $z_i^*(t - 1)$, and perceived constraints $\bar{z}_i(t - 1)$ and $\underline{z}_i(t - 1)$.

Let us now move on to period t. Price makers must first estimate their perceived demand curves. As indicated above, we shall assume that the curves in period t are fitted to the information of period $t - 1$. The estimated parameters for period t are thus $\theta_i(\sigma_i(t - 1))$ and the perceived curves for period t are

$$\bar{Z}_{ih}(p_i, \theta_i(\sigma_i(t - 1))) \qquad \text{and} \qquad \underline{Z}_{ih}(p_i, \theta_i(\sigma_i(t - 1))).$$

The consistency conditions express the fact that the curves in period t are consistent with the observations in period $t - 1$, that is,

$$\begin{aligned}
\bar{Z}_{ih}(p_i, \theta_i(\sigma_i(t - 1))) &= \bar{z}_{ih}(t - 1) &&\text{if} \quad p_i = p_i(t - 1), \\
\underline{Z}_{ih}(p_i, \theta_i(\sigma_i(t - 1))) &= \underline{z}_{ih}(t - 1) &&\text{if} \quad p_i = p_i(t - 1).
\end{aligned}$$

Price maker i will choose a price vector that maximizes his utility, subject to the information from period $t - 1$; $p_i(t)$ will be the solution in p_i of the following program:

Maximize $\quad U_i(x_i, m_i, \sigma_i(t - 1)) \qquad$ s.t.

$$\begin{aligned}
&x_i = \omega_i + z_i \geq 0, \\
&m_i = \bar{m}_i - pz_i \geq 0, \\
&p_h = p_h(t - 1), && h \notin H_i, \\
&\underline{z}_{ih}(t - 1) \leq z_{ih} \leq \bar{z}_{ih}(t - 1), && h \notin H_i, \\
&\underline{Z}_{ih}(p_i, \theta_i(\sigma_i(t - 1))) \leq z_{ih} \leq \bar{Z}_{ih}(p_i, \theta_i(\sigma_i(t -))), && h \in H_i.
\end{aligned}$$

We thus obtain

$$p_i(t) = \mathscr{P}_i^*(\sigma_i(t - 1)) = \mathscr{P}_i^*(p(t - 1), \bar{z}_i(t - 1), \underline{z}_i(t - 1)).$$

A fixed point p^* of this tâtonnement process is obtained when

$$p_i(t) = p_i(t - 1) = p_i^* \qquad \text{for all } i.$$

It is easy to check that the price vector corresponding to such a fixed point and an associated K-equilibrium constitute a K-equilibrium with price makers, as defined in Chapter 9, Section 4.

Appendix M

Multiplier Inefficiency: A Further Example

In Chapter 10, Section 5, we presented an example of a p-inefficient multiplier equilibrium where a direct barter trade was sufficient to reach a p-efficient allocation. We shall now construct an example that again displays multiplier inefficiency but in which a p-efficient allocation can be reached only via indirect barter trades.

The Economy

We shall consider a monetary economy with three markets (1, 2, and 3) and three agents (A, B, and C). The initial endowments are

$$\omega_A = (2, 0, 0), \quad \bar{m}_A = 1,$$
$$\omega_B = (0, 2, 0), \quad \bar{m}_B = 1,$$
$$\omega_C = (0, 0, 2), \quad \bar{m}_C = 1,$$

and the utility functions are

$$U_A = \text{Log } x_{A1} + \text{Log } x_{A2} + \text{Log } m_A,$$
$$U_B = \text{Log } x_{B2} + \text{Log } x_{B3} + \text{Log } m_B,$$
$$U_C = \text{Log } x_{C3} + \text{Log } x_{C1} + \text{Log } m_C.$$

Prices are denoted by p_1, p_2, and p_3. We shall now compute the level of transactions in the region of general excess supply, since we may expect multiplier effects to occur in that case. We shall be particularly interested in the interior of the general excess supply region, which corresponds to the subset of prices defined by

$$p_1 > 1, \quad p_2 > 1, \quad p_3 > 1.$$

214

Determination of Transactions

With excess supply on the three markets, transactions are determined by the demand side, that is,

$$\tilde{z}_{A2} = z^*_{A2} = -z^*_{B2}, \tag{1}$$

$$\tilde{z}_{B3} = z^*_{B3} = -z^*_{C3}, \tag{2}$$

$$\tilde{z}_{C1} = z^*_{C1} = -z^*_{A1}. \tag{3}$$

Agent A's effective demand for good 2, $\tilde{z}_{A2}$, is given by

Maximize $\text{Log}(2 + z_{A1}) + \text{Log } z_{A2} + \text{Log } m_A$ s.t.

$$m_A = 1 - p_1 z_{A1} - p_2 z_{A2},$$
$$z_{A1} \geq \underline{z}_{A1}.$$

The last constraint is binding because A's supply of good 1 is constrained, hence

$$p_2 \tilde{z}_{A2} = \tfrac{1}{2}(1 - p_1 \underline{z}_{A1}) = \tfrac{1}{2}(1 - p_1 z^*_{A1}). \tag{4}$$

We may compute $\tilde{z}_{B3}$ and $\tilde{z}_{C1}$ similarly:

$$p_3 \tilde{z}_{B3} = \tfrac{1}{2}(1 - p_2 \underline{z}_{B2}) = \tfrac{1}{2}(1 - p_2 z^*_{B2}), \tag{5}$$

$$p_1 \tilde{z}_{C1} = \tfrac{1}{2}(1 - p_3 \underline{z}_{C3}) = \tfrac{1}{2}(1 - p_3 z^*_{C3}). \tag{6}$$

Solving the system of equations (1–6), we obtain the realized transactions

$$-z^*_{A1} = z^*_{C1} = 1/p_1,$$
$$-z^*_{B2} = z^*_{A2} = 1/p_2,$$
$$-z^*_{C3} = z^*_{B3} = 1/p_3,$$

from which we immediately compute the final holdings of goods and money

$$x_A = (2 - 1/p_1, 1/p_2, 0), \quad m_A = 1,$$
$$x_B = (0, 2 - 1/p_2, 1/p_3), \quad m_B = 1,$$
$$x_C = (1/p_1, 0, 2 - 1/p_3), \quad m_C = 1.$$

Inefficiency

It is easy to check that the above allocation is not p-efficient in the interior of the generalized excess supply region. Indeed, A would like to acquire good 2 against good 1, B good 3 against good 2, C good 1 against good 3:

$$\frac{1}{p_2}\frac{\partial U_A}{\partial x_{A2}} - \frac{1}{p_1}\frac{\partial U_A}{\partial x_{A1}} = \frac{2(p_1 - 1)}{2p_1 - 1} > 0,$$

$$\frac{1}{p_3}\frac{\partial U_B}{\partial x_{B3}} - \frac{1}{p_2}\frac{\partial U_B}{\partial x_{B2}} = \frac{2(p_2 - 1)}{2p_2 - 1} > 0,$$

$$\frac{1}{p_3}\frac{\partial U_C}{\partial x_{C1}} - \frac{1}{p_3}\frac{\partial U_C}{\partial x_{C3}} = \frac{2(p_3 - 1)}{2p_3 - 1} > 0.$$

Indirect barter

We may also remark that a triangular trade between the three agents would allow the following allocation to be reached:

$$x_A = (2 - p_{min}/p_1, \ p_{min}/p_2, \ 0), \qquad m_A = 1,$$
$$x_B = (0, \ 2 - p_{min}/p_2, \ p_{min}/p_3), \qquad m_B = 1,$$
$$x_C = (p_{min}/p_1, \ 0, \ 2 - p_{min}/p_3), \qquad m_C = 1,$$

where $p_{min} = \min(p_1, p_2, p_3)$. This allocation can easily be checked to be p-efficient, but—and this is the main difference between this example and the example of Chapter 10—it *cannot* be reached through direct barter between agents. Indirect barter is thus necessary. However, this involves all the informational difficulties sketched in Appendix A.

Appendix N

Efficiency Properties of Fixprice Barter Equilibria

In this appendix we shall again consider the "trading post" barter economy studied in Appendix A, this time sketching briefly its functioning when prices do not correspond to those of a Walrasian equilibrium and deriving some efficiency properties for the corresponding fixprice equilibria. We shall find that a fixprice barter equilibrium allocation is p-efficient if the rationing schemes are frictionless. However, as we have emphasized a few times, such a result must be interpreted with the greatest caution. Indeed, the informational problems sketched in Appendix A would make the indirect barter trades leading to such a fixprice allocation almost impossible to find for agents in a decentralized economy when mutual coincidence of wants does not hold.

The Setting

We again consider n agents, indexed by $i = 1, \ldots, n$, exchanging r goods, indexed by $h = 1, \ldots, r$. Agent i's vector of initial endowment is $\omega_i \in R_+^r$, his vector of final holdings $x_i \in R_+^r$. We assume that he has a utility function $U_i(x_i)$.

There are $r(r - 1)/2$ trading posts for the exchange of pairs of goods. We assume that the rates of exchange at these trading posts correspond to a set of numeraire prices $p = (p_1, \ldots, p_r)$. Accordingly the rate of exchange at trading post (h, k) is of $1/p_h$ units of good h against $1/p_k$ units of good k. Denoting by λ_{ihk} the volume of agent i's transaction at trading post (h, k), the final holdings of agent i will be

$$x_{ih} = \omega_{ih} + \sum_{k \neq h} \frac{\lambda_{ihk}}{p_h}, \qquad h = 1, \ldots, r.$$

Fixprice Equilibrium[1]

Since prices do not necessarily clear markets, we must again distinguish carefully between effective demands and transactions. At trading post (h, k) trader i expresses a demand $\tilde{\lambda}_{ihk}$ for good h against good k and realizes a transaction λ_{ihk}^*. This transaction is derived from all effective demands expressed on the market by the n agents, $\tilde{\lambda}_{1hk}, \ldots, \tilde{\lambda}_{nhk}$, through a rationing scheme similar to those studied in Chapter 6. Transactions must balance at all trading posts, that is,

$$\sum_{i=1}^{n} \lambda_{ihk}^* = 0 \qquad \forall \ (h, k).$$

We shall assume that all rationing schemes are nonmanipulable and satisfy voluntary exchange. Accordingly trader i perceives at each trading post (h, k) some constraints on his trades $\bar{\lambda}_{ihk} \geq 0$ and $\underline{\lambda}_{ihk} \leq 0$. These constraints are also functions of the effective demands expressed at trading post

$$(h, k), \text{ that is, } \tilde{\lambda}_{1hk}, \ldots, \tilde{\lambda}_{nhk}.$$

The effective demands of a trader at all trading posts are derived so as to yield the optimal transactions, taking into account all quantity signals.

A fixprice equilibrium will be a set of effective demands, transactions, and perceived constraints that are consistent in the way described in Chapter 7. We shall not describe such a barter fixprice equilibrium in detail but only state a fundamental property (very similar to that given in Chapter 7 for the monetary economy) to be used in deriving the efficiency properties in the next section. That is, at a fixprice equilibrium the transactions of each agent are the optimal ones, given the perceived constraints he faces. Mathematically this means that the transactions λ_{ihk}^* of agent i at all trading posts (h, k) are solutions in λ_{ihk} of the program

$$\text{Maximize} \quad U_i(x_i) \qquad \text{s.t.}$$

$$x_i \geq 0,$$

$$x_{ih} = \omega_{ih} + \sum_{k \neq h} \frac{\lambda_{ihk}}{p_h} \qquad \forall \ h,$$

$$\underline{\lambda}_{ihk} \leq \lambda_{ihk} \leq \bar{\lambda}_{ihk} \qquad \forall \ (h, k).$$

---

[1] The material in this section is an extremely brief account of an argument developed at more length in Benassy (1975a).

The Efficiency Property

We are now ready to state the main efficiency theorem for fixprice barter equilibria.

Theorem N.1 *If the rationing schemes are frictionless at all trading posts, then no Pareto-improving chain exists and the fixprice barter equilibrium is p-efficient.*

Proof Let us consider the above program giving the level of transactions at equilibrium and derive the Kuhn–Tucker conditions associated with it:

$$\frac{\partial U_i}{\partial x_{ih}} \leq \epsilon_{ih}, \qquad \text{with equality if} \quad x_{ih} > 0,$$

$$\epsilon_{ih}/p_h - \epsilon_{ik}/p_k = \mu_{hk}^i.$$

$\epsilon_{ih} \geq 0$ can be interpreted as the exchange value of good h for trader i. It is equal to the marginal utility if the agent consumes a positive amount of the corresponding good.

μ_{hk}^i is an index of rationing for agent i at trading post (h, k):

$\mu_{hk}^i > 0$ if i is constrained in his demand of h against k $(0 \leq \lambda_{ihk}^* < \tilde{\lambda}_{ihk})$.
$\mu_{hk}^i < 0$ if i is constrained in his supply of h against k $(0 \geq \lambda_{ihk}^* > \tilde{\lambda}_{ihk})$.
$\mu_{hk}^i = 0$ if i is not constrained at trading post (h, k) $(\lambda_{ihk}^* = \tilde{\lambda}_{ihk})$.

Because all rationing schemes are frictionless, at any trading post only one side is constrained, and thus the μ_{hk}^i will have the same sign for all agents on a market (h, k). As we shall now see, this property implies the efficiency of barter equilibria.

Let us first consider the simple case where all final allocations are strictly positive. Then $\partial U_i/\partial x_{ih} = \epsilon_{ih}$, and

$$\frac{1}{p_h}\frac{\partial U_i}{\partial x_{ih}} - \frac{1}{p_h}\frac{\partial U_i}{\partial x_{ik}} = \frac{\epsilon_{ih}}{p_h} - \frac{\epsilon_{ik}}{p_k} = \mu_{hk}^i.$$

Since these quantities have the same sign for all i, the equilibrium is p-efficient.

Turning now to the general case, we first note that

$$h(\mathcal{R}_i)k \Rightarrow \mu_{hk}^i > 0.$$

We shall now prove by *reductio ad absurdum* that no Pareto-improving chain of trades exists in the fixprice equilibrium. Indeed, assume that such a chain did exist:

$$h_1(\mathcal{R}_{i_1})\, h_2,\ h_2(\mathcal{R}_{i_2})\, h_3,\ \ldots,\ h_k(\mathcal{R}_{i_k})\, h_1.$$

This would imply

$$\mu_{h_1 h_2}^{i_1} > 0, \ \mu_{h_2 h_3}^{i_2} > 0, \ \ldots, \ \mu_{h_k h_1}^{i_k} > 0,$$

and by the above sign property we would have

$$\mu_{h_1 h_2}^{i_1} + \mu_{h_2 h_3}^{i_1} + \cdots + \mu_{h_k h_1}^{i_1} > 0,$$

which is impossible, since by definition of the μ's the left-hand side is identically zero.   Q.E.D.

Appendix O

Inefficiency and Expectations: A Dynamic Model

We shall construct here a simple model illustrating the ideas put forward by Keynes (1936, Chapter 16). We already formalized this model in Chapter 10, Section 7, but now we shall do so in a dynamic setting. More specifically, we shall present a model where prices are the intertemporal equilibrium prices but where imperfect foresight leads to a "Keynesian" depression.

The Model

We consider a dynamic aggregate monetary economy. Time is discrete and is indexed by t. Agents consist of one firm that lasts forever and of households that live two periods each. At any point in time the agents in the economy are the firm, one "young" household, and one "old" household.

The firm has a production function, the same in all periods, $q = F(l)$, with $F'(l) > 0$, $F''(l) < 0$. It can store at no cost and has a forward horizon of one period.

The household of generation t lives in periods t and $t + 1$. It has an endowment of labor l_0 in period t and zero in period $t + 1$. It starts its life with no money but owns all production of period t. The household chooses its intertemporal stream of consumption $c(t)$ and $c(t + 1)$ according to the utility function

$$U(c(t), c(t + 1)) = \alpha(t) \operatorname{Log} [c(t) + [1 - \alpha(t)] \operatorname{Log} c(t + 1), 0 < \alpha(t) < 1.$$

An Intertemporal Equilibrium

Let us assume first that all generations have the same utility function, with $\alpha(t) = \alpha$ for all t. The intertemporal equilibrium values of wage and price are easily computed as

$$w_0/p_0 = F'(l_0), \qquad p_0 = m_0/(1 - \alpha)q_0,$$

where m_0 is the total quantity of money in the economy and $q_0 = F(l_0)$ the full employment output. In this equilibrium the firm produces q_0 each period and does not store anything. Each household consumes αq_0 in its first period, $(1 - \alpha)q_0$ in its second period. Total consumption in each period is q_0.

In what follows we shall assume that the price and wage are given in all periods and are equal to these intertemporal equilibrium values. We shall consider disturbances that do not modify the intertemporal equilibrium price and wage and see how the economy evolves under different assumptions about expectations.

A Thrifty Generation: Perfect Foresight

Let us assume now that one generation is more "thrifty" than the others; specifically that the utility of generation τ is

$$U(c(\tau), c(\tau + 1)) = \beta \text{ Log } c(\tau) + (1 - \beta) \text{ Log } c(\tau + 1), \qquad \text{with} \quad \beta < \alpha.$$

We notice that this modification does not change the intertemporal equilibrium price and wage. In this "new" intertemporal equilibrium, the firm continues to produce q_0 in each period. All households except that of generation τ consume αq_0 when young, $(1 - \alpha)q_0$ when old. The household of generation τ consumes βq_0 when young, $(1 - \beta)q_0$ when old. We thus see that in period τ total consumption is $(1 + \beta - \alpha)q_0$, which falls short of previous consumption by $\Delta c = -(\alpha - \beta)q_0$. This quantity $(\alpha - \beta)q_0$ is stored by the firm, to be consumed in period $\tau + 1$, where total consumption is $(1 + \alpha - \beta)q_0$. In subsequent periods everything returns to "normal." So what has happened is that the extra "savings" in period τ, $(\alpha - \beta)q_0$, have been matched by an equal increase in investment (in the form of inventory holdings) so that full employment can be maintained.

The above course of events is what will happen in the case of perfect foresight. Indeed, implicit in the above argument is the assumption that the firm knows it will be able to sell in period $\tau + 1$ its full employment production plus the amount of goods stored. We shall now examine what happens if we abandon this "perfect foresight" assumption for a more realistic expectations pattern.

A Thrifty Generation: Static Expectations

Let us assume that the firm forms its expectations historically and, in particular, that it has "static expectations"[1] for demand; that is, it expects demand in the next period to be the same as demand today. It is easy to see that with such expectations the firm will not build up any inventory and will thus produce for current demand only. Production equals sales in all periods.

In period τ the demand consists of m_0/p_0 from the generation $\tau - 1$ plus $\beta y(\tau)$ from the generation τ. Sales and production in τ are therefore determined by

$$y(\tau) = \frac{m_0}{p_0} + \beta\, y(\tau),$$

$$y(\tau) = \frac{1}{1 - \beta} \frac{m_0}{p_0} = \frac{1 - \alpha}{1 - \beta} q_0 < q_0.$$

We see that income is now lower than full employment income. The difference can be written

$$y(\tau) - q_0 = - \frac{(\alpha - \beta)q_0}{1 - \beta} = \frac{\Delta c}{1 - \beta}.$$

The reduction in income is thus equal to the "autonomous" fall in consumption Δc times the multiplier in period τ, $1/(1 - \beta)$. In subsequent periods income returns to its full employment value. What has happened? Exactly what was indicated in our quotation of Keynes (Chapter 10, Section 6): In a realistic economy with few forward markets, a diminution in consumption depresses activity today without giving any signal for increased activity tomorrow. Hence no extra investment takes place and the full effect of multipliers works in the downward direction.

The Two Scenarios Compared

We can compare the two situations by examining the consumption streams of households in the case of perfect foresight and that of static expectations. In both cases, all generations but generation τ consume αq_0 when young, $(1 - \alpha)q_0$ when old. As for generation τ, its consumption patterns are given in Table O.1.

We see that under static expectations generation τ's consumption is smaller than in the perfect foresight case in both periods. We may also note that in the case of static expectations generation τ, which decided to

---

[1] Other "adaptative" patterns would lead to similar, though more complicated, results.

TABLE O.1

	Generation τ		Other generations (both expectations schemes)
	Perfect foresight	Static expectations	
Consumption when young	βq_0	$[\beta(1 - \alpha)/(1 - \beta)]q_0$	αq_0
Consumption when old	$(1 - \beta)q_0$	$(1 - \alpha)q_0$	$(1 - \alpha)q_0$
Total	q_0	$[(1 - \alpha)/(1 - \beta)]q_0$	q_0

save more than the others in order to increase future consumption, ends up consuming less than the others when young, but no more when old. This is still another example of the famous "paradox of thrift."

Appendix P

Income Distribution and Employment

In all the macroeconomic models of Part III we made the simple and traditional assumption that all current profits were distributed to the household and thus that real income was equal to the level of the sales of goods y. We shall now investigate how the results may be changed if we make a different income distribution assumption, namely, that only a fraction δ of profits is distributed in the current period. This will be done for the models without inventories of Chapters 11 and 13. As we shall see, the main changes will be in the effects of wage variations on the level of employment, production, and prices.

The Consumption Function

The change in the above-mentioned assumption will modify our results mainly via the modification of the consumption function. The implicit assumption behind the consumption function used in Part III is that the effective demand for consumption depends positively on real income ρ and initial money balances $\bar{m}$, negatively on prices p and the tax rates τ. When all profits are distributed, real income ρ is equal to y, and the consumption function could thus be written as

$$C(y, p, \bar{m}, \tau),$$

with

$$C_y > 0, \qquad C_p < 0, \qquad C_{\bar{m}} > 0, \qquad C_\tau < 0.$$

If we assume instead that only a fraction δ of profits is distributed, the money income of the household is

$$wl + \delta(py - wl) = \delta py + (1 - \delta)\, wl.$$

Using the fact that in the model without inventories $l = F^{-1}(y)$, real income is thus

$$\rho = \delta y + (1 - \delta)(w/p)F^{-1}(y).$$

225

We note that ρ depends positively on y but now also depends positively on w and negatively on p. Inserting this into the original consumption demand, we obtain a new consumption function, which now depends positively on w:

$$C(y, p, w, \bar{m}, \tau),$$

with

$$C_y > 0, \qquad C_p < 0, \qquad C_w > 0, \qquad C_{\bar{m}} > 0, \qquad C_\tau < 0.$$

We shall now see how the results obtained in Chapters 11 and 13 must be modified.

The Model with Fixed Price and Wage

The determination of the level of sales and employment remains the same as in Chapter 11 for the regions of classical unemployment and repressed inflation. However, in the case of Keynesian unemployment, the equilibrium level of sales is given by the following equation in y:

$$C(y, p, w, \bar{m}, \tau) + \tilde{g} = y,$$

yielding the Keynesian level of sales

$$y_K(p, w, \bar{m}, \tilde{g}, \tau).$$

We notice that y_K, and thus the level of employment $F^{-1}(y_K)$, are now increasing functions of the wage:

$$\frac{\partial y_K}{\partial w} = \frac{C_w}{1 - C_y} > 0.$$

Thus in the Keynesian region an increase in the wage will now increase the level of employment—a result exactly opposite to that obtained in the classical region.

As for the division between the three regions, the picture in $(y_K, w/p)$ space is exactly the same as in Fig. 11.4. In (p, w) space, however, Fig. 11.5 is not valid and must be replaced with Fig. P.1, where, we note, the dividing line between the regions of Keynesian unemployment and repressed inflation now has a positive slope. The values of the Walrasian price and wage p_0 and w_0 are given by the following system:

$$C(y_0, p_0, w_0, \bar{m}, \tau) + \tilde{g} = y_0, \qquad w_0 = p_0 F'(l_0).$$

The Model with Fixed Wage and Flexible Price

As in the model of Chapter 13, we have two regimes, one characterized by unemployment, the other by full employment.

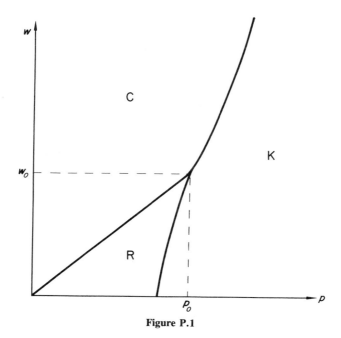

Figure P.1

In the full employment case, p^* and y^* are determined by the following system:

$$C(y, p, w, \bar{m}, \tau) + \tilde{g} = y,$$
$$y = y_0,$$

from which we obtain

$$\frac{\partial p^*}{\partial w} = -\frac{C_w}{C_p} > 0.$$

The equilibrium price is now an increasing function of w. (It was independent of w in Chapter 13.)

In the unemployment case, p^* and y^* are given by the following system:

$$C(y, p, w, \bar{m}, \tau) + \tilde{g} = y,$$
$$y = S(p, w),$$

from which we obtain

$$\frac{\partial p^*}{\partial w} = \frac{C_w - S_w(1 - C_y)}{S_p(1 - C_y) - C_p} > 0,$$
$$\frac{\partial y^*}{\partial w} = \frac{C_w S_p - C_p S_w}{S_p(1 - C_y) - C_p}.$$

The effect of a wage increase on the price level is still positive, but the sign of the effect on sales and employment depends on the sign of the quantity $C_w S_p - C_p S_w$, which may be positive or negative.

Conclusions

Modifying our assumption about profit distribution has mainly changed some results for the effects of wage changes on employment:

• In the model with fixed wage and price, an increase in w increases the level of employment in the Keynesian region. (We found no effect in Chapter 11.)

• In the model with fixed wage and flexible price, an increase in w has a dubious effect on the level of employment. (We found a definitive negative effect in Chapter 13.)

We may remark that we would have obtained the same types of results if we had assumed a higher tax rate on profits than on wages or had assumed two differentiated classes of income recipients, with the marginal propensity to consume being lower out of profits than out of wages.

Appendix Q

The Inflation Model: An Alternative Formulation

To simplify the exposition, in Chapter 14 we developed the model of inflation using the parameter $\gamma = \tilde{g}/y$ as the instrumental variable of the government's demand policy. We shall briefly rework this model here, this time using as a parameter the level $\tilde{g}$ of government demand as in Chapters 11–13. We shall emphasize only the changes affecting the results obtained in Chapter 14. To facilitate comparison, the following subsections correspond to the sections of Chapter 14.

Temporary Equilibria and Dynamics

In a given period, the level of p and y is determined by the intersection of the following "supply" and "demand" schedules derived in Chapter 14:

$$y = \hat{D}(p) = \frac{1}{1 - \alpha(1 - \tau)}\left(\frac{\beta \bar{m}}{p} + \tilde{g}\right),$$

$$y = \hat{S}(p) = \min\left[F\left(F'^{-1}\left(\frac{\epsilon}{\epsilon - 1} \cdot \frac{w}{p}\right)\right), y_0\right].$$

We note that a temporary equilibrium exists if and only if

$$\tilde{g} < [1 - \alpha(1 - \tau)]y_0,$$

which we shall assume in all that follows. Under this assumption, government's demand $\tilde{g}$ and purchases g^* are always equal. We shall denote them both by g.

The dynamic link between successive temporary equilibria is given by the equations describing the evolution of the wage and initial money holdings

$$w(t) = \omega(t)\, p(t - 1),$$
$$\bar{m}(t + 1) = \bar{m}(t) + p(t)\, g(t) - \tau(t)\, p(t)\, y(t).$$

Demand Inflation

The maximum amount of government purchases that can be financed by taxes at full employment is

$$g_0 = \tau y_0.$$

An increase of g above this value will lead to inflation. In the process of demand inflation, temporary equilibria will be of the full employment type. The price in period t is determined by the following equation:

$$\frac{1}{1 - \alpha(1 - \tau)} \left[\beta \frac{\bar{m}(t)}{p(t)} + g(t) \right] = y_0,$$

yielding

$$p(t) = \frac{\beta \bar{m}(t)}{[1 - \alpha(1 - \tau)]y_0 - g(t)}.$$

The equation stating the evolution of money holdings is

$$\bar{m}(t + 1) = \bar{m}(t) + p(t)\, g(t) - \tau p(t)\, y_0.$$

Combining these last two equations, and lagging appropriately, we obtain

$$\frac{p(t)}{p(t - 1)} = \frac{y_0[1 - \alpha(1 - \tau) - \beta\tau] - (1 - \beta)\, g(t - 1)}{y_0[1 - \alpha(1 - \tau)] - g(t)}.$$

The steady-state rate of inflation i can then be computed by taking $g(t) = g(t - 1) = g$:

$$i = \frac{\beta(g - \tau y_0)}{[1 - \alpha(1 - \tau)]y_0 - g}.$$

Applying the same method as in Chapter 14, one can show that public spending in excess of taxes, that is, $g - \tau y_0$, is financed by the "inflation tax" on real balance $i\mu$:

$$g - \tau y_0 = i\mu.$$

Cost Inflation

The cause of inflation is again a rise in the target real wage ω such that it is inconsistent with the pricing policy of the firm, that is, such that $\chi > 1$, with

$$\chi = \frac{\epsilon}{\epsilon - 1} \frac{\omega}{F'(l_0)}.$$

The inflation–unemployment tradeoff curves are determined by the same equations as in Chapter 14:

$$1 + i(t) = \chi(t) \frac{F'(l_0)}{F'(l_0 - u(t))}.$$

The movements and final positions on these curves depend on the dynamics of g. We may consider again an increase of $\chi(t)$ from 1 to $\chi > 1$, accompanied by one of the two following policies: g constant and equal to g_0, or an endogenous stabilization policy modeled as

$$g(t) - g(t - 1) = \eta[u(t - 1) - \bar{u}].$$

Simulations of these two policies yield results fairly similar to those of Chapter 14 (compare Figs. Q.1 and Q.2 with Figs. 14.4 and 14.5). The main difference is that point B, corresponding to the steady state with $\chi > 1$ and $g = g_0$, now displays a *positive* rate of inflation. This occurs because maintaining constant spending in real terms g_0 is not financially neutral: with positive unemployment, $y < y_0$ and the real value of taxes is diminished, thus creating a permanent and inflationary budget deficit.

Steady States

We shall now compute the steady-state values of u and i corresponding to stationary values of ω, g, and τ. In order to do that, let us first rewrite

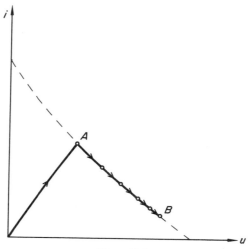

Figure Q.1

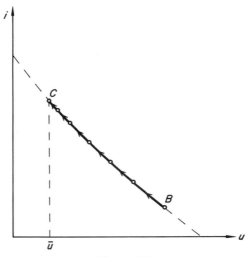

Figure Q.2

the "demand" schedule in a given period t:

$$y(t) = \frac{1}{1 - \alpha(1 - \tau)} \left[\frac{\beta \bar{m}(t)}{p(t)} + g \right].$$

Let us also rewrite the equation of evolution of money holdings:

$$\bar{m}(t + 1) = \bar{m}(t) + p(t) g - \tau p(t) y(t).$$

Combining these two equations and lagging appropriately, we obtain

$$\frac{p(t)}{p(t - 1)} = \frac{[1 - \alpha(1 - \tau) - \beta\tau]y(t - 1) - (1 - \beta)g}{[1 - \alpha(1 - \tau)]y(t) - g}.$$

In a steady state $y(t) = y(t - 1) = y$, so that

$$i = \frac{\beta(g - \tau y)}{[1 - \alpha(1 - \tau)]y - g},$$

which, since $y = F(l) = F(l_0 - u)$, may also be written as a relation between i and u:

$$i = \frac{\beta[g - \tau F(l_0 - u)]}{[1 - \alpha(1 - \tau)]F(l_0 - u) - g}. \tag{1}$$

We obtain another relation between i and u by using the inequality derived from the "supply" curve,

$$\frac{p(t)}{p(t-1)} \geq \chi(t) \frac{F'(l_0)}{F'(l_0 - u(t))},$$

which holds with equality if unemployment is positive. In a steady state with constant χ, this yields

$$1 + i \geq \chi F'(l_0)/F'(l_0 - u), \tag{2}$$

which again holds with equality if $u > 0$. We may combine the two expressions for i, separating the steady states with full employment from those with unemployment:

(a) In the case of full employment, $u = 0$, and Eq. (1) yields

$$i = \frac{\beta(g - \tau y_0)}{[1 - \alpha(1 - \tau)]y_0 - g}.$$

(b) In the case of unemployment, u and i are solutions of the system of

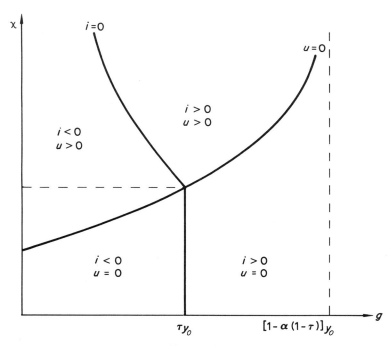

Figure Q.3

equations (1) and (2):

$$i = \frac{\beta[g - \tau F(l_0 - u)]}{[1 - \alpha(1 - \tau)]F(l_0 - u) - g},$$

$$1 + i = \chi\, F'(l_0)/F'(l_0 - u),$$

from which we see that

$$\frac{\partial u}{\partial \chi} > 0, \qquad \frac{\partial u}{\partial g} < 0,$$

$$\frac{\partial i}{\partial \chi} > 0, \qquad \frac{\partial i}{\partial g} > 0.$$

The equation for the separating line between the two regions is obtained by adding $u = 0$ to the system (1) and (2) above:

$$\chi - 1 = \frac{\beta(g - \tau y_0)}{[1 - \alpha(1 - \tau)]y_0 - g}.$$

For a given τ, we can now classify the steady states according to the values of i and u on a (g, χ) graph (Fig. Q.3).

Bibliography

Arrow, K. J. (1959). Towards a theory of price adjustment. In *The allocation of economic resources* (M. Abramowitz, ed.). Stanford Univ. Press, Stanford, California.

Arrow, K. J., and Debreu, G. (1954). Existence of an equilibrium for a competitive economy. *Econometrica* **22**:265–290.

Arrow, K. J., and Hahn, F. H. (1971). *General competitive analysis.* Holden-Day, San Francisco.

Arrow, K. J., Karlin, S., and Scarf, H. (1958). *Studies in the mathematical theory of inventory and production.* Stanford Univ. Press, Stanford, California.

Barro, R. J., and Grossman, H. I. (1971). A general disequilibrium model of income and employment. *American Economic Review* **61**:82–93.

Barro, R. J., and Grossman, H. I. (1974). Suppressed inflation and the supply multiplier. *Review of Economic Studies* **41**:87–104.

Barro, R. J., and Grossman, H. I. (1976). *Money, employment and inflation.* Cambridge Univ. Press, London and New York.

Bellman, R. (1957). *Dynamic programming.* Princeton Univ. Press, Princeton, New Jersey.

Benassy, J. P. (1973). Disequilibrium theory. Unpublished Ph.D. dissertation, Department of Economics, Univ. of California, Berkeley (Hungarian translation in *Szigma,* 1974).

Benassy, J. P. (1974). Théorie néokeynésienne du déséquilibre dans une economie monétaire. *Cahiers du Séminaire d'Econométrie* **17**:81–113.

Benassy, J. P. (1975a). Disequilibrium exchange in barter and monetary economies. *Economic Inquiry* **13**:131–156.

Benassy, J. P. (1975b). Neo-Keynesian disequilibrium theory in a monetary economy. *Review of Economic Studies* **42**:503–523.

Benassy, J. P. (1976a). The disequilibrium approach to monopolistic price setting and general monopolistic equilibrium. *Review of Economic Studies* **43**:69–81.

Benassy, J. P. (1976b). Théorie du déséquilibre et fondements microéconomiques de la macroéconomie. *Revue Economique* **27**:755–804.

Benassy, J. P. (1976c). Regulation of the wage profits conflict and the unemployment inflation dilemma in a dynamic disequilibrium model. *Economie Appliquée* **29**:409–444.

Benassy, J. P. (1977a). A neokeynesian model of price and quantity determination in disequilibrium. In *Equilibrium and disequilibrium in economic theory* (G. Schwödiauer, ed.). Reidel, Boston.

Benassy, J. P. (1977b). On quantity signals and the foundations of effective demand theory. *Scandinavian Journal of Economics* **79**:147–168.

Benassy, J. P. (1978). Cost and demand inflation revisited: a neokeynesian approach. *Economie Appliquée* **31**:113–133.

Benassy, J. P. (1982). Developments in non-Walrasian economics and the microeconomic foundations of macroeconomics. In *Advances in quantitative economics* (W. Hildenbrand, ed.). Cambridge Univ. Press, London and New York.

Böhm, V., and Levine, J. P. (1979). Temporary equilibria with quantity rationing. *Review of Economic Studies* **46**:361–377.

Bronfenbrenner, M., and Holzman, F. D. (1963). A survey of inflation theory. *American Economic Review* **53**:593–661.

Bushaw, D. W., and Clower, R. (1957). *Introduction to mathematical economics*. Irwin, Homewood, Illinois.

Chamberlin, E. H. (1933). *The theory of monopolistic competition*. Harvard Univ. Press, Cambridge, Massachusetts.

Clower, R. W. (1960). Keynes and the classics: a dynamical perspective. *Quarterly Journal of Economics* **74**:318–323.

Clower, R. W. (1965). The Keynesian counterrevolution: a theoretical appraisal. In *The theory of interest rates* (F. H. Hahn and F. P. R. Brechling, eds.). Macmillan, London.

Clower, R. W. (1967). A reconsideration of the microfoundations of monetary theory. *Western Economic Journal* **6**:1–9.

Debreu, G. (1959). *Theory of value*. Wiley, New York.

Drèze, J. (1975). Existence of an equilibrium under price rigidity and quantity rationing. *International Economic Review* **16**:301–320.

Friedman, J. W. (1968). Reaction functions and the theory of duopoly. *Review of Economic Studies* **35**:257–272.

Futia, C. (1975). A theory of effective demand (mimeographed). Bell Laboratories, Murray Hill, New Jersey.

Glustoff, E. (1968). On the existence of a Keynesian equilibrium. *Review of Economic Studies* **35**:327–334.

Grandmont, J. M. (1974). On the short run equilibrium in a monetary economy. In *Allocation under uncertainty, equilibrium, and optimality* (J. Drèze, ed.). Macmillan, London.

Grandmont, J. M., and Laroque, G. (1976). On Keynesian temporary equilibria. *Review of Economic Studies* **43**:53–67.

Grandmont, J. M., Laroque, G., and Younès, Y. (1978). Equilibrium with quantity rationing and recontracting. *Journal of Economic Theory* **19**:84–102.

Grossman, H. I. (1971). Money, interest and prices in market disequilibrium. *Journal of Political Economy* **79**:943–961.

Grossman, H. I. (1972). A choice-theoretic model of an income investment accelerator. *American Economic Review* **62**:630–641.

Hahn, F. H. (1978). On non-Walrasian equilibria. *Review of Economic Studies* **45**:1–17.

Hahn, F. H., and Negishi, T. (1962). A theorem on non-tatonnement stability. *Econometrica* **30**:463–469.

Hansen, B. (1951). *A study in the theory of inflation*. Allen and Unwin, London.

Heller, W. P., and Starr, R. M. (1979). Unemployment equilibrium with myopic complete information. *Review of Economic Studies* **46**:339–359.

Hicks, J. R. (1937). Mr. Keynes and the classics: a suggested interpretation. *Econometrica* **5**:147–159.

Hicks, J. R. (1939). *Value and capital*. Oxford Univ. Press (Clarendon), London and New York. Second Edition 1946.

Hicks, J. R. (1965). *Capital and growth*. Oxford Univ. Press, London and New York.

Hildenbrand, K., and Hildenbrand, W. (1978). On Keynesian equilibria with unemployment and quantity rationing. *Journal of Economic Theory* **18**:255–277.

Howitt, P. W. (1974). Stability and the quantity theory. *Journal of Political Economy* **82**:133–151.

Iwai, K. (1974). The firm in uncertain markets and its price, wage and employment adjustments. *Review of Economic Studies* **41**:257–276.

Kaldor, N. (1956). Alternative theories of distribution. *Review of Economic Studies* **23**:83–100.

Keynes, J. M. (1936). *The general theory of employment, interest and money*. Harcourt Brace, New York.

Keynes, J. M. (1937). Alternative theories of the rate of interest. *Economic Journal* **47**:241–252.

Leijonhufvud, A. (1968). *On Keynesian economics and the economics of Keynes*. Oxford Univ. Press, London and New York.

Machlup, F. (1958). Equilibrium and disequilibrium: misplaced concreteness and disguised politics. *Economic Journal* **68**:1–24.

Malinvaud, E. (1977). *The theory of unemployment reconsidered*. Blackwell, Oxford.

Malinvaud, E., and Younès, Y. (1977). Some new concepts for the microeconomic foundations of macroeconomics. In *The microeconomic foundations of macroeconomics* (G. Harcourt, ed.). Macmillan, London.

Marshall, A. (1890). *Principles of economics*. Macmillan, London (8th ed., 1920).

Michel, P. (1980). Keynesian equilibrium and fix-price equilibria (mimeographed). Univ. of Warwick, England.

Muellbauer, J., and Portes, R. (1978). Macroeconomic models with quantity rationing. *Economic Journal* **88**:788–821.

Negishi, T. (1961). Monopolistic competition and general equilibrium. *Review of Economic Studies* **28**:196–201.

Negishi, T. (1972). *General equilibrium theory and international trade*. North-Holland Publ., Amsterdam.

Negishi, T. (1977). Existence of an under employment equilibrium. In *Equilibrium and disequilibrium in economic theory* (G. Schwödiauer, ed.). Reidel, Boston.

Negishi, T. (1979). *Microeconomic foundations of Keynesian macroeconomics*. North-Holland Publ., Amsterdam.

Ostroy, J. (1973). The informational efficiency of monetary exchange. *American Economic Review* **63**:597–610.

Ostroy, J., and Starr, R. (1974). Money and the decentralization of exchange. *Econometrica* **42**:1093–1114.

Patinkin, D. (1956). *Money, interest and prices*. Row, Peterson and Company, New York (2nd ed., 1965, Harper and Row, New York.)

Robinson, J. (1933). *The economics of imperfect competition*. Macmillan, London.

Samuelson, P. A. (1958). An exact consumption loan model of interest with or without the social contrivance of money. *Journal of Political Economy* **66**:467–482.

Solow, R. M., and Stiglitz, J. (1968). Output, employment and wages in the short run. *Quarterly Journal of Economics* **82**:537–560.

Sweezy, P. M. (1939). Demand under conditions of oligopoly. *Journal of Political Economy* **47**:568–573.

Triffin, R. (1940). *Monopolistic competition and general equilibrium theory.* Harvard Univ. Press, Cambridge, Massachusetts.

Veendorp, E. C. H. (1970). General equilibrium theory for a barter economy. *Western Economic Journal* **8**:1–23.

Walras, L. (1874). Eléments d'economie politique pure. Corbaz, Lausanne (definitive English edition, transl. by W. Jaffé, *Elements of pure economics,* 1954, Allen and Unwin, London).

Younès, Y. (1970). Sur les notions d'équilibre et de déséquilibre utilisées dans les modèles décrivant l'évolution d'une économie capitaliste (mimeographed). Centre d'Etudes Prospectives d'Economie Mathématique Appliquées à la Planification (CEPREMAP), Paris.

Younès, Y. (1975). On the role of money in the process of exchange and the existence of a non-Walrasian equilibrium. *Review of Economic Studies* **42**:489–501.

Index

ECONOMIC THEORY, ECONOMETRICS, AND MATHEMATICAL ECONOMICS

Consulting Editor: Karl Shell

UNIVERSITY OF PENNSYLVANIA
PHILADELPHIA, PENNSYLVANIA